Leisure and Social Inclusion:
New Challenges
for Policy and Provision

Edited by
Gayle McPherson
Gavin Reid

LSA

Publication No. 73

First published in 2001 by
Leisure Studies Association
The Chelsea School
University of Brighton
Eastbopurne BN20 7SP (UK)

A catalogue record for this book
is available from the British Library.

ISBN: 0 906337 84 4

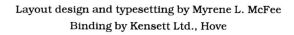

Layout design and typesetting by Myrene L. McFee
Binding by Kensett Ltd., Hove

Contents

About the Contributors

Cara Aitchison is Head of the Leisure and Sport Research Unit at Cheltenham and Gloucester College of Higher Education where she manages graduate education and research in leisure and sport. Her interdisciplinary research addresses leisure and tourism as sites and processes of social, cultural and spatial inclusion and exclusion with a particular focus on gender relations. She has published theoretical papers in leisure journals including Leisure Studies, Leisure Sciences, Annals of Leisure Research, Managing Leisure and Tourist Studies in addition to publications in geography, gender, management and disability studies journals. Cara is co-author (with Nicola Macleod and Stephen Shaw) of Leisure and Tourism Landscapes: Social and Cultural Geographies published by Routledge (2000). Cara has been an active member of the Leisure Studies Association for over ten years. She served for seven years on the Executive Committee with five years as LSA Secretary and was a member of the 1997 and 1998 Conference Organising Committees. She co-edited (with Fiona Jordan) Gender, Space and Identity: Leisure, Culture and Commerce published by the LSA in 1998 and edited LSA Newsletters in 1997, 2000 and 2001.

David Booth is currently Business Development Manager for Sport and Recreation Management at South Lanarkshire Council in Scotland. A former Client Manager, his remit now extends to ensuring that policies and management practices are put in place to deliver Best Value. He is one of the founder members of the South West of Scotland Benchmarking Group for Leisure Services and has presented various papers on benchmarking including to the Annual Conference of the Institute of Sport and Recreation Management (ISRM).

Malcolm Foley is Professor of Leisure Development at Glasgow Caledonian University. His research interests include work and leisure, the experience of working in the leisure industries and the relationship between leisure and other service industries.

Matt Frew is a lecturer within the Department of Media, Language and Leisure Management at Glasgow Caledonian University. He has over 15 years working experience in leisure industry with experience in organisational and personal development, lecturing, and research. His doctoral research is a deconstructive focus on the Scottish public leisure sector, at national and level local, and the inter-relationships and practices between management and staff responsible for service delivery to culturally conflicting customer groups. Other research interests include the commodification and consumption of countryside and aesthetics of leisure.

Debbie Hinds is a lecturer within the Division of Management At Glasgow Caledonian University. Her research interests are in the area of urban planning, development and community issues with particular focus on the impacts of transport policy on the urban environment.

Lindsay King is course leader for the undergraduate Sport Management courses at the University of Northumbria. Within the Division of Sport Sciences her teaching focuses on sport marketing and policy. Previous research has dealt with serious leisure and identity issues, with case studies of volunteers and gay male sport participants. Contributions to journals such as Leisure Sciences and Applied Recreation Research have followed. The main focus of Lindsay's research is a PhD study of the long-term impact of the physical education experience on sport participation and senses of sporting identity in adult life. In her spare time Lindsay is a member of Hexham Rowing club and a devoted fan of the television series 'ER'!

Francis Lobo is Honorary Research Fellow in the School of Marketing Tourism and Leisure at Edith Cowan University. For over a decade Dr Lobo has researched into equitable access to leisure services and facilities for the socially disadvantaged. In particular his research has focused on unemployed seniors and young people. Besides arguing that the unemployed are materially and psychologically deprived, Dr Lobo has provided equitable solutions for effective inclusion and accessibility.

Fiona McCormack is a senior lecturer in the Faculty of Leisure and Tourism at Buckinghamshire Chilterns University College. She completed a PhD in 2000 entitled "Leisure Exclusion? Analysing interventions using active leisure with young people offending or at risk", under the supervision of Mike Collins at Loughborough University. This included two medium term qualitative evaluations of interventions that seek to use recreation to reduce offending. She is currently lecturing in the areas of Youth and Community Recreation, Leisure Policy and Provision and Outdoor Education on undergraduate courses.

Gayle McPherson is a Senior Lecturer in Leisure Management, in the Division of Media, Language and Leisure Management at Glasgow Caledonian University. She publishes mostly in the area of cultural and leisure policy, specialising in the museums sector. Other areas of research interest include exercise referral as part of social inclusion policies for leisure and health.

Geoff Nichols has taught on postgraduate courses in Leisure Management for 11 years. His current research interests include the impact of sports based programmes to reduce youth crime, and this involves four case study programmes. This builds on previous research, including: a national survey of local authority supported programmes conducted in 1998/9; research into the impact of outdoor adventure programmes on drug rehabilitation clients

(1998); research, funded by the Home Office, into physically demanding activities for probation service clients (1997/8); and evaluation of West Yorkshire Sports Counselling, a sports programme for probation service clients, funded by West Yorkshire Sports Counselling Association (1995/6). Geoff has also organised research seminars for the Association for Outdoor Learning and is a member of the advisory panel for evaluation of Fairbridge Drake, a leading national organisation who run developmental programmes for disadvantaged young people.

Susan M Ogden, PhD, is a lecturer within the Business School at Glasgow Caledonian University. Her current research interests focus mainly on service quality management, and the impact of central government policy on local government services and their management. Her recent research has been published in Public Management: An International Journal, Managing Leisure, and the International Journal of Contemporary Hospitality Management.

Kim Polistina is completing her PhD student at the Griffith University, Queensland. She has taught in a variety of leisure subjects, including outdoor recreation, leisure and the environment, introduction to leisure, human communication, and leisure planning. She also tutors at the GUMURRI Indigenous Research Centre, Griffith University. Her personal and scholarly interests focus on cultural studies and environmental and social issues, particularly in relation to outdoor leisure and lifestyles, lifelong learning and the transference of environmental knowledge and values. Her dissertation research focuses on the processes (and constraints to these processes) of transferring environmental knowledge and values which occur in contemporary and traditional appreciative outdoor recreation and Australian Aboriginal communities.

Ashley Pringle was a chief officer in the Community and Recreation Departments of three Scottish Local Authorities — Stirling, Edinburgh and North Ayrshire — from 1988 to 1999 and was an adviser to the Convention of Scottish Local Authorities in 1998 and 1999. He has given visiting lectures to Universities in Teesside, Edinburgh and Glasgow. Ashley Pringle completed a M.A. at the Centre for Contemporary Cultural Studies, Birmingham University in 1973. He is currently undertaking a PhD at Glasgow Caledonian University on the political and social implications of Scotland's National Cultural Strategy.

Gavin Reid is a lecturer in Leisure Management at Glasgow Caledonian University. He gained a BA (Hons) degree in Recreation from Moray House College of Physical Education in 1992 and completed a PhD in institutional economics and leisure contracting in 1996. His research has revolved around a number of leisure policy issues including, most recently, an investigation into the links between charitable leisure trusts and new Labour's 'third way'.

Ronnie Smith is a freelance writer and researcher, having until 2001 been a lecturer in Tourism at the Scottish Hotel School at the University of Strathclyde, Glasgow. He specialises in tourism policy issues and also writes on the relationship between heritage, visitor attractions and tourism. He contributes to the research activities of the Scottish Tourism Research Unit at the University of Strathclyde.

Peter Thompson completed an honours degree in sport development at the University of Northumbria at Newcastle in 1998. With a special interest in research he then went on to do a MSc in social science where he concentrated on the area of homosexuality. Having recently completed the MSc, Peter is looking for research positions in the North East. He now works as a part-time lecturer at the Division of Sport Sciences, University of Northumbria and also contributes to research projects. Peter is committed to qualitative research and is especially interested in the area of homosexuality. This is reflected in his Masters thesis 'Gay men in a straight world', which used in-depth, reciprocal interviews to examine the lives and experiences of ten gay men. Much of his MSc was based around research theory and the examination of homosexuality. In his spare time Peter works as a volunteer for the citizens advice bureau.

Social Exclusion and Policies for Leisure: An Introduction

Gayle McPherson and Gavin Reid

Glasgow Caledonian University

Social exclusion has been defined as "a shorthand label for what can happen when individuals or areas suffer from a combination of linked problems such as unemployment, poor skills, low incomes, poor housing, high crime environments, bad health and family breakdown" (Scottish Office, 1999: p. 5). The relationship between leisure and social inclusion has generated much lively debate within leisure studies. Coalter (2000) has argued that what theorizing has taken place has occurred within a normative citizenship paradigm which unproblematically equates non-participation in public leisure with social exclusion and, implicitly, a threat to societal cohesion. Coalter takes to task a number of leisure theorists for (in his opinion) taking a reproductionist 'society in leisure' approach which fails to critically explore the presumed social consensus underpinning the 'non-participation equals exclusion' view, while also ignoring the nature of that which people are supposed to be excluded from and on what basis. Rojek (1995) also appears to question the inclusive potential of public sector leisure when arguing that its modernist origins — reflected in activities characterised by the need for emotional control and restraint (Wynne, 1998) — result in an underlying ideology increasingly out of date in our postmodern society. Those adhering to this view focus on Le Grand's (undated) contention that an individual can only be excluded from that which he or she would like to participate (Coalter, 2000). Thus, research showing the stubborn refusal of lower socioeconomic groups to partake in public leisure provision, despite changing management approaches and promotional campaigns, gives fuel to the argument that such behaviour has more to do with 'individual' choice than 'structural' exclusion.

To Coalter (2000: p. 172) the failure to adequately theorize social exclusion and its link to leisure means we "risk misunderstanding the nature of leisure and the increased diversity of post-modern societies". The postmodern condition is felt to

1

provide a challenge to the apparent bias within much leisure research that equates the public sector with active citizenship and inclusivity, and the commercial sector with passive consumption and exploitation. To critics, such a view ignores the public sector's previous failure to achieve welfare goals, and the historical evidence highlighting that social engineering, rather than social citizenship, has underpinned much public leisure policy. What is required, therefore, is not merely an assessment of whether 'passport to leisure' schemes can offset social exclusion, but rather a theoretical examination of whether exclusion can actually be alleviated by leisure seen in its widest sense, together with a re-orientation of research agendas towards an examination of leisure experiences (rather than inequalities) via acts (rather than ideologies) of consumption (Coalter, 2000). An understanding of the relationship between leisure and social exclusion is also felt to require an assessment of new modes of inclusion in today's society which Coalter (2000: p. 17) states "may be individual and privatised".

Not surprisingly, these views have been vigorously challenged, with Deem (1999) questioning whether Coalter's argument that non-participation equals choice rests on an uncritical acceptance of the extent of consumer authority in the postmodern era which, characterised as it is by insecure employment and unsocial working hours, leads people to question the merits of consuming. Others critical of the postmodern thesis emphasise that, despite its rightful acknowledgement of profound social, economic and technological changes, the impact of these have not been evenly felt with the existence of cosmopolitan and hedonistic leisure lifestyles co-existing with a continuation of disadvantage, inequality and diminished life chances (Bramham, 1994; Murdock, 1994; Scraton, 1994; Henry, 1995). The language of social exclusion — and even more so 'poverty' — is thus seen as morally more appropriate than the postmodernists' celebration of difference and diversity. Those largely supportive of the public sector's contribution to welfare would find solace in Le Grand's (undated) second conceptual approach to social exclusion, which sees the latter existing if exclusion is deemed detrimental to society, as this chimes with the merit good ideology underpinning much leisure policy (Coalter, 2000). The legitimacy of the link is further acknowledged in Collins and Kennett's (1998) reference to a recent report conceptualising poverty in the 1990s not just in terms of the ability to provide adequate food, heating and shelter, but in terms of the ability to (among other things) join a sports facility or club (Oppenheim and Harker, 1996).

Theoretically, activities in sport and the arts offer a range of physiological, social and psychological benefits that may alter behaviour in ways that alleviate some of the aforementioned linked problems that make up social exclusion. It has been argued, however, that such benefits will not be facilitated if the 'taken for granted' theoretical grounds serve to prevent consideration of the mechanisms, processes and conditions necessary to obtain such advantageous outcomes (Coalter *et al.*, 2000). We thus see the evident link between rigorous theorising and successful practice, with the theoretical benefits of (say) sport unlikely to materialise unless policy-makers pay due attention to the processes that make up sports and their potential to foster/hinder inclusion; to the type of leadership styles required; to the need for a more sophisticated approach to evaluation; to the appropriate length of social exclusion projects and the type of funding necessary; and to the potential clash between the approach of volunteers drawn from excluded communities and mainstream leisure professionals (Coalter *et al.*, 2000).

The above brief discussion highlights that exploring the links between leisure and social inclusion (and vice versa) is not an easy task, particularly as it may force academics and practitioners to confront concepts and relationships that (to them) may have attained the status of common sense.

The papers collected in this volume originated from the authors' presentations to the Leisure Studies Association's July 2000 conference, *Leisure: Centres and Peripheries*, hosted by Glasgow Caledonian University.

A key theme within the conference was the relationship between leisure and social exclusion. The desire of the New Labour government to shift social policy debate from poverty to social exclusion has led to considerable discussion within Leisure Studies over its link to leisure and vice versa. The papers presented here highlight some of the complexities in this relationship, raising theoretical and practical issues in the process.

Fiona McCormack examines the 'Street Sport' initiative in three deprived areas of Stoke-on-Trent. This project was underpinned by a community recreation philosophy with an outreach approach designed to deflect negative behaviour into more constructive activities. The paper assesses the project's impact by drawing on the positive and negative thoughts of participants, local residents, the police, local headteachers, local sports centre managers, parents and youth workers. Key problems were deemed to be: the often short-term nature of these projects; their limited ability to reach 'excluded' females; a heightened awareness among residents of an overall lack of facilities once these projects had finished; and a lack of joined-up thinking between the agencies involved.

Francis Lobo highlights how the predominant paradigm in Australian leisure service delivery changed from a community orientation in the 1960s and 1970s to a business orientation in the 1980s. While acknowledging that there are benefits from this, he embraces the merit good rationale to argue that it ultimately excludes those who need public leisure provision most. In contrast to those who see the commercial sector as a possible vehicle for identity construction and inclusion, Lobo sees public provision as offering a better leisure experience than that obtained when leisure is merely experienced as a commodity in the market. Using an investigation into the delivery of leisure services in nine local authorities in Western Australia — making particular reference to provision for the unemployed — he outlines various steps to generate more inclusive leisure delivery systems.

Ashley Pringle seeks to counter those academics who question the public support for municipal leisure, arguing that its current potential as a vehicle for local democracy and its symbolic role as a manifestation of community solidarity have been undermined by successive cuts in capital and revenue funding. He argues that if the current trend towards externalising public sports facilities to charitable trusts is extended to include the entire Leisure Services function, then this offers the potential to re-connect the service to the local community. Rather than the possibility that, if reduced funding continues, public leisure is left with a purely social exclusion remit, the aforementioned approach offers the potential of greater inclusivity seen in a much wider sense.

Malcolm Foley, Matt Frew and Gayle McPherson critically assess the increasing use of GP Referral schemes in Scotland. Their research found that a range of schemes were in operation throughout Scotland, with council leisure centres facing competition from other facilities (e.g. schools), thus requiring of the former a more proactive marketing approach to enhance their involvement. The likelihood that individuals prescribed an exercise programme by their doctors will come from the group normally defined as socially excluded provides evidence of the local authority's welfare role. Referral schemes offer the opportunity for local authorities to demonstrate their commitment to effectiveness within a Best Value framework, while also obtaining some financial gain — perhaps not surprising given the increasingly fraught financial predicament facing most local authorities.

Susan Ogden and David Booth examine social exclusion from the perspective of benchmarking within a Best Value framework. Drawing on a case study of a public leisure services benchmarking group, the authors highlight the lessons learned from the experience to date, and how this group came to behave as a quality network to meet the challenge of Best Value. While highlighting the role of process benchmarking and strategic benchmarking to the social exclusion debate, recognition is given to the problems in assessing whether Social Inclusion Partnerships (SIPs) are delivering (say) reduced crime and better health. Such problems are deemed to revolve around a lack of expertise, the short-term nature of the projects and limited funding for anything other than basic evaluations.

Geoff Nichols advocates those examining the impact of sports programmes on crime reduction to adopt a research strategy based on a realist approach. This is deemed to offer greater value than evaluations based on the classical (positivist) experimental design. Bemoaning the lack of theoretical underpinning for the use of sport in crime prevention, the realist approach benefits from beginning with a theoretical analysis of the process, together with an emphasis on small-scale research drawing on a range of research methods and an appreciation of the interaction between the participant and the programme.

Lindsay King and Peter Thompson address the 'invisibility' of gay sports clubs in national sports policy and argue for increased attention to gay males in the context of the social inclusionist policies of sporting agencies. The paper examines the reasons for the lack of attention in this area, and explores what inclusion means to those within gay sports clubs. This leads on to a debate concerning whether inclusion is fostered by integrationist strategies or via gay-separatist clubs. The paper concludes by questioning whether gay sports clubs can be inclusive of a socially excluded group, and whether, for some men, these clubs need to feel socially and operationally exclusive.

Debbie Hinds examines the potential of Home Zones in reclaiming the streets for local neighbourhoods, thereby fostering greater social inclusion. Drawing on a number of case studies she highlights the need for effective community involvement for schemes to succeed, while acknowledging that the fostering of inclusion in one area can mean other areas suffering from (say) increased traffic — and hence reduced community interaction. The role of local authorities is also examined in successful initiatives, with analysis made of the ability of Home Zones to provide communities with a greater sense of ownership of their local streets, and their contribution to reduced crime and pollution.

Ronnie Smith examines the relevance of social exclusion to tourism policy. He argues that, generally, tourism has been located within an economic rather than social rationale, with provision for the 'excluded' generally taken to mean the 'disabled'. While appreciating that the 40% of the population who do not take a holiday do so for various reasons, he argues that more thought and action should go into delivering the benefits obtained from holidays to those who wish to take them.

Cara Aitchison provides a number of theoretical reflections on her recent empirical study into the relationship between disability and social inclusion. Arguments are put forward to explain the lack of research into leisure and disability which has had the effect of marginalising the disabled from the mainstream. The author contends that taking a wider view of social and cultural exclusion offers the potential for greater theoretical sophistication within leisure studies.

Kim Polistina assesses how, in Australia, views of appreciative outdoor recreationalists and Aboriginal and Torres Strait Islander people are silenced by dominant social and leisure discourses. For instance, the compartmentalisation of leisure and the governmental emphasis placed on competitive sports in built environments undermines the aforementioned groups' attempts to engage in leisure activities holistically in the natural environment. The inclusion of Aboriginal groups into tourism programmes, while offering the potential for increased recognition, also risks locating the group as a museum artefact, thus excluding their culture from the present.

The Labour Government's apparent desire to widen the welfare debate has raised the profile of the term social exclusion both within and outwith academic circles. The papers published here demonstrate the breadth of areas to which leisure researchers have applied the concept, and the depth of analysis required to inform the debate. Without this rigorous theorising of both social exclusion and (crucially) its relationship to leisure, there is a risk of inappropriate linkages being made which fail to grasp the complexity of both social exclusion and inclusion in the early 21st Century.

References

Bramham, P. (1994) 'Leisure and the postmodern city', in I. Henry (ed) *Leisure: Modernity, postmodernity and lifestyles* (LSA Publication No. 48). Eastbourne: Leisure Studies Association, pp. 83–104.

Coalter, F. (2000) 'Public and commercial leisure provision: Active citizens and passive consumers?', *Leisure Studies* Vol. 19, No. 3: pp. 163–181.

Coalter, F., Allison, M. and Taylor, J. (2000) *The role of sport in regenerating deprived urban areas*. Edinburgh: Scottish Executive Central Research Unit.

Collins, M. and Kennet, C. (1998) 'Leisure, poverty and social inclusion: The growing role of leisure cards in public leisure services in Britain', *Local Governance*, Vol. 24, No. 2: pp. 131–142.

Deem, R. (1999) 'How do we get out of the ghetto? Strategies for research on gender and leisure for the twenty-first century', *Leisure Studies* Vol. 18, No. 3: pp. 157–177.

Henry, I. (1995) 'Leisure and social stratification: The response of the State to social restructuring in Britain', in K. Roberts (ed) *Leisure and social stratification* (LSA Publication No. 53). Eastbourne: Leisure Studies Association, pp. 49–58.

Murdock, G. (1994) 'New times/hard times: Leisure, participation and the common good', *Leisure Studies* Vol. 13, No. 4: pp. 239–248.

Oppenheim, C. and Harker, L. (1996) *Poverty: The facts*. London: Child Poverty Action Group.

Rojek, C. (1995) *Decentring leisure*. London: Sage.

Scraton, S. (1994) 'The changing world of women and leisure: Feminism, "postfeminism" and leisure', *Leisure Studies* Vol. 13, No. 4: pp. 249–261.

Wynne, D. (1998) *Leisure, lifestyle and the new middle class*. London: Routledge.

The Potential of Outreach Sports Initiatives for Young People to Achieve Community Development and Social Inclusion through Leisure

Fiona McCormack

Buckinghamshire Chilterns University College

Introduction

This research was conducted as part of wider study into the role of active leisure based interventions with young people at risk of offending. Many of these young people demonstrate key aspects of social exclusion and one of the research objectives was to examine whether primary level interventions as part of a community development process reduce the problems associated with social exclusion. The case study selected was the Community Services Street Sport initiative based in Stoke on Trent. This paper will review the results of this research by first considering briefly the theoretical background. Then the rationale for the creation of Street Sport and this research design will be summarised before considering the effectiveness of this project and identifying two key factors in the success of this approach.

Background

Welfare philosophy, based on treating the external, or structural, factors causing delinquency, such as poverty and the social residential setting, is the basis for primary intervention. One major example of this is Area Intervention schemes directed at all residents in a specific residential area, which were analysed by Lundman (1993). He suggested that the basic philosophy behind these projects was that:

> ... it makes little sense to focus primary attention on individual juveniles. They are the symptoms rather than the cause. Instead, preventative attention must be directed at high delinquency neighbourhoods generally and delinquent beliefs and traditions in particular. (p. 18)

Local initiatives are important, particularly in deprived inner city areas. Many of these projects are voluntary initiatives supported by some public money: for example, City Challenge. The case for area projects is further supported in Britain by the rise in importance of community development work in social policy. This was demonstrated in the findings of the Policy Action Team's report (DCMS, 1999) and the strategy of the Social Exclusion Unit for neighbourhood renewal (Regeneration Through Sport Conference, 1999). Such initiatives have attracted funding from the Single Regeneration Budget, City Challenge and the urban programmes. A report on Sport and Social Exclusion identified that:

> The English Sports Council has given priority in its lottery funding to deprived districts and wards where a quarter of the population live under its Priority Areas Initiative. (Collins *et al.*, 1999: p. 18)

Traditionally, recreational projects have been included in this type of intervention with the aim of offering opportunities and facilities for local residents, thus improving the social environment by reducing the number of bored young people on the streets. This welfare and education philosophy attempts to ensure that all young people are aware of the opportunities and the method to access these activities.

Constructive leisure activity is a very broad area, but for this research it was defined as leisure activity that conforms to society's norms and offers benefits to the participant. Constructive leisure behaviour can be defined in terms of activities — either participatory such as swimming, or 'creative' activities in arts and music — which offer positive impacts for the individual and society. Non constructive use of leisure time includes activities such as vandalism and drug abuse which harm society or the individual. Constructive leisure behaviour continues to be encouraged through public sector subsidised provision and contracted services from private companies.

Politicians and government policy in recent years have embraced the theory that constructive leisure is a tool to reduce delinquincy and develop communities. The Scarman Report (1982) suggested that the Brixton riots were closely linked to a lack of constructive leisure opportunities for young people. In the 1990s this argument was supported by the high levels of youth unemployment in Britain, which leaves thousands of young people with no direction, little money and plenty of free time. However preparing young people to benefit from this free time has generally been ignored by both schools and the youth service. This has left the responsibility for leisure education to the family. In most families this was adequately provided, but in the often chaotic family structures of many socially excluded communities this process cannot be relied upon. For these young people the assimilation of positive and constructive use of leisure time from a supportive family is unlikely. Many socially excluded families will have little experience of the choices and processes by which leisure opportunity is accessed. This may result in their exclusion from a process that enables "individuals to enhance the quality of their lives in leisure" (Mundy and Odum,

1979: p.2). and should result in "increasing the individuals' options for satisfying quality experiences in leisure" (Mundy and Odum, 1979: p.13).

Constructive leisure participation offers benefits in terms of interest, opportunity for self expression, and social interaction. Unlike sport and physical recreation, constructive leisure need not test physical ability, nor offer an enforced sense of competition. Examples of leisure education and community-based constructive leisure can be found in the USA, as identified by Witt and Crompton (1996). Their study included the example of Madison School Community Recreation department who, through providing multiple strategies for reaching at-risk youth, demonstrated improvements in a number of protective factors for at-risk young people including greater participation in activities, attention to school study and increased the amount of time spent with adults and peers in positive activity.

The Case Study — Street Sport, Stoke on Trent

Street Sport was an example of an outreach sports intervention operating at primary level. It provided single two-hour sports sessions across the city, in locations where young people were known to gather. The sessions were held each week and young people could attend free of charge for as long as they wished.

Street Sport was the result of a successful funding application to the West Midlands Sports Council. In April 1994 outreach services were launched with a three year start-up grant. The roots of the project had been developed in the 1970s, through detached youth work provided by the Hanley Youth Project. The philosophy of this work was summarised by Kevin Sauntry, Manager of Community Recreation, in a June 1997 interview:

> ... there is a negative lagoon of drugs, crime, prostitution and victimisation. Youth work must be preventative and work upstream of this lagoon, with the objective of getting inter generational talking going and a network of community support.

The response to this need was a combination of community development and recreation services which were described as a programme of activities including play schemes, play training, community events, establishing residents associations and formal community networks.

The concept of Street Sport was closely linked to community development objectives as demonstrated by the following statement:

> Intended to provide an insight into the effectiveness of recreation outreach work on young people in terms of deflecting negative behaviour into constructive activity.
>
> A pilot project directed towards exploring ways of using play as a gateway to introducing sport to infants and juniors so that they may develop an appetite

for it through their lives.

A project directed towards exploring methods of using recreational activities with young people as an approach to promoting harmony in communities. Intended to offer a valuable indication as to how we can have a significant effect on improving relationships between communities and adolescents in our further recreational strategies. (Leisure and Recreation Committee, 1995)

There were also clear guidelines to what should be expected of Street Sport:

"Street Sport is not ... A mass participation in sport scheme At this point in time a service available in all areas of the city. A quick fire, immediate problem solving project. Able to meet the total recreational needs of all young people in the City. (Leisure and Recreation Committee, 1995)

Although Street Sport did not provide a regular head count for sessions, diary entries and observations suggested that average attendance was 12 participants. There were 7 sessions a week, weather permitting. This would imply an average of 84 young people a week involved in Street Sport, and total annual attendance of 4200 based on operating 50 weeks per year.

Street Sport was not actively marketed, and it did not aim to bring more young people out on the street. Rather, it aimed to contact and provide for the recreational needs of young people already on the streets. In this way it directly addressed a significant cause of community friction in young people 'hanging about'. Such young people are often seen as the cause of friction and crime, but they are also vulnerable to becoming victims of crime. Street Sport sessions were provided in locations around the city from Monday to Friday evenings all year round, with additional day-time sessions throughout the school holidays.

As an outreach initiative Street Sport used mobile sports equipment, such as temporary football goals, to facilitate sessions on agreed sites. The evening sessions were supported through the use of a converted transit van equipped with gas powered telescopic spotlights. The Community Services Department was also responsible for parks and playgrounds, and this led to the concept of Sports Courts, multi purpose hard courts developed from the concept of 'Kick About Areas' reported in the Sports Council research working paper 20 (Boothby *et al.*, 1981). The Stoke on Trent sports court design included a hard court area marked out for various sports including football and basketball, and provided fixed goals, basketball posts and timed lighting for evening use. The courts also include a seating area for young people. They were funded by community bids for lottery grants and SRB funds and were used by the Street Sport sessions once developed, thus freeing the transit van to support new sessions.

Research design

The evaluation was conducted over six visits, each lasting 3 days over a one-year period (1999). The visits were spaced 8 to 10 weeks apart in February, March, May, July, September, and November. Contact was maintained with the sports leaders between visits by regular reviews of documented diary evidence. Visits were made Monday through Wednesday which allowed three sessions to be observed at the same sites, Stanfields, Bentilee and Cobridge.

Three community groups working with young people were identified during the study: NACRO Moves, Bentilee Volunteers and Youth Action. These community based projects were not leisure-based interventions but provided other support mechanisms for young people at risk of offending. Visits to these projects contributed the views of non-participant young people on the potential of Street Sport, and more general leisure profiles. The structure for each group of interviews was designed to gain a similar range of information while allowing flexibility.

Overt observation of Street Sport sessions was used to assess group dynamics and peer pressure at the Street Sport sessions. A number of sessions for each group were observed and any patterns or changes derived from the records. A session observation *pro forma* was used to note details in a consistent format. Interviews with young people were conducted during the sessions observed in July and September. This timing was identified to allow some trust to have been established with both staff and participants, and because it was likely to provide the best weather for outdoor interviews. The new youth bus, a mobile youth centre, was used to attract interest in the research. It was driven as close to the session site as possible and soft drinks or coffee were provided. The entrance to the bus was used to introduce the research topic through a series of exhibition boards. A video made two years earlier, which covered similar issues, was also played to provoke discussions in a group situation.

Social exclusion, young people and Street Sport

Risk factors related to delinquency in young people have been defined in terms of personal, social and environmental factors (e.g., Witt and Crompton, 1996), and many of these factors are linked to social exclusion. The case study areas — Bentilee, Cobridge and Stanfields — demonstrated a number of these features for young people. All the areas had high levels of unemployment, associated poverty and poor housing.

On the Bentilee estate a detached youth worker suggested that key issues for young people were drugs, unemployment and a lack of leisure opportunity. Bentilee was the largest council housing estate in Europe when it was built in the post war years. It is still a large and sprawling development of mainly terraced and semi- detached houses. The estate consists of a number of 'villages' and recent initiatives have centred on this theme to encourage a stronger sense of community spirit. The area suffers from particularly high levels of unemployment and most of the young people contacted had experienced short or long term unemployment, either personally or in their families. The estate also had a large proportion of young single parents. This may be a contributory factor in explaining the lack of young women at the sessions. For those who had children, their leisure opportunities were significantly reduced. During one observed session, two young women both with children under five watched as their partners played. Although they expressed no desire to take part in this male-dominated session, they also suggested that free time for leisure was almost non-existent for them due to a lack of childcare.

There were a number of play schemes and youth clubs which addressed the needs of the younger children, but as they grew out of these activities there was no acceptable alternative. Hendry (1993) showed that for his sample of young people the transition from structured leisure activity at 13 or 14 presented similar problems:

> This seems like the classic no win situation. A number of respondents claim that the rules at leisure clubs, youth clubs and sports clubs were too strict. On the other hand lack of supervision was clearly not appreciated. (Hendry, 1993: p. 56)

This resulted in young people hanging around areas such as the shops, causing a disturbance for other residents. This situation was reiterated by the manager of the Youth Action Project in the local High School:

> ... young people in this area suffered from the effects of poor housing, low parental support, poor leisure opportunity, drugs and unemployment [which led to] a culture of low aspirations and poor expectations. (Interview, May 1999)

There was a similar situation in Cobridge, which was further strengthened by negative media coverage of young people: "young criminals are making life a misery for families on the Grange estate in Cobridge" (*The Sentinel*, September 7th 1999). The situation was further complicated by the multi cultural nature of the community in Cobridge. The young people from ethnic minorities were seen to be breaking away from the strict family control that had been especially associated with these communities and were now "Involved in petty crime and the drug dealing, as well as some cross cultural conflict" (Manager Cobridge Community Centre, May 1999).

In Stanfields, where young people faced high unemployment and low economic prosperity, there was also the poorest level of facility provision in the three areas. Stanfields was the only area to receive 2 sessions each week, this being achieved through external funding. Stanfields was a small low-rise council housing estate to the north of Burslem; it was on the edge of its ward, which had problems of urban deprivation, crime and unemployment extenuated by a lack of local government funding. The 1991 census provided the most up-to-date population data for this area. Unemployment in the area was 10.9% with lone parent families accounting for 3.9% of the total population. There was a significant population of young people; those under 30 years accounted for 59% of all the residents — thus Stanfields had a large proportion of young people and low economic prosperity.

Observation of the area revealed pockets of run-down housing and few leisure resources for adolescents. There was a large area of open space next to Port Vale Football Club, which Street Sport used during the summer months. The High School provided a number of community activities outside school hours but had little to offer in terms of a drop in environment for the adolescent population. The school allowed Street Sport to use an all-weather surface for the winter session, which had the advantage of basketball posts and a hard surface suitable for roller blades.

Table 1 Young people's concerns about their community

	Bentilee	Cobridge	Stanfields	Non Participants
Drugs	2	5	2	7
Crime	3	3	3	4
Personal Safety	3	0	2	0
Lack of employment	3	2	5	1
Friction	0	2	1	0
Lack of local venues	4	5	5	2
totals	15	17	18	14

Since the project aimed to address community development, young people were asked about their communities. Their concerns are shown in Table 1, and unsurprisingly drugs were the most commonly identified concern.

Young people were also asked in the interviews about their experiences of crime. Only five Street Sport and seven non participants gave full answers. Of these, four reported being stopped or cautioned by the police, two being victims of crime and five being involved in minor offences such as vandalism. One participant admitted significant involvement in drug related offences. [It is believed that these reported levels of involvement in crime were lower than the true level, since people underestimate sensitive issues (Foddy, 1993).] Seven of the young people interviewed felt that boredom caused youth crime and that leisure provision would help to prevent them offending; the Audit Commission sample (1996) gave a similar response.

The impact of Street Sport on participants and their communities

The success of Street Sport in providing sustainable leisure opportunity for socially excluded young people was closely linked to the effectiveness of leisure education. The outreach workers took time out of the sports session to mingle with spectators and those not currently involved in the sports. This was demonstrated to be effective in building a positive relationship with participants and in providing ongoing support.

There was no cut-off for the Street Sport project and, as long as participants integrated well in the session, they could attend for as long as they wished. This theme of on-going support produced examples of education which could meet the changing needs and abilities of groups and individuals. One example of this work was observed at Stanfields where the participants wanted to set up a junior league football team. The workers helped them to establish a team and win a set of kit through a local competition. The team demonstrated the workers' role as enablers in their leisure education.

However, the role was not simply one of leisure education but also covered social education. This was best demonstrated by the individual case history shown below. The participant, now in his early twenties, had attended regularly for over four years. He had experienced a number of problems in adolescence including drug abuse, unemployment and crime. He was now making an effort to review his lifestyle and attributed this, in part, to the continued support of the Street Sport team. He identified the importance of regular sessions, which accepted people as individuals, and did not exclude those who failed to meet the standards of play, but which pointed to the need for certain behaviour in any ordered activity. This gentle approach to counselling and youth work had helped him to survive difficult years, and had given him a new perspective on lifestyle options.

In a wider analysis of reported leisure time activity for participants and non participants in Street Sport, the quantitative data revealed some significant differences in behaviour. The sessions targeted young people who congregate on the street. The interview questions sought to establish how common this was, as shown in Table 2.

Table 2   Reported leisure venues for young people Activity

	Participant n =14	Non participant n =11
At home	3	3
Hanging around	8	10
Pubs	4	4
Leisure Centres	1	
Parks / sports courts	7	3

Young people who spend their time 'hanging around' on the streets are at greater risk of offending for a number of reasons. Residents and the police said that young people congregating in groups resulted in nuisance calls to the police, whether or not justified. The presence of these groups was synonymous for older residents with the threat of crime, as shown in the interview with a Stanfields resident:

> The problem of petty crime and vandalism must come from the groups of youngsters who are always on the streets. When they are there in big groups at night, older residents are frightened to go out. (Resident A, Stanfields, September 1999)

The fear translated to nuisance calls to the police as reported in an interview at Burslem LPU:

> We get quite a lot of petty nuisance calls regarding young people causing a disturbance. We have to address this and respond to the residents but this creates friction between us and the young people as we are always moving them on. From this situation there is a risk that problems can escalate. (September 1999).

Young people gathering on the streets are also vulnerable to negative influences from their peer group and others. Therefore, if Street Sport altered leisure behaviour and moved the young people off the street then this was a positive outcome. The information in Table 2 would suggest that participants in Street Sport are less likely to hang around in the street. Only 57% of participants reported this as a significant feature of their leisure, whereas 90% of non-participants did so. It would be naive to suggest that there is a direct link between Street Sport and reduced hanging around. However, since Street Sport operated through outreach work, all the young people involved had been hanging around before participation. This was confirmed by a female participant in Stanfields:

> I found out about Street Sport through my friends when we were just hanging around. ... I don't hang around on the streets as much any more, in summer I prefer to play sport in the parks in winter I only go out now if my friends are there. (female, 16: interview Stanfields, September 1999)

The evidence from interviews with participants who had been involved in Street Sport for more than 6 months indicated that the project had altered leisure behaviour. There was greater use of parks for informal sports activity among Street Sport participants as shown in Table 2, and this was confirmed by interviews with established players at both Stanfields and Bentilee:

> Before Street Sport we might kick a ball around in the streets but we rarely met at the park and organised a kick around. Now we have the team and meet to practice regularly, there is less time to hang around. (male, 18: interview Stanfields, July 1999)

> ... the sports area is open all the time and we sometimes play outside the sessions. (male, 16: interview Bentilee, July 1999)

Reported leisure patterns for this group were varied and included football, tennis, snooker, golf, rounders, cinema, pubs and play schemes. In 30% of the sample participation in these activities was as part of a family group. The remainder were with their peers. They wanted to participate in recreation primarily to socialise and for the enjoy-ment. Competition and exercise were secondary motivations.

Therefore it would appear that, for participants who regularly attended Street Sport sessions for more than 6 months, there was a change in leisure patterns: they all reported playing some sport outside the sessions and there was reduced incidence of hanging around on the streets. There was a discount card scheme called Recreation Key in Stoke on Trent which gave reduced prices to those on low income. Only one Street Sport participant had heard of this scheme, so there is little evidence of improved knowledge among participants of the leisure opportunities available.

An important aim of Street Sport was to support the Community Services work in terms of community development, through reaching young people and improving communication with these age groups. A summary of the perceptions of community representatives are presented here.

Street Sport was generally supported by the local schools. The head teacher at Hay-wood High School was particularly supportive of the Street Sport project. She com-mented that the majority of her pupils were well-disciplined and motivated; problems associated with young people, such as crime and vandalism, were restricted to a minority. Her pupils needed somewhere to play and meet outside school time, preferably with some adult support, as this was sometimes missing in the home environment. Street Sport had, she felt, reduced vandalism in the school grounds by allowing legitimate access. The project leader of Youth Action at Mitchell High School commented that friction in the community was caused by a lack of mutual understanding. He sup-ported the concept of Street Sport, but felt that more frequent sessions were needed.

In Stanfields the local councillor was concerned about the lack of activities and support for young people in the Stanfields area. She pointed out that both Street Sport and detached youth work had an important role, but that something more permanent was needed. When asked whether the proposed sports court would address this, she commented that this would depend on the management of the facility.

Two female residents were also interviewed about the Stanfields estate, young people and Street Sport. They commented that young people were constantly hanging around in the streets and they attributed this to both a lack of venue and working parents. These young people caused disturbances, were seen to be responsible for crime and were a threatening presence when these residents considered going out at night. The age range of these young people was between 10 and 14 years. On this basis, and the fact that many drove cars to the Street Sport session, led these residents to conclude that Street Sport was not really addressing the problem created by young people hanging around on the Stanfields estate.

In terms of crime and policing, the community police regarded burglary, drugs and car crime as the most serious problems facing this area. They acknowledged that the fear of crime in this community was very high. This could then be linked to reported friction between groups of young people and the older community. The police reported considerable friction caused by noise, vandalism and football in the streets. They felt that some of these issues were linked to poor levels of leisure provision in the area. They acknowledged the important role that Street Sport played in reducing community tension but felt that more was needed. They identified a need for Street Sport scheme to run alongside play schemes during the holidays, as this was a time of increased crime and tension. The problem facing young people in this area was that, particularly in winter, there was nowhere to play football when Street Sport was not in operation.

Community workers in Stanfields regarded the physical environment, most aspects of community services and economic prosperity as poor. Street Sport was seen as a positive move to reducing friction but since the hard court was unavailable outside of the fixed session the project could only be seen as a short-term diversion. The other perception of Street Sport was that it was a dedicated football scheme aimed at young men. The young men were generally causing greatest friction but young girls were increasingly seen as a problem, not addressed by Street Sport.

In Cobridge there was a new community centre, equipped with meeting rooms, a fitness room, changing rooms, hall, kitchen and a bar. The centre was well used by older members of the community from all cultural groups. The community centre manager was interviewed about young people and community issues. The manager highlighted the need for an all-weather surface for sports since the open grass pitches were unusable at night and in adverse weather. He felt that the young people needed something for themselves. He reported that there had been great enthusiasm by young people about the community centre, but this had turned to disillusionment and aggression when they realised that the centre was mainly targeted at adults. He felt that Cobridge lacked sports provision for young people who generally came from families that offered minimal support and exerted little control over them. Street Sport was therefore an important solution to some of these issues.

A mother in Cobridge was interviewed about the Street Sports session that her sons were attending. She felt that young people and their parents would value any casual activity session. There had been hope that the community centre would provide something for young people with or without their parents. However, with the exception of occasional sessions this was not the case. Parents in Cobridge found it difficult to support positive leisure patterns when there were so few facilities within the community.

The interviews with youth workers demonstrated the feeling that Street Sport was a good concept, but was viewed as an isolated attempt to introduce football to a limited audience of young men. Generally the Street Sport session, although well established with the participants, had limited impact in terms of community development or acceptance. There were a number of agencies, both voluntary and statutory, working in this area and this could explain the community's view of Street Sport and other initiatives as another "limited quick fix solution to a complex problem" (Youth Worker, interview Willfield CEC, May 1999).

To summarise, the Street Sport project represented a serious attempt at community development work with adolescents. The impacts were difficult to measure, but in each area the sessions were known about by older residents, and seen as a positive move for young people. If nothing else the sessions had convinced some of the residents of the needs of young people and the possibility of reducing friction by providing for this group. This was exemplified by the comment of one resident in Stanfields: "We need somewhere for youngsters go and some activities for them.... Unless this is addressed they will continue to cause trouble on the streets" (Resident B, interview Stanfields Inter Agency Meeting, September 1999).

Factors affecting the impact of Street Sport on community development and social exclusion

Two key aspects of the project were identified as important in achieving a positive outcome in terms of community development and reducing the problems associated with the quality of leisure opportunity in socially excluded communities. These were the nature of the service organisation and the process of implementation.

Organisation: The Community Services Department evolved from an independent community-based initiative, the Hanley Youth Project. The ideals and work of this organisation were incorporated into the new Community Services Department. The Community Recreation Team was able to provide non facility-based services in local communities, drawing on a range of funding opportunities such a SRB (Single Regeneration Budget) and lottery money for community bids.

To create the Community Services Department several different functional areas were brought together: parks, greenspace, playgrounds, special needs, children's play, community art, events, outreach and environmental conservation, as shown in Table 3. These very different service areas were combined, with an emphasis on involving communities and enabling individuals by providing training opportunities. The focus for these activities was on using local parks and open spaces.

Implementation: In Street Sport the criteria were simple; the outreach workers should meet the demands of young people using community resources. This process was identified as a continuum of provision from childhood, through adolescence to adulthood. Initially community recreation reached children within their communities through play services, and a comprehensive delivery of holiday play schemes directed at children up to 12 years of age. The play service was an important element in community recreation for two main reasons.

(1) The ethos and policy for play provision in terms of equality; opportunity and community involvement were used to shape subsequent initiatives such as Street Sport.

Table 3

Section	Responsibility
Community Development	'Bringing communities together in partnership with the City Council'
Play Services	'Providing a variety of play opportunities'
Play ground Provision	'Provision and maintenance of open access play areas'
Play training	'For play scheme leaders, schools, community groups'
Special Needs	'Integration throughout all service areas'
Outreach Services	'Connecting with young people — Street Sport'
Community Art Services	'Support communities' art and promotional needs'
Event and Support Services	'Infrastructure for all other services'
Event Training	'Community training to manage events'
Environmental Conservation	'Involvement of people in the wildlife management and practical conservation throughout the parks and green spaces'
Courses	'Training opportunities for all services'

Source: City of Stoke on Trent Community Services Poster

(2) The play service reaches 48 districts within Stoke on Trent and makes
    contact with parents and children in these areas. The approach involves
    creating partnerships with local people, which provides important contacts
    for other initiatives. In 1998/9 partnerships were established with 33
    community groups through play schemes. (Interview, July 1999)

The play schemes were high profile services which provided a popular distraction for
primary age children. In this way the p in June 1997 lay schemes provided an important
basis to create a more positive community image for children. This positive energy and
enthusiasm generated in children required direction and encouragement in adolescence.
        The community recreation team had sought to offer a transition from play scheme
activities to community involvement in adulthood. The delivery was conducted in three
ways: outreach sports workers; hang out shelters alongside sports areas; and the Sports
Court Network. This three-pronged approach ensured that the delivery was seen not
simply as another football session, which simply provided a few hours diversion, but
as part of a planning process to meet the needs of young people within their communities. The process engaged young people in visible positive activity, usually in the
form of a football session. This process aimed encourage a positive dialogue with the
community and increased recognition that the needs of these young must be addressed.

The internal documentation for Street Sport demonstrates a clear process for service delivery with distinct approaches or methods at each stage. The overall process is demonstrated in the diagram in Figure 1. The diagram demonstrates how the process of service delivery relies on consultation with both young people and their communities at every stage. The documentation pointed out that: "An important factor in the initial development work was to utilise and strengthen existing links within the community" (Street Sport, 1994: p. 2).

Initial contact was made with a small group of teenagers: this stage is described as 'reconnaissance'. The reconnaissance collected evidence under the headings 'People and Services' (quantitative data) and 'Values and Attitudes' (qualitative data). The values and attitudes data identified social boundaries and problem areas, and was collected by "involvement and communication with the neighbourhood through a broad range of approaches ...Working with schools, 'Street Sport', linking in to Residents Associations gaining acceptance into any social gathering — pubs, clubs, celebrations etc." (Proposal for Street Sport, 1994).

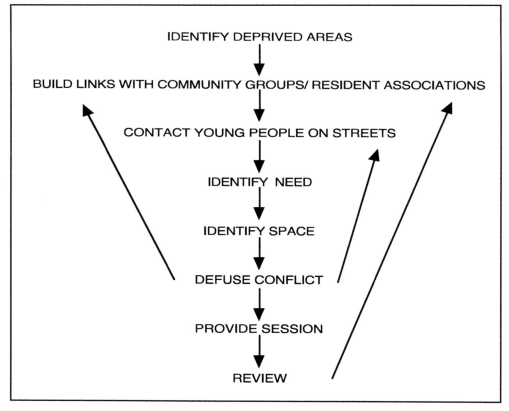

Figure 1   Street Sport consultation process

Contact with young people was made through outreach techniques developed by the youth service for detached workers. Outreach workers made contact with young people "where they naturally congregate — on street corners, outside shops, in parks etc., engaging in conversation, to enable us to learn how we can serve them best" (Internal document 'Why Street Sport?', undated).

In preparing staff for this method of working, Street Sport adhered to the methods of operation and management as recommended by the National Federation of Detached Youth Work. Once established in the team, workers were supported through regular team meetings to explore issues and provide training or guidance.

When the reconnaissance was complete then sessions were provided on a regular basis, usually one evening per week, at a selected site. The choice of site was based on capacity, physical access and suitability for the activity. Once established, the sessions were often well attended by a regular core group. However if numbers were low the staff reverted to the reconnaissance work with young people to re establish the session. The process was one of continual review and consultation both with older community members and young people.

Conclusions

The results demonstrated the importance of local solutions involving the community, feedback from community members and young people. Observation suggested that despite the recommendations by Cooper (1989) for the use of partnerships, there was little evidence of multi-agency provision. Despite claims of inter-agency initiatives, there were problems in establishing links with other providers. Street Sport dedicated considerable resources to community liaison and consultations, which was observed to form over half of the day time work of the two full time members. However, despite the potential for active links with youth work, differences in working practice had led to friction rather than co-operation in many cases.

Leisure has been shown to be part, but is unlikely to be all, of the solution to juvenile delinquency and social exclusion. Therefore, better links, partnership and inter agency work are needed to achieve the goal of 'joined up' provision proposed by the Social Exclusion Unit and the PAT 10 report (DCMS, 1999). This was shown in Street Sport to require allocation of resources in terms of staff work load, and therefore has significant cost implications.

References

Audit Commission (1996) *Misspent youth — young people and crime*. Abingdon: Audit Commission.

Boothby, J., Tungatt, M., Anderson, F. and Glyptis, S. (1981) *Kick about areas, Sports Council Research Working Paper 20*. London: The Sports Council.

Collins, M., Henry, I. P. and Houlihan, B.M.J. (1999) *Sport and social exclusion*. London: DCMS.

Cooper, B. (1989) *The management and prevention of juvenile crime problems*. London: Home Office.

DCMS (1999) *PAT 10 report*. London: DCMS.

Foddy, W. (1993) *Constructing questions for interviews and questionnaires: Theory and practice in social research*. Cambridge: Cambridge University Press.

Hendry, L (1993) *Young people's leisure and lifestyles*. London: Routledge.

Lundman, R. (1993) *Prevention and control of juvenile delinquency* (2nd edition). Oxford: Oxford University Press.

Mundy, J. and Odum, L. (1979) *Leisure education: Theory and practice*. New York: Wiley and Sons.

Lord Scarman (1982) *The Scarman Report*. London: Penguin.

Social Exclusion Unit (1998) Bringing Britain Together. London: Cabinet Office.

Street Sport (1994) *Annual report*. Stoke on Trent City Council.

Witt, P. and Crompton, J. (1996) *Recreation programs that work for at risk youth: The challenge of shaping the future*. Pennsylvania: Venture Publishing.

Delivering Public Leisure Services: Integrating People, Places and Partnerships

Francis Lobo

Edith Cowan University, Perth, Western Australia

Introduction

The paper traces the development of leisure services delivery in Australia over the past fifty years. As times and economic circumstances have changed, the service delivery paradigm shifted. Rolling back the Welfare State towards hard nosed economic rationalist policies have ensured inequitable access of leisure services to many classes of citizens. The paper briefly analyses transient stages from community development models to more commercial orientations, including Compulsory Competitive Tendering and Best Value approaches. Through a case study approach of unemployed young adults a strategy is proposed integrating people, places and partnerships towards a more equitable service delivery system. The following sections of the paper examine the leisure service delivery paradigm, and researches leisure delivery in nine local authorities in Western Australia. Leisure delivery is examined through seven variables: organisation philosophy; personal philosophy; economic demands; contracting services; equity measures; unemployment programs; and types of programs. Pseudonyms are used for the seven local authorities to preserve their identity. *Info*

The leisure service delivery paradigm

Over the past fifty years, the leisure service delivery paradigm has been characterised by several approaches. They include: community service and development; marketing and commercial; humanitarian and humanistic; benefits based; social action; compulsory competitive tendering; and best value.

In its early formulations 'recreation and park administration' was community service based. It was viewed as an important governmental function, one that had the potential for considerable good within a community. As early as 1948, Meyer and Brightbill succinctly summarised this approach as:

> Recreation had no peer, with the possible exception of a desirable family environment, in strengthening and preserving the best in children and youth stabilising family and community living ... It is the first line of opportunity in preventing social ills ... (pp. 6–7)

This approach characterised recreation and leisure service delivery in the United States and Australia during the 1960s and 70s. Characteristic of this approach was the idea that human service was the essential function of government, and although various agencies and organisations might have specific human service functions, delivery was based on linkages between agencies to provide a broader base of services than any one agency could provide (Niepoth, 1983). It came to be known as the community development approach.

During the 1980s there was a change in the prevailing philosophy of leisure service delivery. A declining tax base, inflation, and increased operational costs made it necessary for many leisure service agencies to make dramatic cutbacks. Along with these austerity measures came a more business-oriented approach to leisure service. Modelled after commercial recreation ventures, public agencies began to adopt a 'marketing approach' (Howard and Crompton, 1980; Crompton, 1987) to service delivery. Torkildsen (1992) summarised this change as follows:

> Public sector marketing is a hybrid of approaches which evolved historically and are caught up with commercial approaches, primarily to limit subsidy or help the facilities pay for themselves. (p. 343)

This commercial orientation to recreation has several major benefits. It makes management more accountable, it encourages more efficient use of resources and personnel, and it encourages more public visibility through marketing and advertising. It, however, is not without drawbacks — chief of which is its tendency to exclude from service the very people who need it most. Furthermore, there is also a legitimate concern that the values and traditional philosophy of the recreation profession will give way to business philosophy where profit is the motivation for service, and the bottom line the principal criterion for success.

Perhaps the main weakness of the marketing approach to leisure is that it is based on a logical positivistic philosophy that is clearly materialistic and linear in nature. Such a philosophy takes a narrow view of leisure, viewing it in quantitative terms. This perspective, born out the Puritan Work Ethic, subscribes to the notion that leisure is discretionary or excess time. From this perspective, the leisure service agency is primarily concerned with marketing activities and programs that have appeal to the paying public. Murphy (1980) warned about this approach to service delivery:

> Utilising a discretionary time perspective as the only philosophical basis for leisure service programming is nearsighted. It serves only to keep people where they are; it perpetuates the myth of an industrial rhythm of life; it limits the development of human potential and reduces the prospects for a high standard of quality of life ... (p. 198)

What Murphy was calling for was a humanistic approach to leisure service delivery. He argued that leisure service should be concerned not just with the provision of leisure activities, but with human and community development. His view of a leisure service was expansive and holistic. For Murphy leisure service had to include the remediation of factors that prevented individuals from meaningful involvement in the community, limited their capacity for self-expression, and hindered their opportunities for rich and varied leisure experiences.

The harsh economic reality of the 1980s in the Western world did little to promote Murphy's view of humanistic leisure service delivery. The marketing model seemed to predominate the thinking of most planners throughout the 1980s. With the 1990s came the realisation that the business approach to public recreation was eroding the place of the recreation professional. Godbey warned that unless leisure service included a humanistic component, it would soon "cease to exist ..." (Kraus, 1997: p. 389).

In Australia reforms in the name of economic rationalism have failed to increase choices for most people or to fulfil the utilitarian principle of the greatest happiness for the greatest number. They have failed to redistribute income equally. Instead, there has been a significant redistribution of income upwards; that is, the richer have got richer (Pusey, 1991). The counterfeit of economic rationalism is massive unemployment. Unemployment not only causes economic disadvantage to children, but they also experience the trauma their parents are going through (Langmore and Quiggin, 1994). The recreation of these children is adversely affected (Lobo and Watkins, 1995). Young unemployed males and females are restricted in their leisure as a result of material, psychological and social deprivation (Lobo, 1997). Other disadvantaged segments of society face similar problems. Consequently, some leisure scholars have denounced the market approach. Roberts (1999) notes that the market experience has been a proven failure in the promise of a satisfying life. He suggests that we are driven more powerfully by more socially induced wants than by a more basic nature. Parker (1999) supports Roberts in that people who use their leisure capital creatively and pleasurably, by themselves or in the company of others have better leisure experiences than those who turn to the market to consume leisure as a commodity.

In the United States, there is a blending of the old and the new. The human services approach is coming together with the marketing approach to produce a more benefits based delivery system. Although, not full-circle, this return to a more humanitarian perspective has produced in some leisure service agencies, a promising blend of the best elements from the marketing orientation with the social commitment of the early community development model. But when it comes to the needs of the invisible minority, such as the unemployed, this new hybrid model of leisure management may not be enough. Perhaps, another dimension needs to be added to the mix — social action.

The main attribute of social action is advocacy, and this essentially means to champion a cause or group. Edginton, Hanson, Edginton and Hudson (1998: p. 39) describe the social action strategy:

> It presumes that there is a disadvantaged population, great injustice, and a need to force the system, institutions, organisations, and agencies to change the ways they are distributing resources, hence services.

Edginton *et al.* (1998) believe that a leisure service agency can serve as an agent for social change in several ways. Advocacy can be identified by several roles (Edginton and Compton, 1975). Initiator, planner and organiser roles identify the problem, serve as a catalyst and outline a plan of action. The investigator role calls for organising facts and information in support of the group or cause. Help in resolving disputes between the disadvantaged and others can be achieved through the negotiator role. The lobbyist represents the needs of the disadvantaged by influencing decision-makers to make decisions favourable to the disadvantaged group. Counsellor and resource specialists can match individuals and groups with resources and help facilitate desired changes. The educator role assists with awareness of the plight of the disadvantaged and educating the disadvantaged to utilise resources that help themselves. Evaluation steps can be used to determine the degree of change that has occurred and if necessary new strategies that might be introduced to further newly introduced intended changes.

In the early 1980s and the early 1990s the need for the leisure market to become more competitive brought in a new approach to service delivery through Compulsory Competitive Tendering (CCT). With increasing consumerism and competition as a result of CCT, leisure managers had to win CCT contracts and had to meet requirements of CCT specifications. In order to be competitive leisure managers had to adopt quality management procedures and deliver quality programs (Robinson, 2000). Economy, efficiency and effectiveness were the performance indicators of CCT (Williams, 2000).

The flow-on from CCT was the Best Value approach that took hold in the late 1990s and into the new millennium. Through Best Value local authorities are expected to search continuously "… to improve the quality, efficiency and effectiveness of all its services…" (ILAM, 1997: p. 1). Driven by the need to monitor service performance, Best Value relies on the 4Cs principle of challenge, compare, consult and compete. The new approaches are laudable and appropriate for citizens who have the ability to pay for services. But what about those who seek value, but do not have the means? The following sections describe how nine local authorities in the Perth metropolitan area delivered their leisure services.

Method, sample and procedure

Nine providers of sport and recreation services were be selected to be interviewed in-depth to examine strategies to deliver services taking into account the material and psychological deprivations of the unemployed. Special attention was paid to the removal of barriers to participation and sensitivity towards the management, promotion and flexibility to varying and changing needs of the unemployed as well as the providers. The composition of the nine providers included recreation coordinators and senior officers in local authorities in the Perth Metropolitan area and at least two on the city-rural fringe.

Providers' perceptions for services to the unemployed were structured around seven variables. These included organisational policy, providers' philosophy, economic demands, contracting services, equity measures, unemployment programs and types of programs. Based on these variables a profile for local authorities of Wentworth, Shenton, Bradford, Melton, Cranston, Brinkley, Preston, Oakwood and Ravenswood are presented. The foregoing names are pseudonyms for those of local authorities that were studied.

Results

The variables that formed categories in the questionnaire to public providers were: organisation policy; personal philosophy; economic demands; contracting services; equity provisions; unemployment programs; and program types. The similarities and differences are given below.

Organisation policy: The policies of the nine local authorities were fairly consistent in that they wished to be inclusive of the whole community in the provision of facilities and services. Providers had their own way of implementing local authority policy. In the case of Wentworth, they would do so by direct services and supporting self-help agencies and associations. Equity in planning, coordinating, and promotion of services was a valued ideal for Shenton. Melton formed partnerships with clubs and associations. Cranston provided for health and enjoyment outcomes. Brinkley's program was to enhance the quality of life and Oakwood planned for a variety of activities. Only one authority, namely, Preston linked its objectives with financial viability, by providing

Table 1: Organisation policy

Local Authority	Organisation policy
Wentworth	Provision of leisure opportunities to all sectors of the community by direct and supportive self-help services.
Shenton	To plan, manage, co-ordinate and promote services, facilities and resources on basis of equity.
Bradford	Constant communication with the community to satisfy perceived community needs.
Melton	Leisure provision viewed as a community service; philosophy of partnership between council, clubs and organisations.
Cranston	Provision of opportunities for access to all forms of recreation to stimulate and encourage health and enjoyment.
Brinkley	Recognises leisure to enhance quality of life of residents; equality of access seen as important.
Preston	Planning, facilitating of cost effective services with widest possible community access.
Oakwood	Optimise the leisure potential of the community by providing a variety of recreational activities.
Ravenswood	No written policy, but flexibility exists for service delivery.

cost-effective services. Ravenswood had no written policy, but was flexible enough to encourage change. Individual responses to organisational policy are listed in Table 1.

Although philosophies of each local authority were inclusive, they had various methods of implementing policy. If these fragmented approaches were integrated they would form a basis for a coordinated policy for local authorities in the Perth metropolitan area.

Personal philosophy: The personal philosophies of the nine recreation officers were consistent with the policies set out by their local authorities. However, each one made a qualifying statement. At Wentworth, the recreation officer said he was responsible for driving policy. The focus of Shenton was on localisation of facilities and services to encourage accessibility. At Bradford, the policy did little for youth and needed coordination and integration. It was hard to put a dollar value on all recreation services in Melton. Brinkley would like direct delivery of services, rather than the mere provision of facilities. There was disappointment in Preston as policies weren't being implemented. Oakwood experienced conflicts between service delivery and business

Table: 2 Personal policy

Local Authority	Personal policy
Wentworth	Agency policy consistent with the interviewee's position; responsible for driving leisure service delivery and defining performance
Shenton	Consistent with that of employer; leisure seen as best provided at local level, accessible in places where people live and work.
Bradford	Current policy does not cater of the younger population as much as it should; more integrated and co-ordinated approach required.
Melton	Consistent with council policy; not always possible to put a dollar value on a human service.
Cranston	Consistent with that of council, while adding mental to physical health.
Brinkley	Consistent with council policy; would like to see services rather than just facility provision.
Preston	Philosophy consistent with council policy; but stated policies not always implemented.
Oakwood	Consistent with council philosophy, but some inconsistency with service delivery and business efficiency.
Ravenswood	Service delivery policy consistent with those of local authority.

efficiency. In Ravenswood, service delivery was totally consistent with local authority policy. Table 2 indicates the personal philosophies of the recreation officers responsible for the delivery of services.

There were inconsistencies between organisation and personal philosophies of recreation officers. The emphasis of services and manner in which they were delivered varied in each case. Thus organisation and philosophies did not have a good fit.

Economic demands: Services in seven of the nine local authorities were affected by the national competition policy. In Wentworth, Council had to be more accountable for financial losses. Services were assessed against the national competition policy in Shenton. Economic rationalisation had a big effect on services, budgets and quality of services in Melton. It also meant reassessment of services and fees and charges in Cranston. In Brinkley contracting out was a preferred option, while Preston was constrained in facility development because of budget cuts. Oakwood was required to more competitive with public recreation outlets. The small local authority of Bradford

Table 3: Economic demands

Local Authority	Economic demands
Wentworth	Services affected by current economic climate; Council accountable for financial losses resulting from 'national competition' policy.
Shenton	Services affected by economic climate; services assessed against the background of national competition policy.
Bradford	Current economic climate has little impact on service delivery; council provides funds for service delivery.
Melton	Economic rationalism having an influence on budgets and quality of services offered, but assistance still offered 'start up' new clubs.
Cranston	Economic climate requires reassessment of service delivery in relation to charges and use of leisure contractors.
Brinkley	National competition policy taking effect in council's decisions; contracting of services preferred if financially advantageous.
Preston	Affected service delivery; constraints on capital works and budgets requires subsidies from external sources.
Oakwood	Big effect as the council has shifted strategy to more competitive modes of service delivery.
Ravenswood	More emphasis on 'making the dollar go further'; pay as you use system introduced to counter difficulties in paying up-front fees

and Ravenswood, a rural shire on the City fringe did not report the national competition policy affecting services. The various ways in which local authorities responded to economic concerns are listed in Table 3.

The national competition policy influenced how services should be delivered. Concerns about being competitive in the leisure services market consumed local authorities and inclusion of deserving people may have been overlooked.

Contracting services: The local authorities of Shenton, Cranston, Brinkley, Preston and Oakwood had some services leased out to private contractors. Wentworth was in the process of contracting out services. Bradford, Melton and Ravenswood had facilities and services controlled by the Council. In each case where services were contracted out, the objectives of the contractors had to comply with those of the council. If the objectives of contractors were not consistent with those of Council, a contract would not be awarded. However, there were instances at Oakwood and

Table 4: Contracting out

Local Authority	Contracting services
Wentworth	Plans underway to lease out services to private contractors, but contractors' economic interests must be balanced with community interests.
Shenton	Outsourced services should benefit contractor and council; only those with mutual benefits are leased out.
Bradford	No services or facilities are leased out; services directly delivered.
Melton	No leases to private clubs.
Cranston	Some aspects contracted out on a commission basis; objectives of contractors must be consistent with those of the council.
Brinkley	Many services leased out to private contractors; financial objectives often in conflict with social objectives.
Preston	Some services contracted out; objectives of contractors and council not always congruent; biases towards certain sports.
Oakwood	Some services contracted out, especially those where greater efficiency is recognised by a private operator.
Ravenswood	Facilities maintained by council, but services may be leased out.

Brinkley, where financial objectives conflicted with social ones. Attitudes towards contracting out are listed in Table 4.

The data revealed that contracting out was embraced by the majority of local authorities. This was done for purposes of efficiency. However, although some local authorities made contractors comply with council objectives, it was felt that financial objectives conflicted with social ones.

Equity provisions: All of the nine local authorities had some sort of equity provisions at least for certain sections of the community. Seniors came out best in Wentworth, Melton, Cranston, Brinkley, Preston and Ravenswood. In Wentworth, juniors were not charged with fees. Except for Melton and Preston, young unemployed people were not

Table 5: Equity Provisions

Local Authority	Equity provisions
Wentworth	Concessions for services exist for senior citizens, juniors and individuals using specific services; no concessions for young unemployed.
Shenton	Concessions and subsidies for events are available to the community; young unemployed not targeted specifically.
Bradford	No concessions to any sectors of the community, but hire of facilities by interest groups are considerably discounted.
Melton	Concessions available to disadvantaged, including unemployeds; off-peak rates available to the general community; sliding scale rates available.
Cranston	Concessions and discounts available to some community segments, but none exist for unemployed people.
Brinkley	Concessions made for certain segments, such as seniors, but no specific steps taken for the unemployed
Preston	Range of concessions offered — discounts and free access; concessions extended to young unemployed.
Oakwood	No direct concessions as services are heavily subsidised; bulk tickets provide further discounts.
Ravenswood	Reductions for seniors, 'season tickets' are available, but nothing for young unemployed.

given concessions. At Bradford no concessions were awarded to individuals, but groups were treated on a merit basis. The status of services on an equity basis is listed in Table 5. Equity provisions were in place for seniors and in some cases for juniors. Just two local authorities took into account the interests of the unemployed. This indicates that this class of people are either not taken into account or authorities find it difficult to identify and process them for services.

Unemployment programs: All the local authority recreation officers supported the promotion of healthy lifestyles for young people. However, none conducted specific programs for the unemployed. Melton encouraged participation at its facilities during off-peak periods. Cranston encouraged no cost activities by promoting the use of parks and the river. The authorities of Brinkley, Wentworth, Shenton, Bradford and Oakwood

Table 6: Unemployment Programs

Local Authority	Unemployment programs
Wentworth	Favours mainstream and specific programs; cost is a factor; if external funding is available, there is no problem running programs; no steps taken to identify the unemployed.
Shenton	No specific programs for the unemployed, but they can be set up with partnership with other or private agencies.
Bradford	No specific programs exist, but existing costs are not prohibitive. Council would support specific programs if funding is available.
Melton	Healthy lifestyle encouraged; off-peak participation designed to promote participation.
Cranston	Although healthy lifestyles are encouraged, there are no specific programs for the unemployed; use of river facilities and parks are supported.
Brinkley	Healthy lifestyle programs exist for youth, but not specifically for the unemployed; with funds available, council would implement.
Preston	Healthy lifestyles should be encouraged, but council do not have the means and the group is not a focus for them.
Oakwood	No programs exist for unemployed people, but council would consider if funds were available.
Ravenswood	Young unemployed people should be encouraged to lead healthy lifestyles, but no programs exist.

would conduct programs for the unemployed if external funds were available. Shenton would do it in partnership with private agencies. Responses for programs for the unemployed are listed in Table 6.

Specific programs for the unemployed were non-existent. However, there was a willingness to conduct programs or include the jobless if appropriate funding was available.

Program types:. The preferences for program types are listed in Table 7. Most local authorities favoured mainstream programs for the unemployed. Shenton, Bradford, Melton, Cranston, Brinkley and Oakwood expressed a mix of mainstream and specific programs. Specific programs were meant to be stepping stones for integration into mainstream programs. The Officer for Brinkley suggested specific programs for skill

Table 7: Program Types	
Local Authority	Program types
Wentworth	Young jobless need access to facilities and services; finance and time availability should be assessed.
Shenton	Support for mainstream in preference to specific programs; use of passive space for those who do not wish structured leisure services.
Bradford	A balance between specific and mainstream programs; mainstream programs are more integrative and specific ones seen as a 'stepping stone'.
Melton	Combination of mainstream and specific programs preferred.
Cranston	Support for both specific and mainstream programs, with the former seen as the first step to the latter.
Brinkley	Supports integration into mainstream, but sees some advantages in specific programs e.g. Skill development, empowerment.
Preston	In favour of mainstream programs which incorporate concessions.
Oakwood	Specific and mainstream programs favoured.
Ravenswood	Specific programs seen as unsuitable; lack of numbers and motivation seen as problems.

development and empowerment. The Bradford representative saw specific programs as an integration into mainstream ones

There was overwhelming preference for mainstream programs with specific programs being run as stepping stones into mainstream leisure. However, mainstream leisure was seen not for skill development at purpose built facilities, but also in the natural environment.

Implications for equity and inclusion

Research shows that unemployment excludes people in their leisure. However, unemployed people do not react passively to job loss. Through personal agency in varying degrees many cope with unemployment by engaging in activities by drawing on their leisure capital. Concern is expressed for young people who are severely and adversely affected by unemployment. Although many have good coping leisure skills, their frame of mind disables them from engagement in leisure activities. For those affected in this way, they need to know how to access counselling services and be made aware of leisure programs that are affordable to them.

Public providers of leisure should be cognisant about difficulties unemployed persons face in participating in leisure programmes. No plea is made for segregated activities, but rather that unemployed people should be integrated in mainstream programs. With young people Evans and Haworth (1991) suggest that the main activity of the unemployed person be identified. These may include a wide range of things like listening to and playing music, training for marathons, compiling a low budget cookery book, participating in fringe theatre, visiting friends, and casual repair work. Engagement in these activities instils in young people a sense of accomplishment, the chance to use their abilities, to be creative, to use their own judgment and to keep them busy. The main activity would help them to attain and maintain high levels of self-esteem and extend their social networks.

With psychological and financial deprivations weighing heavily on the unemployed, it is recommended that public providers integrate equity into their service delivery policies. They may do this through five distinct strategies (Lobo, 2000).

- Providers of leisure service delivery services should make every attempt to identify and encourage the unemployed to use local sport and leisure facilities through awareness campaigns.
- If discounted rates are offered during off-peak times, then these should be advertised at places that the unemployed frequent, such as job clubs and training agencies.
- Working in partnership with employment and training agencies, providers of sport and leisure services should seek subsidies and arrive at agreements to supply

standard entry cards for services offered at public facilities at no financial
disadvantage to the individuals affected.

- Equity provision for participation of unemployed people in sport and leisure
  should not only feature in policy statements, but must be seen to be promoted and
  implemented.

- Mainstream programs are supported, but if specific programs are conducted for
  the unemployed, they should act as stepping stones towards social integration and
  assimilation into the general community.

The integration of the foregoing recommendations into service delivery policy
documents should ensure that people, places and partnerships will merge and form
inclusive leisure delivery systems that will only take account of unemployed people,
but also others who are likewise disadvantages materially and psychologically.

References

Crompton, J. L. (1987) Doing more with less in the delivery of parks and recreation
    services. State College, PA: Venture.
Edginton, C. R. and Compton D. M. (1975) Consumerism and advocacy: A conceptual
    framework for the therapeutic recreator. Therapeutic Recreation Journal, 9 (1),
    271–29.
Edginton, C. R., Hanson, C. J., Edginton, S. R. and Hudson, S. D. (1998) Leisure
    programming: A service-centred and benefits approach. Boston, Massachusetts:
    WCB McGraw-Hill.
Evans, S. T. and Haworth, J. T. (1991) Variations in personal activity, access to
    categories of experience and psychological well-being in unemployed young
    adults, Leisure Studies, 10, 249–64.
Howard, D. R. and Crompton J. L. (1980) Financing, managing, and marketing
    recreation and park resources. Dubuque, IA: Wm. C. Brown.
ILAM (1997) Best Value: a definition and process, fact sheet 97/10. Goring upon
    Thames: ILAM.
Kraus, R. (1997) Recreation in modern society. (5th ed.). Menlo Park: Benjamin
    Cummings.
Langmore, J. and Quiggin, J. (1994) Work for all: Full employment in the nineties.
    Carlton, Victoria: Melbourne University Press.
Lobo, F. (2000) Youth unemployment: impediment or catalyst to leisure and human
    development. Paper presented at the 6th World Leisure Congress, University of
    Deusto, Bilbao, Spain, July 3–7.
Lobo, F. (1997) Young people, leisure and unemployment in Western Australia. World
    Leisure and Recreation. 39 (4), 4–9.

Lobo, F. and Watkins, G. (1995) Late career unemployment in the 1990s: It impact on the family. Journal of Family Studies. 1 (2), 103–113.

Meyer, H. D. and Brightbill, C. K. (1948) Recreation administration: A guide to its practices. Englewood Cliffs, New Jersey: Prentice-Hall.

Murphy, J. F. (1980) An enabling approach to leisure delivery. In T. L. Goodale and P. A. Witt, (Eds.), Recreation and leisure: Issues in an era of change, pp. 197–210, State College, PA: Venture.

Niepoth, W. F. (1983) Leisure leadership. Englewood Cliffs, NJ. Prentice-Hall.

Parker, S. (1999) Socialist views and experiences. Leisure Issues, 2 (2) pp. 2–3.

Pusey, M. (1991) Economic rationalism in Canberra. Cambridge: Cambridge University Press.

Roberts, K. (1999) Do we know what leisure is good for people? Leisure Issues, 2 (1): p. 2.

Robinson, L. (2000) Following the quality strategy: the reasons for the use of quality management in UK public leisure facilities. Leisure Studies Association Newsletter, No. 55, March: pp. 26–36.

Torkildsen, G. (1992) Leisure and recreation management. London: E & FN Spon.

Williams, C. (2000) Monitoring of public sector leisure services by best value. Leisure Studies Association Newsletter, No. 55, March: pp. 37–40.

Leisure Services and Local Government in Scotland — Time for a Divorce?

Ashley Pringle

Glasgow Caledonian University

Introduction

This paper considers the current position of Leisure (or 'Cultural and Leisure') Services in Scottish Local Government. The question it seeks to address is the inverse of the one being asked of Leisure Services by others in Local Government, with growing insistence. That latter question is — what can Leisure contribute to the strategic priorities of the Scottish Parliament, and of Local Government itself? Foremost amongst these priority areas is that of 'social inclusion' and the contribution of leisure services here became the subject of renewed interest and generated a period of intense research activity, within both UK and Scottish Governments, in 2000. For example:

> DCMS is looking at ways to promote social inclusion elements in culture and leisure policies for the benefit of poor communities ... DCMS published a report that showed the valuable contribution art and sport made to delivering key outcomes of lower long-term unemployment, less crime, better health and better qualifications. (DCMS, 2000)

In Scotland, the autumn of 2000 saw the publication by the Scottish Executive of two substantial reports, focusing on the role of, respectively, the arts and sport in regenerating deprived urban areas (Coalter *et al.*, 2000; Kay and Watt, 2000) Both reports call for 'new ways of working' or 'a change in attitudes' amongst leisure service providers and others, and anticipate a significant role for local authorities as key delivery agents.

This paper, however, asks a much more fundamental — and much older — question: whether Local Government in its current condition is the most appropriate vehicle for delivering 'adequate' Leisure Services, or whether the trend to their externalisation, currently happening in a patchy, ad hoc manner, should not now be actively embraced as the first choice. Without this basic 'adequacy' of provision, it is difficult to see how local government can be regarded as having the essential resources to deliver effectively on the social inclusion agenda, or on any other national policy priority.

The paper refers mainly to the situation in Scotland, where both legislation and the pace of change differ from the rest of the UK, but it seems reasonable to suppose that there are parallels and resonances of interest outside Scotland. One of the distinctive features of leisure provision by local authorities in Scotland is its statutory basis. The Local Government and Planning (Scotland) Act of 1982 requires councils to "ensure that there is an adequate provision of facilities for the inhabitants of their areas for recreational, sporting, cultural and social activities" (p. 2).

Although this appears to encourage a commitment to the service, it has long been recognised as inherently problematic. What constitutes 'adequate' remains unexplained, and, short of action being brought to the courts, no clarification appears to be in prospect. In theory, the local authority could deem that it need provide nothing directly, as the commercial and voluntary sectors, however limited, are between them providing an 'adequate' range of leisure opportunities, even if located outside their area. Bookshops, hotels, fitness clubs, cinemas and private sports clubs could be seen, in the absence of indications to the contrary, as sufficient for the perceived needs of the populace.

Legitimacy and credibility

A current strand of thought on this subject is exemplified by the Audit Commission's recent report 'The Price is Right', which questions the legitimacy of the subsidy entailed in public sector leisure provision. An exposition based on this report comments:

> One may ask whether public leisure services are provided in the interests of the public or for the greater glory of members and officers. There seems to be an absence of objective evidence supporting the case for public leisure provision. (Holmes *et al.*, 2000: p. 17)

As a former Chief Officer in three Scottish local authorities, I would not argue that members and officers are congenitally above such tawdry self-interest: survival in uniquely vulnerable circumstances necessitates a modicum of this quality[1]. However, the view that public-funded leisure facilities are foisted upon reluctant communities bears little scrutiny. In fact, closer to reality are the experiences of, on the one hand, appeasing voluble local demand from communities for new or improved facilities, while on the other, struggling to acquire a share of increasingly scarce capital funding for leisure in the face of contending priorities in Education, Social Work, Transport etc. In truth, such favour as Leisure receives is, arguably, owed to its characteristically local locus. Since other services are specified in detail by national government, local democracy has little room to exercise its prerogative in their delivery. Leisure Services, meanwhile, are seen by communities as functions they can influence directly. The threat to close, or failure to provide, a local swimming pool, library or playing field, invariably produces a voluble stakeholder reaction as intense as any issue confronting local politicians. At such times, members' commitment to public-funded leisure is liable to attain heights of hitherto unsuspected passion!

Public support

The decline in usage figures, particularly at such 'flagship' leisure centres as the Magnum, Irvine, might, in a highly reductionist way, be cited as evidence of the redundancy of local authority leisure provision. As other leisure opportunities, particularly in the commercial sector, increase in range and modernity, it is inevitable that the regional multi-purpose centre will have to at least change its role, and decide how to live with lower attendances — their life-cycle is likely to be relatively short. However, while attendances remain at a level of several hundred thousand per year, closure panics are likely to be premature, unless serious alternatives are offered.

The anti-subsidy argument, however, is more moral and political than practical. It appears to assume a consensus that subsidy should be rigorously targeted only to the disadvantaged/socially-excluded, and therefore public-funded facilities are to be seen as 'providers of last resort'. I would argue a somewhat different case, that, apart from the regional facilities mentioned above, most local authority leisure provision fulfils a key symbolic role in local communities, at least equally important as its defined function. Swimming pools, community sports centres, playgrounds, libraries, local museums, even outdoor sports pitches are valued as foci, giving palpable authentication of a community's integration.

Such a concept is difficult to validate with hard evidence. However, the high level of public support, relative to that for other public services, for the wide range of public sector leisure provision has been evident in national surveys conducted in the 1980s and 1990s by MORI and others.

In two recent consultation exercises conducted by Scottish local authorities, this support was echoed in different contexts:

- In 1997, Fife Council consulted with 6700 local people on a range of options for budget 'savings'. Of 16 options presented, which also included charges for, or reductions in, various education, social work and roads services, 'Cut leisure centre hours' was by far the most unpopular, with a ratio of 6 to 1 against (Accounts Commission, 1998).
- In 1998, a representative survey of 1800 North Ayrshire residents considered their views on each of the services provided by the Council. 91% regarded Leisure Centres as one of the Council's 'foundation services', with 93% regarding outdoor sports facilities likewise. Both these services were placed by residents in group "A" ('important services, well-delivered') of four divisions into which their rating of the Council's services fell. (Ashbrook Research and Consultancy, 1998)

On a more anecdotal level, there is evidence from the now annual round of local authority budget cuts, which has bitten deep into Leisure Services, as discussed in more detail below. It is an oft-repeated scenario for vocal public opposition to these to manifest itself as a form of 'consumer-power', where elected members, taken by surprise at the volume and public awareness of the opposition, are forced to rescind their decisions cutting direct Leisure Services (they usually then blame the officers for them).

Decline

This vocal opposition is most often directed at cuts involving facilities, however: opening hours, threatened closures or, less often, increased charges. Behind this, a significant decline in investment in local authority Leisure Services is going on in Scotland. As the following charts for overall capital and revenue spending illustrate, this can be directly linked with the Scottish Local Government reorganisation of 1995–96, as shown in Figures 1 and 2.

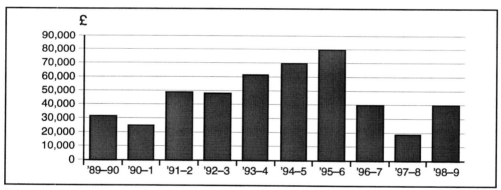

Figure 1   Scottish Local Authority Capital Expenditure on Leisure and Recreation (£000s)

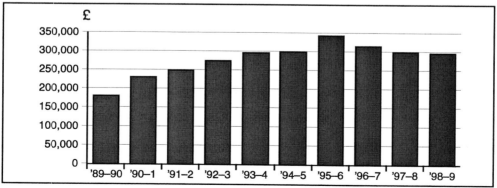

Figure 2   Scottish Local Authority Revenue Expenditure on Leisure and Recreation (£000s)

When compared to trends in overall local authority capital and revenue expenditure (the 'General Fund'), the table below, showing the % percentage spend on Leisure and Recreation, also confirms their relative decline, as shown in Figure 3:

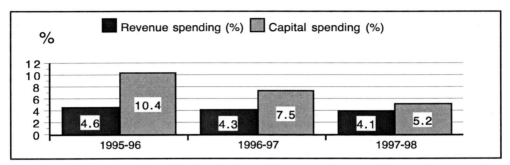

Figure 3   Scottish Local Authority Expenditure on Leisure and Recreation as a Percentage of the 'General Fund'

The impact of this sudden and drastic downturn on provision and participation has not been investigated, despite calls for a systematic audit from COSLA, sportscotland and others. Again, however, the anecdotal evidence is consistent: investment in new and refurbishment of established facilities of all kinds is much reduced and the infrastructure is noticeably decaying. Participation levels, especially amongst children, are reported to be in free-fall. These trends, combined with the vigorous challenge to the professional credibility of leisure providers referred to above, indicate that the health of Leisure Services in local government has never been worse (see Pringle and Cruttenden, 2001 for a detailed analysis).

Other features of the current local government scene can also be regarded as threatening or at least unhelpful distractions, to Leisure Services. Compulsory Competitive Tendering (CCT), an expensive and almost wholly futile exercise in Scotland, where not a single Leisure contract attracted outside competition, has given way to the Best Value Regime (BVR). Although seen as an opportunity to engage public consultation, performance review and 'continuous improvement', the cuts sustained by Leisure Services over the years have contributed to making Best Value a bureaucratic monster. Data collection, interpretation and presentation have assumed such monumental scale that they dwarf the primary function of service delivery. In retrospect, Best Value, like CCT, was always more about the mistrust of central government for local authority autonomy, in a climate where councils have primarily functioned as convenient scapegoats. It is a game where civil servants hold the cards, and use them to reinforce their own status.

Much the same can be said of the culture of Performance Measurement, which has increased exponentially in the public services under this government. Where Performance Indicators (P.I.s) for waste disposal, exam passes or homelessness may have varying degrees of relevance and validity, the P.I.s for Leisure have hitherto featured the crudest of raw data. These typically pertain, for example, to the cost of maintaining a given area of sports turf or swimming pool — of limited interest or relevance, and effectively demeaning to the nature of the service.

Leisure Services in Scottish local government have fallen away from their positive image in their heyday of the late 1970s/early 1980s as the 'good news' of local government. They are now more like the infant cuckoo in the nest, screeching with starvation and rejected by indifferent parents. Local government is, of financial necessity, retrenching to what it considers its 'core functions' of Education, Social Work, Housing and Cleansing. The next stage could see even these externalised through various mechanisms, en-route to the 'enabling council', dreamed of by successive governments.

Externalisation

It is in this context that the externalisation of Leisure Services management into Trusts, Limited Companies or Industrial and Provident Societies (a.k.a. 'Workers' Co-operatives') has been gradually extending throughout Scotland. Something of this kind now exists in Edinburgh, West Lothian, East Lothian, Perth, Highland, Clackmannanshire, Moray, East and North Ayrshire. Initially, Councils entered into many of these for the short-term expedient of savings on rates and VAT on income. It has since become apparent, however, that further advantages develop, e.g.:

- Involvement of community representatives and professional expertise on management boards.
- Enhanced capacity to attract external funding for investment in the service.
- Escape from the dead hand of Council's central departments (who have often pursued their own agenda rather than that of the service they nominally support)
- Escape from the short-termism of political interference
- Circumvents the tortuous bureaucracy of the Best Value regime.
- Increased sense of 'ownership', with consequently improved morale, amongst staff.

Of these, it is the first, which, I would suggest, is the most interesting. As argued earlier, Leisure Services historically emerged from and have since drawn support from their local character. This new opportunity which externalisation represents, to 're-connect' with the community, creates the conditions both for the increased relevance of the services and a more general re-vitalisation of grass-roots democratic participation.

Here also lies potential for a more fruitful relationship with the commercial sector. Rather than a spurious 'competition' between public and private provision, because Trusts etc. are more open to outside involvement, the sectors can speak more constructively to each other, complement each other's role, and operate more flexibly to serve the local community. The boundaries are being removed (see Simmons, 2000).

One particularly interesting extension of the beneficial externalisation of Leisure Services, and a model that Scottish Local Authorities should be contemplating, is the London Borough of Hounslow. Here, the entire Leisure Services function has been externalised into a 'Community Initiatives Partnership' (CIP) (London Borough of Hounslow, 1999). This comprises a central Board with a number of subsidiaries corresponding to the different areas of service — Sport, Arts Libraries, Parks/Countryside etc. Each draws on community representatives with a particular interest or expertise in each area. Hounslow has gone beyond anything attempted so far in Scotland, where externalisation has mainly been restricted to Sport and Leisure Centres, where the greatest financial saving is made. The 're-connection with the community', referred to above, is expanded much further in a CIP than a more restricted Trust arrangement. The opportunity to rejuvenate the benefits of a comprehensive and integrated Leisure Service should therefore attract Scottish Councils, especially in the context of Community Planning, which seems likely to be their core role in future (for an analysis of the initial stages of Community Planning in Scotland, see Rogers *et al.*, 1999). The future of this growing trend towards Trusts is, however, largely dependent on their capacity to attract ongoing investment, in order to repair and expand provision that has in many places deteriorated under local authority control.

Conclusion

Leisure Services in Scotland's local authorities have for several years been suffering decline that could ultimately be terminal. At best, years of unequal struggle with Councils' internal bureaucracy, circuitous procedures and political expediency have knocked the stuffing out of them. Constantly forced on to the defensive, creativity is dulled and a beleaguered cynicism can replace the enthusiasm, innovation and social-consciousness, which have historically been the characteristic virtues of those working in Leisure Services. Professional credibility is under challenge as never before. Progressive cuts have meant that, by default, the service is being squeezed out of direct provision by Councils. The time is ripe, therefore, to make a virtue of necessity, seize the moment and pursue forms of structural innovation which could take Leisure Services wholesale outwith direct local authority control and back into the heart of the communities they serve.

Hounslow's Community Initiative Partnership is of particular interest because of the radicalism of its structural innovation. It is not necessarily a blueprint that should be directly replicated in Scottish contexts: rather what are needed are strategies appropriate to particular local circumstances. There is now an opportunity to define that tantalising statutory 'adequacy' of provision which should give Scotland's Leisure Services an advantage.

Longer-term, what could the trend towards externalisation lead to? Part of the answer to this should begin to emerge from the publication in August 2000 of the Scottish

Parliament's 'National Cultural Strategy', 'Creating our Future … Minding our Past'. If this initiative is to be more than mere rhetoric, and coherent action is to follow, the Parliament itself will surely have to take a more direct hand in the future development of Scotland's Cultural and Leisure Services. If the recent flurry of research and apparent government interest genuinely indicate their conviction that Leisure Services have a significant part to play in facilitating social inclusion and other policy priorities, then concerted action of the kind called for in 'The role of sport in regenerating deprived urban areas' will be required:

'The ingredients of success are a varying combination of an outreach, bottom-up approach; the use of local facilities; building on existing structures and traditions; recruiting local people; adopting a needs-based rather than a product-led 'sports development' approach; addressing issues wider than sport and physical recreation.'

However, to depend on already struggling local authorities for anything requiring additional investment will soon be exposed as an unrealistic demand. It is possible, then, that the comprehensive re-structuring of the sector that has begin with externalisation could move on apace, and new consortia, voluntary and public/private partnerships emerge to replace, or at least complement, Local Authority Leisure departments. If so, then direct funding to such bodies from the Parliament, with a proportionate reduction in Council's grant-aided expenditure, could ensue. Such a move could present an opportunity to implement national strategies directly, through detailed contractual arrangements with these new structures. Consequently, a coherent strategy for linking leisure provision with, for example, the social inclusion agenda, may be better facilitated than has been possible in the existing local authority climate of resource depletion and policy confusion. Nowhere, in my view, demonstrates the potential for this better than the holistic Hounslow model, but it is important that those involved in the services and community stakeholders together help guide this process in the appropriate a direction appropriate to local circumstances. If they are able to take on this role, then today's sporadic formation of Leisure Trusts can be regarded as the light at the end of a very long, dark tunnel.

References:

Accounts Commission (1998). *The challenge of charging*. Edinburgh: Accounts Commission for Scotland.

Ashbrook Research and Consultancy (1998) *North Ayrshire Council Residents Survey*.

Audit Commission (1999) *The Price is Right? Charges for Council Sevrvices*. London: Audit Commission .

Coalter, F, Allison, M, and Taylor, J. (2000) *The role of sport in regenerating deprived urban areas*. Edinburgh: Centre for Leisure Research (for Scottish Executive).

DCMS (2000) (http://www.culture.gov.uk)

Holmes, G., Christie, M. and Higgins, L. (2000) 'Is the price right?', *Leisure Manager* (July).

Kay, A, and Watt, G. (2000) *The role of the arts in regeneration*. Edinburgh: Scottish Executive.

Local Government and Planning (Scotland) Act 1982.

London Borough of Hounslow (1999) 'Hounslow Community Initiatives Partnership' Information papers. http://www.cip.org.uk

Pringle, A. and Cruttenden, T. (2001) *Sport and Local Government in the New Scotland*. Edinburgh: Convention of Scottish Local Authorities.

Rogers, S., Smith, M., Sullivan, L. and Clarke, M. (1999) 'Community Planning in Scotland — an evaluation of the Pathfinder Projects', Convention of Scottish Local Authorities (June).

Scottish Executive (1999) *Celebrating Scotland — a National Cultural Strategy. Consultation Document*. Edinburgh: Scottish Executive.

Scottish Executive (2000) *Creating our future ... Minding our past. The national cultural strategy*. Edinburgh: Scottish Executive.

Scottish Office (1996) *Scottish Local Authority Expenditure*. Edinburgh: Scottish Office.

———— (1997) *Scottish Local Authority Expenditure*. Edinburgh: Scottish Office.

———— (1998) *Scottish Local Authority Expenditure*. Edinburgh: Scottish Office.

Simmons, R. (2000) 'Partners in Trust — a study of the "New Leisure Trust" options for local leisure services', *Leisure Manager* (January): p. 17.

Exercise Referral Schemes in Scotland: Is it 'Joined-up Policy'?

Malcolm Foley, Matt Frew and Gayle McPherson

Division of Media, Language and Leisure Management, Glasgow Caledonian University

Introduction

General Practitioner (GP) Exercise Referral Schemes enable local GPs to refer patients to a designated sports / leisure facility for a 'prescription' of exercise rather than medication. Such initiatives have, since 1990, involved alliances between health and leisure services. In Scotland it is evident that there is no standard approach to the operation or strategic development of these schemes. The level and type of provision is varied across the country, with many schemes operating at local level with GPs and leisure facilities, others between Primary Care teams and the Education Department, and others at the Area Health Board and Unitary Authority level. There has been no national direction or strategic direction from Health Education Board for Scotland (HEBS), Council of Scottish Local Authorities (COSLA), or Sportscotland. Recent evidence suggests that, increasingly, Area Health Boards are using the facility of General Practitioner (GP) Exercise Referral Schemes to address issues of obesity, heart disease, high blood pressure and stress among their patients (Bowler, 1995).

The referral schemes involve a GP or other Primary Care Specialist (e.g. Practice Nurse) prescribing a course of exercise at a local leisure/sports facility which delivers the course (usually) at a reduced cost for a fixed period. These initiatives are based upon some well-established, and widely accepted beliefs in the benefits of exercise in promoting longer life expectancy and better quality of life. In some cases, exercise referral schemes have been targeted at working-class beneficiaries in parts of Scotland where diet and lifestyle have contributed to chronic problems of the type described above. For example, Glasgow City Council runs three exercise referral schemes, two of which are situated in areas of priority treatment (APT). Contemporary literature on this topic — and this study's findings — have revealed that there is no standard approach to the operation of exercise referral schemes; they operate to various criteria and are driven by differing policy and income objectives across Scotland. This paper will explore the use of such schemes as a marketing tool for leisure centre managers, and the possibility that greater alliances between health and leisure professionals would promote wider access and at the same time satisfy policy and income objectives for both services. This study found that of the thirty two local authorities throughout Scotland, fourteen are currently operating exercise referrals, and thirteen of the remaining eighteen are considering introducing such schemes.

Methodology

The study consisted of a postal questionnaire to all unitary authority leisure and recreation departments (n=32) and to all Area Health Boards (n=16) in Scotland, conducted over the holiday season months of June and July 1997. It was concerned with strategy and policy rather than operational issues. A 100 per cent response was achieved after follow-up calls and reminders. There is a low number of Area Health Boards and Unitary Authorities, so to present an accurate picture of Scotland, it was important that a full response was achieved. The postal surveys of the health boards and unitary authorities consisted of similar questions about the operation, strategy and origin of the schemes, the marketing of them and the amount of collaboration between the two services in relation to their policy-making processes and marketing. In addition, opinions were sought on how successful the schemes were in attracting new users to the leisure centres and on their continued adherence to exercise. For those who did not operate schemes, information was sought on why this was so, whether and when they were hoping to introduce schemes, and if there had been any past attempts. The postal survey method was selected to gain general information on a large scale in the short space of time that was available. From these surveys, an overall picture of the location, operation and marketing of the Scottish schemes was obtained. Information on the working nature of leisure and health alliances was also obtained.

   In addition to the postal survey, a case study was analysed of patients' experiences of an 8–10 week referral scheme in the Borders — 551 patients were questioned on starting, and the 247 patients still on the scheme at the end were questioned again. The Borders' survey of patients provides quantitative data of a mainly rural area which has had an exercise referral scheme in operation since 1994 — one of the longest running in Scotland. The survey of patients in the Borders was carried out by Borders Health Board between September 1994 and the end of 1997 and analysed during 1998 by Glasgow Caledonian University, using the Windows SPSS system. The survey highlighted what the referral patients wanted to gain from exercise; their main barriers to exercise participation; the activities they wanted to take part in; and what encouraged them to continue exercising.

A further case study utilising semi-structured interviews with leisure managers in Glasgow provided qualitative information on the operation of exercise referrals in an urban setting — the largest unitary authority in Scotland. Because of the high instances of heart disease in the area, this council has a stated policy commitment to health and fitness promotion and further alliances between leisure services and health agencies (Glasgow City Council, 1993). They are also currently reviewing the schemes with a view to introducing them on a wider basis. The Health Education Board for Scotland (HEBS) has also added their opinions and comments on exercise referrals based on their policies/strategy on physical activity which provides valuable information from a national agency. The Glasgow case study involved interviews with two facility managers operating referral schemes; two facility managers who were not operating a scheme; interviews with Health and Fitness Development Officers responsible for the development of referral schemes in Glasgow; and an interview with the Greater Glasgow Health Board (GGHB) Senior Health Promotion Manager for Physical Activity. Other interviews were carried out with personnel responsible for exercise referrals in the Borders and Argyll and Clyde areas. This part of the study took place throughout 1997 and 1998. With little in-depth knowledge of the schemes available at he time, a qualitative approach was adopted, with Glasgow chosen because of its large population and the large-scale leisure provision in the area.

The aim was to critically review and evaluate these schemes at policy level, rather than to analyse operational practices. Additional data on evaluations and promotional activity for schemes in Highland, Tayside, Argyll and Clyde, Glasgow and the Borders has been collected which will contribute to understanding of issues such as adherence. The case study of Glasgow provided perspectives from leisure personnel, while the Scottish survey enabled the gathering of information about where and how exercise referral schemes are operating. Furthermore, the case study of the Borders Region adds considerably to the policy debate by providing a perspective from the patients themselves.

These schemes sit alongside local authority leisure policies and plans which focus on many of the communities specified above, and which attempt through marketing and other outreach strategies to persuade citizens to participate in active recreation. Such concerns are based upon preoccupations with recreational deprivation and the use of recreation as a strategy to promote welfare in communities and to address individual and collective leisure needs. Local governments in Scotland have a statutory obligation to provide "adequate" recreational and cultural opportunities for their populations (HMSO, 1982). However, in recent years, sport and recreation management in local authorities has been subject to compulsory competitive tendering — a process which has tended to accentuate commercial over welfare values (Bailey and Reid, 1993). In particular, sports centre managers are now more conscious of market segmentation, relationship marketing and yield management when making decisions about provision,

Thus there is the potential for senior management to use GP referral schemes as a means of encouraging greater participation at off peak hours. The area's increasing popularity is shown by the number of "Exercise Referral Officer" appointments made in some local authority recreation departments (e.g. two posts in Glasgow City Council in 1999) as well as posts within health boards (five in Glasgow in 2000).

The state of health and fitness in Scotland

The benefits of exercise are well documented (Fenton *et al.*, 1986) with the message spread via promotional activities such as the 'Fit For life' campaign and the "Gavin Hastings" (HEBS) advertisement. Supporters would claim that the success of these messages is shown by, for example, the Allied Dunbar National Fitness Survey (Sports Council, 1992) in which 80 percent of the UK sample expressed a strong belief in the value of exercise to health and fitness; and by various studies on GP exercise referral schemes reporting the success patients have achieved (Januarius, 1993; Giles, 1994; Turner, 1994; Nutley, 1994; Bowler, 1995; Scottish Borders Health Board, 1995).

Table 1   Self Reported Physical Activity Levels for Men and Women: England, N. Ireland, Scotland

Activity level	Men			Women		
	England	Ireland	Scotland	England	Ireland	Scotland
5.	14	21	17	4	6	6
4.	12	9	12	10	9	9
3.	23	22	8	27	31	8
2.	18	8	17	25	17	17
1.	16	18	18	18	17	23
0.	17	21	28	16	20	37
Total (%)	100	100	100	100	100	100

KEY TO ACTIVITY LEVEL
5.   12+ occasions of vigorous activity in the previous month
4.   12+ occasions of a mix of vigorous + moderate activity on the last month
3.   12+ occasions of moderate activity in the last month
2.   5–11 occasions of a mix of moderate + vigorous activity in the last month
1.   1–4 occasions of a mix of moderate + vigorous activity in the last month
0.   No moderate or vigorous activity in the last month (light activity only)

Sources: Allied Dunbar National Fitness Survey (1991); Northern Ireland Health and Activity Survey (1993); Health Education Board for Scotland (1993)

This paper, however, concentrates on the effects and experiences of GP referrals schemes on public leisure centres in Scotland. Background research revealed little information on the benefits of exercise referrals to leisure centres. It thus sought to complement reports on English based projects such as the Oasis Project (Horsfall Turner, 1995) where the Lagoon leisure centre (which served the scheme) indicated increases in facility usage (15%) and in revenue (£50,000 per annum) (Simmonds, 1994). From the self-reported activity levels for men and women in England, Ireland and Scotland (Table 1) it would appear that health and fitness agencies in Scotland have a lot more work to do.

Referral schemes in Scotland also exhibit major operational differences from their English counterparts, including the decision-making, activity times available, who deals with the participants, the sources and uses of funding. Nevertheless, national similarities do exist, the most striking being the lack of leadership in strategic direction by any of the agencies involved with leisure or health services, despite policy statements encouraging greater alliances. Such fragmentation in policy and strategic direction is ironic, given that twenty one percent of unitary authorities view GP exercise referral schemes' single most important opportunity being to encourage alliances with the health service.

Increase in GP Exercise Referral Schemes

Cropper (1995) reported that GP referrals for exercise were on the increase. A study commissioned by The Health Education Authority into the extent and nature of physical activity promotion by the primary health care team in England found that at the end of 1993 there were at least 121 primary health care programmes promoting physical activity in England, with at least another 52 planned for 1994. Of these programmes there were two main types, one of which is GP referrals. Cropper (1995) suggested that these figures were an underestimation; Giles, (1994) argued that there might be over 1,000 exercise referral schemes in Britain. This study, however, has managed to provide much clearer information on the geographical operation of such schemes throughout Scotland.

Local government reorganisation in Scotland has meant that the 15 Health Boards operate on a wider basis than the 32 local authorities. Therefore, Health Boards often incorporate more than one unitary authority. At present there are twelve main areas in Scotland which operate exercise referral schemes in some capacity, but not always with the knowledge of both the health board and local authority. These include, Ayrshire and Arran, Argyll and Clyde, Borders, Dumfries and Galloway, Fife, Forth Valley, Glasgow, Grampian, Highland, Lothian, Tayside, and Western Isles. Initially it appears that almost the whole of Scotland is operating these schemes, but further analysis shows otherwise. For example, Ayrshire and Arran Health Board Area operate only one scheme in one unitary authority area — North Ayrshire — while the Health Board area covers two other unitary authority areas. Overall, 9 of the 15 Health Boards (60%) and 15 of the 32 unitary authorities (44%) operated exercise referral schemes in 1998 (Glasgow Caledonian University, 1998).

Unlike the Health Education Authority for England, the Health Education Board for Scotland has done no research into the existence of exercise referral schemes in Scotland. This is despite there being evidence to suggest that GP exercise referral schemes have been operating in Scotland at least since 1993 and that, compared to England and Northern Ireland, much higher proportions of men and women in Scotland are inactive or engage in light forms of activity (HEBS, 1995). Furthermore, given one of HEBS' policy aims is to "stimulate policies which promote physical activity as part of everyday life" (p. 7), which the majority of Health Promotion Units within the Health Boards in Scotland are using to encourage activity, the lack of research into referral projects demonstrates some degree of inconsistency. This is surprising as there are numerous reasons why and how HEBS could be of benefit to operators of exercise referral schemes throughout the country.

For example, HEBS policy highlights the aim to develop safe environments for active living. Ensuring that the leisure facilities the patients are being referred to are suitable and safe could be one area where guidance to the Health Boards is given. Another area includes the training of suitably qualified staff. This has proved a

Table 2   Benefits patients found from exercise programmme

HOW HAS EXERCISE HELPED YOU ?	%
Less stress, sleep better etc.	15
Generally fitter	28
Raised awareness of how and why to exercise	5
Psychological improvement / positive outlook	7
Feel a lot better in general	14
Weight loss	7
Non response	23

Table 3   Patients' perceptions of lifestyle improvements as a result of the exercise programme

HOW HAS EXERCISE HELPED YOU ?	%
Eating habits	39
Sleep patterns	20
Social life	17
General mood	31
General Health	44

real concern, not only for Health Boards, but for Leisure Services who hope to receive patients. This is suggested since "the developing of professional skills necessary to enable the promotion of physical activity" is another stated objective of HEBS (1995: p. 6).

Results of the follow-up patient survey revealed that eighty nine per cent of the respondents felt that their exercise programme had been of benefit to them. The main ways patients felt they had benefited are listed in Table 2. These findings emphasise clear benefits to people's feelings of general well-being. Although there are different priorities within different areas, it is argued that the lifestyle changes of patients (see Table 3) should provide encouragement for those unitary authorities not already operating referral schemes to consider the benefits to their communities.

Regardless of ability to quantify such perceived benefits, it is in the interests of HEBS, health boards and unitary authorities to take note. For this situation presents opportunities of reciprocal benefit for those within the bio-medical fraternity and leisure services. The maximisation of such benefits, however, necessitates closer alliances between health and leisure.

Change in marketing of public sector leisure facilities — CCT

Until the last ten or so years, marketing skills and strategies were largely unknown in local government (Cornwell, 1987) with provision supply-led rather than demand-driven. Furthermore, Cornwell (1987: p. 5) has argued that before this time there was "No major evidence of marketing being applied to local authority recreation and sports centre planning and provision". He also urged, however, that the absence of substantial marketing may not necessarily be a bad thing: a standardised approach may end up satisfying no-one's needs.

Some argue that the organisational structures in the public sector are not suited to responding to the market place with service delivery dominated by slow moving bureaucracy, departmentalisation and political short-termism. Others argue that this is not what they are there to do, with their objective being to meet the needs of citizens not market consumers. General constraints such as these have made it difficult for local authorities to adapt to a marketing approach.

However, others (e.g. Coalter, 1990) argue that positive discrimination is necessary because certain groups will always be under-represented if demand-led strategies are used, as they fail to cater for the whole community. Those most likely to be recreationally disadvantaged may not be represented because, for example, it is the middle class who mainly use sports centres (Audit Commission, 1989) and join voluntary groups (Coalter, 1990). On the other hand, Gratton and Taylor (1985) argue that segmentation and targeting groups does not work because little attention has been paid to the recreation preferences of the manual worker as a target group, with preferences of non-manual workers catered for more fully.

Despite the 1975 White Paper's (HMSO, 1975) designation of leisure services as part of "the general fabric of the social services they have occupied an ambiguous position between ideologies of welfare ('need') and ideologies of the market ('demand' or 'profit')" (Coalter, 1990: p. 23). This has become most evident since the beginning of the Thatcher era because the Conservatives, committed to a reduction in public expenditure, placed primacy on the market in the allocation of most goods and services (Hoggett, 1987). The 'New Right' emphasise the importance of moving away from a dependency to an enterprise culture, underpinned by a minimalist government, advocating a reduced role for the state in the economy, and social policy and greater power to market forces (Allison, 1993). Coalter (1990) argued that Conservative policies such as CCT had the potential to transform the rationale for, and practice of, local government leisure provision by constructing a greater defence of welfare via the introduction of throughput figures to disadvantaged groups in the contract specifications. That this didn't occur marked CCT down as a lost opportunity. The ambiguity over the status of leisure services is possibly, in part, due to an ideology of leisure being a private sphere in which individual choice and responsibility is paramount, and in which the notion of 'need' (the basis of welfare provision) is difficult to define (Coalter, 1990). Consequently, due to the underlying ideology and income generating pressures of policies such as CCT, public authority sport and recreation centres have developed various marketing and promotional initiatives intended to attract and retain customers as well as improving their fitness. Now most leisure facilities perform basic marketing activities: for example, leaflets within the centre or at other council buildings; local radio; adverts; local press; exhibitions; or the use of banners outside the building. Marketing is also being used to attract non-users with (say) information about 'women only' nights being promoted at community centres or local crèche facilities or nurseries.

With the growth of the fitness market over recent years, leisure services are now focusing on the inactive groups (non-users of sports facilities). In view of the aims of policy makers, exercise referral schemes offer one way of reaching this target group (because target groups such as women and over 50s are well represented among those referred). Examples of leisure service's use of health as a marketing tool to reduce participation barriers include Glasgow City Council's 'Women In Sport' literature, designed to appeal to the target group.

Additionally, leisure services assist in addressing council policy objectives of increasing physical activity to reduce poor health records. With the new Labour Government signalling the end of CCT, and its replacement by a 'Best Value Regime' (BVR), a more flexible contract culture is emerging "that allows leisure professionals to focus on quality of life issues" (ILAM, 1998: p. 2). However, although the focus is changing to effectiveness and the quality of local services, economy and efficiency issues brought about from the introduction of CCT in leisure services are here to stay (ILAM, 1998).

Health and leisure alliances

Literature reveals the current topical nature of health and leisure alliances but this is not a new phenomenon as, historically, leisure and health have been linked via state legislation. For example, the Baths and Wash-Houses Act of 1846 was initially introduced on the basis of public health issues of hygiene (Clarke and Critcher, 1985).

It is evident that health and leisure services could work together since their policy aims and objectives are similar. This, however, may lead to potential duplication of effort as both have policies aimed at promoting and providing opportunities for people to lead an active and healthy lifestyle, based on need (Glasgow City Council 'Sport Recreation Strategy Document', 1993; HEBS, 'Policy Statement' 1995). One example could be that of health promotion by both services. Despite Glasgow City Council's (1993) policy to "seek to develop joint initiatives and closer links with health agencies, such as the GGHB's Health Promotion Department" (p. 31), and their recognition that adopting a more co-ordinated approach to campaigns and events and the sharing of information and research with the Health Board would be beneficial, there has been little collaboration until recently on the GP referrals initiative. Evidence, perhaps, of the practical difficulties the two services have in working together and, some might say, of ideological differences.

Further evidence of this inability of leisure and health services to work together, despite similar objectives, is highlighted in more recent literature on exercise referrals which criticises leisure and health services as merely and jumping on the GP referral bandwagon (Health Club Management, May 1996). This particular article states that good communication and co-ordination are prerequisites to successful schemes. The conflict arises because of the dual role of jobs in the health and leisure services to improve the health of the population by encouraging and providing the opportunities to exercise and satisfy a need (Glasgow City Council, 1993; HEBS, 1995). The view of Ayrshire and Arran Health Board is that their scheme is successful because of very good communication links. However, there is contrasting evidence from Forth Valley Health Board that alliances are clearly difficult and, in this case, impossible, as they state that they have tried to work with leisure departments in the past but found it impossible.

In Lothian, another issue emerges with the health board aiming for their scheme to get further away from the leisure facility model. It appears then that leisure facilities in some cases are not able to accommodate exercise referral schemes in a manner that health boards would like. They favour a more holistic approach where exercise includes work in and around the home as well as in leisure centres. Furthermore, Fife Health Care, who do not operate a scheme, are very interested in exercise referrals although they have a problem with "committing themselves to prescribing", which may also indicate that their reluctance is due to liability issues for GPs.

From the patient survey (see Table 4), it is evident that leisure centres are necessary to the long term success of a scheme, since the majority of patients (52%) want a mix of activities around and outside the home whilst others (31%) preferred organised activities.

Although leisure managers must realise that they need not all be facility based activities. Evidence demonstrates (see Table 5), that health boards can benefit their patients by listening to their wishes and working with leisure services where possible. There is a need for them to work together.

It is possible that leisure centres are not adapting well to the new physical activity messages of HEBS which promote 'active living' in terms of fitting exercise into everyday life (HEBS, 1995). Using examples from the Borders' patient survey and an

Table 4   Types of exercise patients prefer

TYPE OF EXERCISE	%
Home Based Only	12.2
Organised Activities Only	31.2
A Mix Of Activities Around and Outside The Home	52.3
Non Response	4.3

Table 5   Particular activities patients prefer

PARTICULAR ACTIVITIES	%
Aquaerobics	23
Dancing	10
Walking	57
Cycling	37
Swimming	54
Weights	29
Bowling	6
Aerobics	17

Table 6   Borders GP Referral Scheme — Age and Sex of Participants

AGE RANGE	18-24	25-34	35-44	45-54	55-64	65-74	75>
MALE %	1.5	3.6	8.3	10.2	5.3	2.7	.9
FEMALE %	3.6	10.2	13.8	19.6	13.1	3.8	.7
TOTALS %	5.1	13.8	22.1	29.8	18.4	6.5	1.6

interview conducted with GGHB, the patients both before and after participating on the scheme viewed work commitments as the main barrier to participation in exercise. GGHB's view is that leisure centres need to adapt to people's busy everyday lives by having more flexible programmes.

However, despite some practical difficulties, it is argued here that GP referrals are an ideal initiative for health and leisure services to work together to meet similar policy objectives such as encouraging a main target group (e.g. women) to exercise more. This is emphasised further with survey results indicating that both health and leisure services throughout Scotland have the over 50s as a main target group. For example, findings from evaluation of referral rates (see Table 6) show many more women than men on the schemes, and the most representative age-group was 30–64 years.

Further enhancing the alliances debate, is the fact that HEBS have clear aims and objectives with regard to physical activity promotion in Scotland, which include encouraging "co-ordination and consistency of action by the many agencies in Scotland with a part to play in physical activity in Scotland" (HEBS, 1995: p. 12).

Despite this, and the fact that their policy also states that "The aim is to maximise interagency networking and communication to enhance partnerships for physical activity promotion at national and local levels" (p. 13), in practice this is not happening with regard to exercise referral schemes. However, it should be noted that there is a relationship there between HEBS and the Scottish Sports Council (SSC) and Fitness Scotland in relation to more general physical activity issues at strategy level, but the SSC have no policy on exercise referrals. The opinion from HEBS is that, this is an area in which they are keen to build upon although, at present, there is little infrastructure that would support it. The HEBS policy also states that inter-agency alliances are important to encourage more physical activity, especially at local level with Health Boards, Councils and local leisure facility providers, in order to meet objectives such as stimulating policies which promote physical activity. However, findings revealed that these alliances have been slow to take exercise referral schemes on-board, despite pilot schemes being introduced by local authorities.

Results from leisure services revealed that many of the schemes originated from the leisure services whether at local or strategic level. This contrasts with the Health Board's responses, which are biased towards schemes originating from either health boards or GPs. Questions over ownership and origin of schemes highlights the variety of ways and different services involved with exercise referrals in Scotland. This not only shows how the schemes are being introduced to the public but, also, the types of public services concerned with getting people to be more active. It also raises more questions about alliances between these services and the role of public sector leisure services which could be threatened by other environments such as schools, or clinics (which the survey showed to be operators of some schemes) and could be less threatening environments for inactive groups.

The indication from the case study was that schemes were mainly operating at a locally based level without much strategic direction or help from the Health Boards at a regional level. This is also borne out in the survey results which indicate that they are mainly operated at a local level whether it be by GPs, Leisure Centre Managers or the others mentioned above. Many of the schemes (43%) are socially inclusive, adopting a stakeholder approach, making policy decisions via steering groups, made up of representatives from leisure and health services and sometimes including patients. However, there are clear indications of non-co-operation between health and leisure. If such restrictions are not rectified and alliances built, then health benefits for patients will be limited and marketing opportunities for leisure will be lost.

Relationship marketing

In line with the introduction of CCT in leisure services in 1992, relationship marketing — which is particularly suited to service organisations because of the longer term relationships with customers it creates — has seen increased acceptance. This is due to the need to retain current customers rather than attract new ones. Relationship marketing is a move away from the 'new customer only' approach of marketing which is criticised for being wasteful because it may cost more to acquire new customers that retain or build up existing ones. With regard to exercise referrals, the study revealed (see Table 7) that, for 43% of the leisure facilities, GP referral schemes provided a marketing opportunity to attract non-users. Relationship marketing, therefore, is an ideal tool for leisure managers: once a patient has been referred by the GP, they can build on the individual needs of the patients, and are in touch with the customer on a regular basis by phone or weekly appointment. Without the referral, the leisure centre would have been unlikely to attract this person to the centre.

Table 7   Opportunities for leisure facilities provided by Exercise Referral Schemes

MOST IMPORTANT OPPORTUNITY	%
Enhances Activity Programming	0
Marketing Tool To Attract Non-users	43
Increase Revenue	0
Encourages Alliances With Health Service	21
Meeting Council Policy Social Objectives	29
Not Applicable To This Scheme	7

Source: Glasgow Caledonian University (1998)

Exercise Referral Schemes also offer the opportunity for leisure services to build on their alliances with the health service by making themselves more attractive to health service needs in order to obtain referral patients. For example, the literature (Ramrayka, 1995; Anstiss, 1997; Hillsdon, 1997) and this research show that patients' adherence to the schemes, and to exercise once the referral period has ended, is problematic. Relationship marketing could be employed beneficially. Firstly, for leisure managers, information on adherence would be useful in the longer term: as Simmonds (1994) reported, there is potential revenue from the 60 per cent of 'referred patients' who continue to use the centre after the course has ended. Secondly, certain Health Boards expressed interest in the effectiveness of schemes since long-term change in physical activity health indices is unlikely to occur simply as a result of referral — adherence to the referral programme and continuation after it has ended are required.

There have been some positive results, with some schemes claiming 60 per cent adherence after six months (Simmonds, 1994: p. 74). This is highly successful when compared with other initiatives such as the "Gavin Hastings" advertisement evaluation (HEBS, 1995) which indicated no change in influencing adult behaviour. Exercise referrals appear an excellent way to achieve, at least, an introduction to exercise and, at best, more regular and ongoing involvement in physical activity, enhancing individuals' quality of life. Therefore, relationship marketing has an important role, not only in exercise referrals in particular, but public sector leisure facilities in general.

As the health and fitness industry expands, the public sector is caught up in this competitive environment due to the fact that so many local authorities have invested in 'state of the art' fitness gyms, which match many private gyms. Consequently, there is a need to create more flexible delivery systems. This has become evident from the study of patients who have completed a ten week programme. They cited specialised services — such as advice on how to exercise safely, personal exercise programmes with targets and goals set and someone to encourage them ... as the main reasons they were able to continue/adhere to their exercise. The argument for increasing flexibility means that leisure managers operating exercise referrals need to tailor products and services to the precise needs of individual customers or segments. Referral patients are one of the segments that leisure managers cannot be complacent about, especially since, as the literature (Osbourne, 1996) and this study indicate, leisure managers view exercise referrals as a panacea for their problems of 'dead' times during the day and as a way of generating income.

However, as Osbourne (1996: p. 23) states:

> ... if the measure of success is finance, forget it. There are easier ways of generating income ... access to exercise referrals in a non-threatening environment is essential for wellness programmes which provide proactive health development.

Leisure facilities must adapt their range of activities and services to their new users (referral patients) if they want to keep them: especially since, as the patient survey shows, the top activity this inactive group preferred (57%) was a non-facility based activity — walking.

What enhances the role GP Exercise Referral Schemes in the marketing of leisure facilities is the necessity for qualified personnel to administer advice, instruction and information on exercise, diet and lifestyle issues. For instance, Wallace (1995) emphasises that "Safety and competence with a recognised qualification are imperative within a medical referral programme" (p. 30). This study also highlights the necessity not only of qualified staff, but also those suitably sensitive to the particular needs of 'unfit' people.

Much of the usual marketing processes can be used for internal marketing, although the main ones relating to leisure managers and exercise referral schemes might be communications programming, product modification, and market research (e, 1995). Managers must find out what (their supplier of patients) the Health Board and Primary Care team want from them in terms of staff service and quality. The product (job) of exercise consultant can be modified by changing the role of the job to better fit the requirements of different segments. Formal communications' programming, designed to shape work attitudes and behaviour, could be an important element of an internal marketing strategy for exercise referral schemes. For example, to encourage Fitness Consultants, Development Officers and Attendant staff to be aware of, and to understand the sensitive nature of referral patients and their needs, compared with other users of the leisure facilities.

Part of the marketing task for Leisure Managers operating exercise referral schemes is thus to encourage internal customers to perform and external customers to buy. In summary, it's about performing the service in the right way by creating an organisational climate in general, and job products in particular. Furthermore, the results of the patient survey (see Table 8) reveal that the majority (66%) of the inactive group studied had in their past experience usually enjoyed exercise, and (54%) were very interested in becoming more active.

Table 8   Referral Patients Main Experience of Exercise

MAIN EXPERIENCE	%
Always enjoyed it	26
Enjoyed it most of the time	40
Enjoyed it only sometimes	21
Never really enjoyed it	9
Non response	4

These findings indicate that, although the referral patients generally reported quite enjoying exercise, there appear to be barriers to their becoming more active. One of these barriers may be that leisure facilities fail to suit people's everyday leisure needs: they might for example offer shorter exercise classes to fit in with people's lunch hours.

Evaluation of adherence

A key issue emerging from this study has been the evaluation of adherence. It is important that the reasons for non-adherence to exercise are identified, and that the ability of GP referrals to encourage adherence be considered. This study was able to identify that monitoring of adherence levels was recognised as an important issue throughout the schemes in Scotland. The majority of unitary authorities viewed failure of patients to adhere to exercise as the single most important threat to the success of exercise referral schemes. Although adherence to exercise for the duration of the scheme is being monitored in all the unitary authorities and almost all the health board areas in Scotland that operate schemes, there is a significant drop-off rate for the monitoring of physical activity beyond the referral period.

There are also varying methods being used to evaluate adherence: the Borders scheme measures adherence levels at various stages of the programme and looks at patient attitudes and reasons why they were hindered or helped to continue. In short, they concentrate on those who do continue to exercise. By contrast, Argyll and Clyde concentrated more on those who did not complete the course, and the reasons why they did not. If operators were to evaluate adherence to their exercise referral schemes, from both the perspectives just mentioned and over a longer period, then more detailed and clearer factual information about GP referral schemes in general could be obtained. This would result in less confusion for leisure managers, GPs and Health Boards embarking on the implementation of GP referral schemes.

Financial issues

Funding for the running of the schemes in Scotland varies, ranging from Urban Aid to The Scottish Office, but most schemes are funded by health boards and unitary authorities. Some schemes are 'self-sufficient', meaning that they do not have reduced rates for participants. Funding usually covers the costs of providing the service free of charge or at a reduced rate. Sometimes it is used to employ a member of staff to develop and operate the schemes. Funding for qualified, motivated staff can be unequal within one area health board or unitary authority. For example, Glasgow's Drumchapel exercise referral scheme has not received Urban Aid Funding, while the Castlemilk scheme has, so Castlemilk does not have a staff member allocated specifically to this former project. This situation will continue, even with Scottish Office funding for the Health Board, because the scheme in Drumchapel will still be self-funded while the Castlemilk scheme will receive more funding to retain staff already obtained with Urban Aid funds. This issue of funding may highlight the conflicting interests between the Unitary Authority and the Health Board such as the issue of qualified staff and their training.

Opinions also vary on whether the reduced rates for patients are important to their choice to take part in exercise. The findings from the patient survey indicate that financial concessions are not as important as other variables in helping people become more active. However, it is important to note that over fifty per cent of participants on that particular scheme were in employment of some sort. Argyll and Clyde Health Board view the reduced rate as having minimal effect because "it is roughly the same as the reduced rate they would get at the leisure centre anyway " (Hammond, 1997) — i.e. low income groups already receive lower rates. This is based on the assumption that those referred, because they may live in APT areas, are not working or are on low income. Yet there is a lack of primary research to prove or disprove this.

Furthermore, evaluation would help assess the financial value of GP referrals for exercise to a Direct Services Organisation (DSO) Manager and aid the Health Promotion Units who wish to know whether GP referrals are worth the effort in terms of adherence to exercise for long term health benefits. Findings also indicate that there could be financial gain for leisure managers since patients tend to bring along their family and friends with them for support, who perhaps also are not frequent users of the facilities and may not receive the reduced rate the patient gets. Other Leisure Managers argue that the social benefits (for example, mental health) are more important. But this is difficult to quantify, and although the managers don't mention it, it must satisfy policy objectives of providing for leisure needs.

Activity programming

Clearly there are resource implications in operating exercise referral schemes. Since one of the main issues of this study is to assess the effects on the leisure facility, it should be noted that it is the belief of some Leisure Managers that increased usage at off-peak times has been made possible due to exercise referrals. No evaluation has been carried out, but he increase in usage at off-peak times is consistent with the literature findings.

Another interesting finding in relation to activity programming is that referral patients are not interested in aerobics (Table 5). Since aerobics is one of the major activities provided by many public leisure facilities, this factor needs to be considered.

Staffing

Evidence suggests that GPs are still reluctant to refer patients to the schemes due to their concerns over quality of staffing, the 'liability factor' and, as suggested by Nutley (1994), their 'territory' being 'invaded'. Concerns about lack of trained staff are beginning to be addressed by the Dundee medical foundation who launched the first national GP referral programme to ensure consistent standards across the country, (Ramrayka, 1995). At present, staff in Glasgow involved with referrals are degree-qualified in Sports Science; and in the Borders and Argyll and Clyde, full training is given on how to deal with people who have never exercised, and on dietary advice. The survey also found that fifty five per cent of health boards operating schemes have created new posts specifically for exercise referrals.

In Glasgow, the Health Board's Draft Guidelines (1997) for the proposed new exercise referral schemes in Glasgow have already set out requirements for staff qualifications. The leisure services could see this as an infringement on their territory since this document states that "Practice Nurses will also be trained in fitness assessment, activity guidelines and exercise consultation" (p. 6). However, it is the conflict of objectives and aims of each of the services involved that cause most problems. This is evident from the fact that the health boards aim to increase the physical activity levels in certain practice populations, whereas the Leisure Services have various aims mentioned previously, one of which is ensuring the financial viability of exercise referral schemes.

This leads to opposing priorities with regard to evaluation. For example, the GGHB in particular wish to carry out psychological assessments, but this may not be as high a priority for leisure managers who will need to assess the frequency of customers' visits, the activities they do, how much they spend and how many companions they bring with them. This is the case in Renfrewshire where the leisure services conducted a survey into how much those still exercising after the scheme were spending. This was reported as an average £10 per week. The range of activities available also seems to be an area that the Health Board want to influence, which will raise issues of staffing levels, finance and GPs reducing costs in fund holding practices.

Conclusion

This study has produced some interesting and controversial findings for leisure services and leisure facilities. Key implications include the need for relationship marketing to improve adherence levels of patients after the prescription period. Exercise perception is also a key area for the marketing of exercise referral schemes because of the sensitivity of inactive groups to exercise, and to sports centres and the 'sporting image' in general. Other barriers to participation were also analysed to ascertain whether they were being addressed by leisure facilities in order to render them more attractive to non-users. The findings also revealed that potential candidates wanted to participate in exercise, highlighting they were not doing it just because their GP prescribed it, or to cure their ailments, but to increase their opportunities for socialising, losing weight and feeling fitter.

Main conclusions drawn from the research are that across Scotland the schemes are varied in their operation and levels of policy-making. Health Boards may use other facilities (e.g. schools), so leisure services must adapt to needs of the inactive if they want to reach this (potentially lucrative) market. Not all facilities will be able to adapt to this. Relationship marketing is one strategy that can provide leisure managers with information to target and maintain previous non-users. Exercise referrals are seen as marketing tool by leisure services, but it may not be being used to full advantage since the survey suggests that some schemes are not promoted as well as they could be. There is also the suggestion that, for some local authorities, monetary imperatives may be as important as the social objectives. However, although there is some evidence of 'joined-up' policy at a local level between the health professionals and the leisure professionals, intra-agency collaboration at the national level appears to be still non-existent.

Nevertheless, as with governmental policy initiatives such as Best Value (Foley *et al.,* 2000; Filkin, 1997), hopes of joined-up policy reflect a pragmatic concern to advance a 'rights and responsibilities' agenda. This policy approach reflects the attempt of third way politics to re-invent collectivism through individualism. It advocates a new way, one that will "find a balance between individual and collective responsibilities" (Giddens, 1998: p. 37). Here the agency expressed in individual consumption and lifestyle patterns is balanced with concern to take responsibility for such action and its utilitarian impacts upon the local community and wider society.

However, such pragmatic policy approaches often ignore or forget the structural relations of the individuals involved in the GP referral process. Individuals act within worldviews or cultural contexts where physical and dietary actions are holistically intertwined with factors of background, gender, ethnicity, economy and education. Health d's not sit in isolation but operates within a web of structural or objective conditions. The referred are the excluded economically, socially and more often, politically. Housing, jobs, income and education provide a snare to the health and even health aspirations of the individuals concerned. The advocacy of rights and responsibilities negates such a web of structural relations and their influence on the dietary and physical habits of the individuals therein. Aspirations of decentralised policy and subsidiarity (D', 1997; Giddens, 1998) must take in to consideration the objective relations that individuals find themselves in. Moreover, policy processes, if they are to be effective require practical mechanisms of reinforcement. Behavioural change takes time and referral schemes require the real support of resources as much as the rhetoric and persuasive power of the policy makers.

Therefore, as highlighted, in conjunction with any sustained or strategic programme, the need for professional skills to promote physical activity must incorporate the cultural dimension. Practitioners, whether in the GP surgery or within the leisure facility, must develop a series of 'soft skills' or 'reflexive techniques' (Greenaway, 1993) that will enhance communication, empathy and, thus, cultural sensitivity. Through such efforts, policy objectives become practically married and heighten the possibility of producing an awareness and understanding of cultural diversity that will engender the seeds of behavioural change. Here professionality as much as the policy process is problematised. For scientific methods and professional qualifications become meaningless if practitioners, from all sides, fail to appreciate the objective conditions in which many of those targeted for GP referral schemes find themselves. Given this, it is essential that policy makers and practitioners recognise the privileged knowledge and culture positions that they occupy when dispensing their pearls of wisdom. Without such recognition (and the ability to suspend value judgements of taste), relationship marketing techniques, medical science/leisure service collaboration and the hope of joined-up policy may be lost.

However, and more importantly, losing the opportunity to facilitate behavioural transformations in the lives of, more often than not, the disadvantaged, would be a heavy price to pay. Surely, if it means simply making a difference, the bureaucracy of policy and professional pride must be set aside, or consistently challenged, in favour of a pragmatism that acknowledges the cultural diversity and difficulties of the disadvantaged.

Acknowledgements

The authors would like to thank Claire McAteer for her work as a research assistant on this project. The authors would also like to thank Imelda Corry, GP Referral Coordinator for Borders Health Board and Borders Regional Council for access to data provided in this paper. Access to staff in both the Health and Leisure sectors made this project possible.

References

Allison, L. (1993) *The changing politics of sport*. Manchester: Manchester University Press.

Argyll and Clyde Health Board and Renfrewshire Council (1996) 'Living Plus GP Referral for Exercise Programme', Final Evaluation Report.

Bailey, S. and Reid, G. (1993) 'Contracting Out Municipal Sports Management: The British Experience', Discussion Paper No 20. Department of Economics, Glasgow Caledonian University.

Borders Health Board (1995) General Practitioners Exercise Referral Scheme Report On First Twelve Months.

Bowler, I. (1995) 'Activity Alliances for Health', *Leisure Manager* Vol. 12, No. 12 pp. 32, 33.

Clarke, J. and Critcher, C. (1985) *The Devil Makes Work: Leisure in Capitalist Britain*. Macmillan.

Coalter, F. (1990) *Social Policy Analysis and Leisure Policy*.

Cornwell, J. (1987) *Leisure Policy Now*. Association of Metropolitan Authorities.

Cropper, S. et al. (March 1995) 'Promoting Health and Profit', *The Leisure Manager* Vol. 13, No. 1: pp. 24, 26.

Department of the Environment (1975) *Sport and Recreation*. London HMSO.

Department of the Environment (1997) *New duty of best value for local authority services*. London.

Fenton, P. H., Bassey, E.J. and Turnbull, N.B. (1986) *The Living Case for Exercise*. London: Sports Council.

Filkin, G. (1997) *Best Value for the Public*. London: Municipal Journal Limited.

Foley, M., Frew, M., McPherson, G. and Reid, G. (2000) Healthy Public Policy: a policy paradox within local government, *Managing Leisure* 5, 77–89.

Giddens, A. (1998) *The Third Way: The Renewal of Social Democracy*. London: Polity Press.

Giles S (May 1994) 'Take This Prescription to the Gym', *The Independent*.

Glasgow Caledonian University, Survey of Unitary Authority Leisure and Recreation Departments and Area Health Boards in Scotland 1998.

Glasgow City Council (1993) 'Sport for Life' Sport and Recreation Strategy.

Glasgow Health Board (1997) Draft Guidelines.

Gratton, C. and Taylor, P. (1985) *Sport and Recreation: An Economic Analysis*. Spon.

Greater Glasgow Health Board and Glasgow City Council (1997) Draft Guidelines for Exercise Referral Programmes in the Primary Care Setting.

Greenaway, R. (1993) *Playback: a guide to reviewing activities*. Edinburgh: the Award Scheme Limited.

Hammond, I., Brodie, D. and Buldred, P. (1997) Exercise on prescription: guidelines for health professionals, *Health Promotion International*, 12(1): pp. 33–41.

Health Education Board for Scotland (1993) *System 3 Scotland Panel Study, 1993*.

Health Education Board for Scotland (1995) 'The Promotion of Physical Activity in Scotland — A policy Statement'. Edinburgh: HEBS.

Hillsdon, M. and Thorogood, M. (1996) 'A Systematic Review of Physical Activity Promotion Strategies', *British Journal of Sports Medicine* Vol. 30, No. 2: pp. 84–89.

HMSO (1975) *White Paper on Sport and Recreation*. London: HMSO.

Hoggett, P. (1987) *Decentralisation and Democracy: Localising Public Services*. University of Bristol.

Horsfall Turner, I. (1995) *The Oasis Programme Evaluation*. London: Sports Council.

Institute of Leisure and Amenity Management (ILAM) (1998) Best Value for Leisure Services: The development of a Test of Best Value, discussion paper, Basingstoke, ILAM.

Januarius, M. (1993) 'Healthy Profits: Health and Leisure', *Leisure Management* Vol. 13, No. 5: pp. 75, 77.

Northern Ireland Health and Activity Survey (1993).

Nutley, M. (ed) (1994) 'Exercise Just As the Doctor Ordered', *Leisure Week* (November) Vol. 6, No. 5: p. 3.

Osbourne, M. (1996) 'Live and Learn', *Leisure Manager* (May) pp. 17, 19.

Ramrayka, L. (November 1995a) 'Doctors' Orders', *Leisure Week* Vol. 7, No. 419: p. 8.

Ramrayka, L. (February 1995b) 'Doctors' Orders: Health and Fitness Special Report', *Leisure Week* Vol. 6, No. 10: pp. 22, 23.

Scottish Borders Heath Board (1995) *Health Board Report*.

Scottish Health Service (1990) *Prevention of Coronary Heart Disease in Scotland*. HMSO.

Simmonds B (1994) *Developing Partnerships in Sport and Leisure*. Longman.

Sports Council (1992) *Allied Dunbar National Fitness Survey*. London: Sports Council.

Taylor, A (1996) *Evaluating GP Exercise Referral Schemes: Findings from a Randomised Controlled Study*. University of Brighton: Chelsea School Research Centre Topic Report 6.

Wallace, J. (995) 'The Health of A New Nation', *The Leisure Manager* (September) pp. 30, 31.

A Realist Approach to Evaluating the Impact of Sports Programmes on Crime Reduction

Geoff Nichols

**Leisure Management Division,
Sheffield University Management School**

Introduction

Criticisms of previous research into the causal relationship between sports programmes and a reduction in 'anti-social behaviour' and crime have been that:

- sport and 'anti-social behaviour have been poorly defined, which makes it difficult to aggregate the results of different studies (Coalter, 1996);
- research has not built on a theoretical understanding of either the causes of such behaviour, or how programmes might prevent or reduce it (Coalter, 1996; Robins, 1996);
- "Advocates of such programmes are often propelled by a sort of aggressive optimism which acts as a defence against the helplessness felt when confronting the destructive nihilism of criminalised youth", and policy has been led by this rather than by evidence that such programmes are effective (Robins, 1996: p. 26).

However, such programmes continue to be prominently promoted: for example, by Sport England (1999) and the Policy Action Team 10 (1999) in their report to the Social Exclusion Unit.

This paper considers the extent to which criticisms of previous research are related to their source within the classical experimental tradition. From this tradition, some criticisms may be almost impossible to overcome, as valid research demands a methodological rigour which is beyond the capabilities of most programmes and researchers. However, these criticisms may also be being made from a research paradigm which is itself flawed. The paper considers whether the approach of 'scientific realism' advocated by criminologists Pawson and Tilley (1997) can overcome some of these limitations. Practical and theoretical limitations of research which attempts to use the

71

classical experimental design are illustrated with reference to research into the impact of adventure education courses on participants, but the illustrations could as well be taken from research into crime reduction programmes. While some of these criticisms can be overcome by the 'scientific realism' advocated by Pawson and Tilley, their approach can still be criticised.

Problems with previous research which has used the classical experimental design

Figure 1 illustrates that 'classic experimental research' starts with two identical groups. One group is given the treatment, and one group is not. Research is looking for measurable outcomes of a programme in the experimental group, and comparing them to the control group who have not experienced the same programme. If the group that had the treatment changes and the control group does not, it is deduced that the treatment caused the change. If numbers in the two groups are large enough, it can be ascertained whether the evidence of a causal relationship is statistically significant. Causation between the programme and intermediate effects, or the final outcome, is inferred from the repeated succession of similar effects after similar programmes.

	Pre-test	Treatment	Post-test
Experimental group	O1	X	O2
Control group	O1		O2

Figure 1   The Classic experimental design
             (source Pawson and Tilley, 1997: p.5)

Much previous research in criminology, and on the impact of sports programmes, has been based on this model, although it may not have applied it with methodological rigour. As long ago as 1979, a systematic review of research into programmes using outdoor adventure concluded that very few were conducted with a rigour which allowed them to produce valid results (Gibson, 1979). This paper is concerned to challenge the validity of these criticisms, so as to challenge the validity of the research paradigm of the classic experimental design from which they are made.

Practical problems with attaining the standards required by the experimental research design

Gibson (1979) summarised potential limitations of research conducted using the classic experimental framework as:

- Bias in sample selection;
- Small sample size;
- Lack of adequate control group;
- Questionable validity of assessment instrument (for example, a questionnaire may not have been validated as measuring a phenomena; its construction may have been ad hoc);
- Insufficient description of outcome criteria (poor definition of outcomes);
- Inadequate statistical analysis of data (to show a significant relationship);
- Lack of follow-up investigation (monitoring outcomes over a longer period than just after the programme).

These potential criticisms build on those of Coalter (1996) above. Immediately one can see many practical difficulties in the average local authority supported sports programme achieving this degree of methodological rigour in measuring their outcome. However the main focus of this paper is with challenging the theoretical base from which these criticisms are made rather than the impracticality of the high methodo-logical standards they require. Once the objectives of research broaden to consider *why* a programme has an effect, rather than just *if* it has an effect, then a more sophisticated model is required (see Figure 2).

1 Type of participant	2 Process of getting involved	3 Programme content and process	4 Intermediate effects	5 Main objective — reduced propensity to take part in crime.

Figure 2   The elements of the process of a crime reduction programme in sequence (source: author)

Figure 2 illustrates that research is trying to show a causal relationship between elements of boxes 1–5. It is not as simple as showing that participants on any one programme appear to experience a particular outcome, while non participants do not (Figure 1). The process of the programme is far more complex, and involves several different variables.

This illustrates the importance of basing research on theory, because the model has already assumed that the type of participant, the process of becoming involved in the programme, and the varieties of programme content and process will all determine intermediate effects. Further, there is an assumed relationship between particular intermediate effects and the final outcome, here defined as a reduction in the propensity to take part in crime. If we are not able to measure final outcomes in box 5, we will have to use theory to inform the intermediate outcomes we chose to measure in box 4.

So, a theoretical base becomes more important if we want to find out *why* a programme has an impact. However, even if we are only interested in *if* it has an impact, we may have to use theory to make the links between intermediate and final outcomes. Thus, only research which seeks no understanding of causality can avoid criticism if it does not build on theory.

An implication of the classic experimental research design is the potential value of a meta-analysis in combining independent empirical research results to gain greater statistical validity and identify independent causal variables. However, aggregated results from 96 studies of outward bound courses (Hattie *et al.*, 1997) illustrate that it is still extremely difficult to isolate the individual causal variables in a process. This analysis claims to have found that the three variables which explained the most variance of outcome were age of participant [adult or student], length of programme [long or short] and whether or not it was provided by Australian Outward Bound. However, a criticism of this analysis is that it was attempting to 'add up' results from programmes which were dissimilar in content and which had different objectives.

It is very difficult to determine the effect of individual variables in a single process. It is also very difficult to set up experiments to isolate them. For example, it would be difficult, although not impossible, to ensure that all participants on one programme [box 1, Figure 2] were black, middle class and male; and then to compare an identical programme on which all participants were black, middle class and female. Even if this were accomplished, all the other potentially relevant variables, such as facilitator skills, would need to be held constant.

The variable of the way in which participants become involved [box 2] is particularly difficult to eliminate. Where programme participation is voluntary there is always the problem that participants are more likely to gain benefit from it not because of the programme itself but because of their own attributes: for example, a willingness to try new experiences in general, or a predisposition towards the type of activities in that particular programme. The effect of voluntary involvement is very difficult to isolate if one is attempting to use a control group. Where programme participation is voluntary there have been attempts to set up a control group who thought they were volunteering for the same programme, but this is difficult to arrange.

So, one set of criticisms are that it is just not practical to live up to the standards of methodological rigour demanded by the classical experimental approach. Research is limited by resources and the practicalities of the research situation.

Theoretical problems with the experimental research design, and the way they are overcome by 'scientific realism'

Hattie *et al.*'s (1997: p. 78) meta-analysis of evaluations concluded that their approach revealed little about the process of the programmes. This is related to the general criticism that in the classic experimental design the notion of causality is 'one-way'.

A programme causes an effect. This takes no account of human agency, and is reflected in the dominance of quantitative methods over qualitative ones.

This is in contrast to the approach Pawson and Tilley (1998a) have called 'scientific realism'. They also propose that "it is not programmes that work, but the generative mechanisms that they release by way of providing reasons and resources to change behaviour"(1997: p. 79). Their epistemological position is that causation in a programme cannot be understood through deducing from statistical regularities how a programme works. One has to understand why actors involved in the programmes chose to change the way they act. Causality has to be understood as a combination of human agency and its reaction to new opportunities and resources. For example, to understand a programme offering sports activities to probationers, one would need to understand not only the new range of opportunities offered by the course, but also the resources and attitudes the participants brought with them, and how these changed as the course developed. The two together would help explain the outcome. From a realist perspective it is necessary to understand the interaction between the programme and the participant; between structure and agency.

This perspective is valuable because it takes into account the dynamic relationship between participant and programme. The participant changes in response to the programme, and therefore sees the programme in different ways at different stages of involvement. Practically, this means that as involvement progresses, the participant may be able to take advantage of a greater range of opportunities offered by the programme, and may in fact only see them as opportunities after some period of involvement. This was illustrated in a sports counselling programme evaluated by Nichols and Taylor (1996) in which the participants progressed through a range of increasingly demanding opportunities offered by the programme.

A second criticism of the classical experimental approach is ontological. The approach assumes the existence of an objective reality, external to and independent from the observer. For Pawson and Tilley, social reality is stratified (1997: p. 64). If we are to understand causality as a combination of human agency and its reaction to new opportunities and resources, we need to understand the social world as perceived by the programme participant. We need to understand how the social actor sees the programme — that is, how it is 'embedded' in their particular level of social reality. Only in this way can one understand the mechanism by which a programme has an effect: "Social mechanisms are ... about people's choices and the capacities they derive from group membership" (1997: p. 66).

The mechanism has to be understood as embedded in its particular level of social reality. This provides a context on which it is contingent. Some programmes will work with some participants, in some contexts, but not in others. An example is from the author's research (Nichols, 1999) into the place adventure activities took in the rehabilitation of long-term drug addicts. It was found that a key to successful rehabilitation was the ability to start a new life among new peers in a new area. The area could be thought of as the context. If, having gone through rehabilitation (a process as long as 12 months) a former addict moved back to their former home area, then the pressures and opportunities to become trapped in a cycle of drug taking and crime were often too hard to resist.

While Pawson and Tilley's' approach criticises the understanding of social reality upon which classic experimental research is based, it still seeks to explain regularities. The three elements of mechanism, context and regularity are drawn together in Figure 3 below. Methodological implications are that research must start from theory. This informs hypothesis generation about context, mechanism, regularity configurations. It is necessary for the researcher to develop an *understanding which includes hypotheses about their subjects' reasoning within a wider model of their causes and consequences* (Pawson and Tilley, 1997: p.163, emphasis in original). These hypotheses can be tested with a combination of quantitative and qualitative methods, the combination of which is justified by an epistemological position that causation in a programme cannot be understood through deducing how a programme works externally through statistical regularities (as discussed above). One has to understand why actors involved in the programmes chose to change the way they act. This is in contrast to the pragmatic avocation of mixed methodologies (e.g. Tashakkori and Teddlie, 1998).

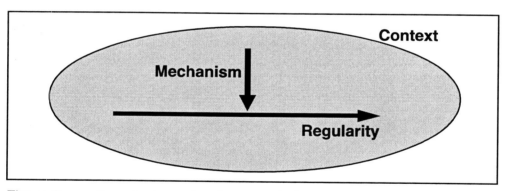

Figure 3   A context, mechanism, regularity configuration (source, Pawson and Tilley, 1997)

How does this solve the problem of producing research that is methodologically valid but practical to conduct?

Pawson and Tilley's' approach appears to imply that a series of case studies of CMR configurations can 'add up' to a better understanding of what works for who in what circumstances. Construction of hypotheses about CMR configurations still has to proceed from existing theory. While a combination of quantitative and qualitative methods is justified, they would both be subject to the normal standards of validity.

Although one might be using both quantitative and qualitative research, in quantitative research one would still aim to avoid bias in sample selection, obtain a sufficient sample size to show statistical significance, use valid questions and conduct a follow-up some time after the programme had been completed. There is less need for a control group, as causality is not deduced from differences between two groups.

Pawson and Tilley may offer a solution to conducting practical valid research by showing that any case study, however small, has the potential to add to existing understanding if it systematically develops hypotheses to add to existing knowledge of CMR configurations. Research methods must be designed according to the resources available to conduct them. If the resources to conduct a large quantitative survey are not available, then conduct a small number of case studies of individual participants, and that will be methodologically valid. The study can still be designed to build on existing theory. This implication partly arises from Pawson and Tilleys' willingness to use qualitative research evidence.

Criticisms

From positivist and interpretivist positions

This leads into criticisms of the scientific realist approach. The approach has mainly been seen as a criticism of the predominance of positivistic research in criminology, and those who favour this approach have engaged in fierce debate over the validity of qualitative evidence (Pawson and Tilley: 1998b; Farrington, 1997; 1998). However, one might equally well make a criticism from the interpretivist tradition that Pawson and Tilley assume that there is some sort of reality that the researcher can get closer to than the actor. This is implied in the use of the word 'stratified' in that the researcher is implied to understand a 'level of reality' superior to that of the actor, rather than just alternative to that of the actor. This may seem a reasonable view, given the researcher's superior knowledge of theory, but one could argue that Pawson and Tilleys' understanding of 'reality' may be no nearer to some ideal ultimate reality than the view of the actor. It could be an alternative view, rather than one based in a higher 'strata'.

To take this further, the very questions that Pawson and Tilley ask are framed within their own social reality and this is why they are important to them. 'What works', in other words the objectives of policy, are determined by Pawson and Tilley, and those funding the research.

So, Pawson and Tilley tread a delicate line between the positivist and the interpretivist position. They have avoided the social relativism of interpretivists at the cost of imposing their own conceptual framework on the research, in order to provide policy solutions, and build on theory. They want to know what works and why, and in what circumstances, because they want to advise policy makers.

What is 'adequate' knowledge of a CMR configuration?

For Pawson and Tilley, the outcome of research will be generalisations — 'It is likely that this type of programme will achieve this type of outcome in this situation'. But, as they accept, research can not produce universal laws. Case studies are designed to build on theory. They move towards an improved understanding because they build on existing theory. However, firstly, how does one define when observation of outcomes is sufficient to constitute a 'regularity'? Does one still aim for statistically significant results? Secondly, if one takes crime reduction programmes as an example, the range of contexts is infinite. The types of mechanisms are also infinite in variety, if we get down to the fine detail. The outcomes are also infinite in variety, if again we consider the details. At what point do we decide that understanding is sufficient for the level we require, or sufficient for use in the way we want? How different from the hypothesised position does a result have to be to challenge the original theory? To return to the example of a drug rehabilitation programme that only worked when the participants were able to move away from the place where they were initially involved in drug taking (Nichols, 1999), how far do they need to move away? Could they move into another social context, but in the same location? Pawson and Tilley do not consider that the degree to which we discriminate between different context, mechanism or outcome permutations is determined by views of what is 'adequate theory'.

What is new?

How much more does scientific realism add to social science research which already uses a combination of methods to ask both what happens and why? It is accepted by many researchers that qualitative and quantitative methods complement each other, and can do so in precise ways. As such, one could still design small scale qualitative research which would build on and extend existing theory. Is the major attraction of scientific realism that it will allow us to do 'valid' research into a complex social situation with limited resources? In which case, how valid is it to just ask a participant in a programme why he or she felt the programme had kept him away from crime? Questions could be structured from theory, and sensitive interview technique used. But would the result be valid as it stood, or would one have to complement it with the participant's offending record? And if the record still showed that he or she had offended after the programme, would one then conclude that the respondent was not truthful, or that the programme had reduced his propensity to be involved in crime, but not to the extent that he did not do it?

Conclusion

Many of the previous criticisms of research into the relationship between sports programmes and crime reduction are valid: it is extremely difficult to conduct research which meets the criteria of validity in the classic experimental paradigm. However, this paradigm can be criticised because it can not give us an adequate understanding of why a programme has a particular effect. The approach of scientific realism offers the chance that small scale research, systematically conducted, can contribute to the bigger picture, as long as one accepts the validity of a range of research methods.

However, policy makers do not judge validity by the same standards as academics. Even if the academic position accepts the validity of certain methods, policy makers, guided by political criteria, use different standards. Practitioners are likely to remain motivated by "aggressive optimism which acts as a defence against the helplessness felt when confronting the destructive nihilism of criminalised youth" (Robins, 1996: p. 26). They have to be.

References

Coalter, F. (1996) *Sport and anti-social behaviour — Sport 2005 working paper*. Edinburgh: Scottish Sports Council.

Coalter, F. (1990) 'Sport and anti-social behaviour', in J. Long (ed) *Leisure, health and well being* (LSA Publication No. 44). Eastbourne: Leisure Studies Association, pp. 145–154.

Farrington, D. (1998) 'Evaluating "Communities that care"', *Evaluation*, Vol. 4, No. 2: pp. 204–210.

Gibson, M. (1979) 'Therapeutic aspects of wilderness programs: A comprehensive literature review', *Therapeutic Recreation Journal* (Second quarter): pp. 21–33.

McGuire, J. and Priestley, P. (1995) 'Reviewing what works: Past, present and future', in J. McGuire (ed) *What works: Reducing offending*. Chichester: Wiley.

Nichols, G. (1999) 'Is risk a valuable component of outdoor adventure programmes for young offenders undergoing drug rehabilitation?', *The Journal of Youth Studies* Vol. 2, No. 1: pp. 101–116.

Nichols, G. and Taylor, P. (1996) *West Yorkshire Sports Counselling, Final Evaluation Report*. Halifax: West Yorkshire Sports Counselling Association.

Pawson, R. and Tilley, N. (1997) *Realistic evaluation*. London: Sage.

———— (1998a) 'Caring communities, paradigms polemics, design debates', *Evaluation* Vol. 4, No. 1: pp. 73–90.

———— (1998b) 'Cook book methods and disastrous recipes: A rejoinder to Farrington', *Evaluation* Vol. 4, No. 2: pp. 211–213.

Robins, R. (1996) 'Sport and crime prevention: The evidence of research', *Criminal Justice Matters* No. 23: pp. 26.

Policy Action Team 10 (1999) *A report to the Social Exclusion Unit*. London.

Sport England (1999) *Best value through sport: The value of sport*. London: Sport England

Tashakkori, A. and Teddlie, C. (1998) *Mixed methodology*. London: Sage.

"... limp-wristed, Kylie Minogue-loving, football-hating, fashion victims ..." *

Gay sports clubs — providing for male members, challenging social exclusion?

Lindsay King and Peter Thompson

Division of Sport Sciences, University of Northumbria at Newcastle

Introduction

In 2000 the first UK Gay Sports festival was held. The event was endorsed by the Council of Waltham Forest and backed by a £15,000 grant from the UK Millennium fund (Dermody, 1999; BGLSF, 2000). In 1999, London Amateur Wrestlers (with a predominantly gay male membership) were awarded the BAWA Winter Games III and set out development plans in the UK for *all* wrestlers (Dermody, 1999). At the same time, Stonewall Football Club, perhaps the UK's best recognised gay sports club, added a third team to cope with the demand from players (BBC Radio, 1998). There are many other examples that illustrate the change in visibility and apparent recruitment explosion in the number of separatist gay sports clubs and events. Thousands of athletes are now joining clubs and are participating in high profile European and global games. The British Gay and Lesbian Sport Federation (BGLSF) had over 40,000 members in the late 1990s (Clarke, 1998)[1], and team UK finished 4th in the Gay Games, held in Amsterdam, 1998. The increasing publicity given to gay clubs is of interest in itself. However, these two examples also illustrate signs of a relationship between some of the so-called 'separatist' and 'autonomous' clubs, with the mainstream of governing bodies, local authorities and national funding for sport.

Whilst recognising that there has been academic attention paid to gay sport, this has tended to concentrate on lesbians. Lesbians, whilst also facing discrimination, appear to be more visible in sports and sport studies than gay men (Lenskyj, 1990, 1991; Squires and Sparkes, 1996; Clarke, 1998; Hall, 1998). A few authors have dealt with gay men's experiences in mainstream sports (Rotella and Murray, 1991; Messner,

---

* This stereotypical view of gay men as non-sports oriented was expressed by one club organiser interviewed in this study.

1992; Woog, 1999). Only Pronger (1990) and to a lesser extent Messner (1992) have examined the issue of male participation in alternative gay sports clubs. This existing literature is North American focused. In the UK, there is a gap in quantitative research on participation rates and trends in such clubs, Likewise, few have explored the alternative experience offered by these sports clubs. Previous research sees gay sports clubs and festivals as peripheral. This invisibility in itself reflects sport's masculine tradition (Pronger, 1990). As was noted in a response to the 1998 North American Society for the Sociology of Sport conference "…if anything is noticeably absent, it is theoretically and experientially based analyses of gay males in sport" (Hall, 1998: p. 3). It is recognised that researching the participants will allow an understanding of the experience. However, it is important to examine the frameworks within which that experience takes place.

As many organisers of Gay Sports Clubs observe, a commonly asked question is 'why have an alternative club, why not just play for mainstream clubs?'. This paper sets out to address that question. The gay sport club's *raison d'être* and philosophy are examined. The organisers' perceptions of club culture are discussed. In turn, the contribution of clubs to the gay and wider community is briefly explored to address the question, 'Are clubs an integrated part of the UK sport network or are they left outside?'. The relationship of the clubs to UK sport is also noted.

Related literature

Gay Sport

Gay sports clubs in the UK have been inspired by the Gay sport culture in North America. The Gay Games, set up by Tom Waddell, is the most well known gay sporting alternative[2]. Whilst the original Gay Games in 1982 included the word 'Olympics' in its title, philosophically it was set up as an alternative to all that the Olympics stand for. As Waddell, in later years, commented (quoted in Young, 1995: p. 133):

> The Olympics are racist, the Olympics are exclusive, they're nationalistic, they
> pit one group of people against another, and only for the very best athletes.

In the Gay Games, the traditional 'competitive' value system has been reconstructed to reflect feminist and gay liberationist ideals of equality and universal participation. The ethos is said to be an ideal that *does* translate into practice — 'it's the taking part that counts'. UK athletes travelled to the US to participate in the Gay Games and on returning home set up their own gay sports clubs. On occasion these were established as separate clubs — an alternative to the bar culture; at other times they were an 'arm' of a general gay social club (Kruger, 1999).

'Why the Gay Games?', the title of an article by Dermody (1999), could be linked to another question: 'Why the Gay Sports Club?'. To begin to answer this question, the experience of gay men in mainstream sport needs to be considered. Many gay athletes are seen as 'late bloomers', having suffered humiliation in group sport whilst growing up gay. This may be more so the case for gay males than for gay females. As Hekma (1998: p. 2) observes:

> Gay men who are seen as 'queer' and 'effeminate' are granted no space what-soever in what is generally considered to be a masculine preserve and a macho enterprise. Lesbians seen as 'masculine' and 'butch' are, on the other hand, well represented in women's sports.

Gender stereotyping applied to gay men apparently defines their position in the sport culture. This awareness of 'position' is often developed at an early age:

> ... early childhood sports gatherings are often the first places we hear the word 'fag' being tossed about, usually to describe some less-than-perfectly-co-ordinated boy. (Weilder, 1998: p. 11)

Negotiating masculinity in straight sport?

Participation in sport strengthens the male bond through displays of traditional hetero-sexual masculinity. Sport is the venue where 'boys learn to be men' and to maintain this position. Physical activity celebrates qualities associated with "icy, uncompromising masculinity" (Tatchell, 1996: p. 80): namely competitiveness, aggression and dom-ination. Through aggressive play and verbal sparring, boys are forced to create an identity which conforms to a narrow definition of masculinity. Associated definitions of physical ability and the body provide a training ground for gender-appropriate be-haviour (Lenskyj, 1990). Likewise, this leads to inferences of gender-appropriate sport participation. 'Sport typing' was noted in boys' judgements on the 'transgressions' of men who crossed gender boundaries into women's sports or codes of sport (Kane, 1995 cited in Laberge and Albert, 1999). Through participating in the 'right sport', in the 'right way', masculinity can be displayed. Messner (1994: p. 198) comments on this:

> Boys learn through sport to place great value on competition and winning, to 'take' physical pain and 'control' their emotions, to view aggression and violence as legitimate means to achieve one's goals, to accept uncritically authority and hierarchy and to devalue women as well as any feminine qualities in males.

The expectations in mainstream sport are echoed in Parker's work (1999). Homophobic taboos, misogyny, objectification of women and impoverished emotional relations with other men are tickets to acceptance. Consider then the position of gay athletes within this myth of masculinity. If they are open about their sexuality they break the bond and face outcasting. The alternative is to remain silent in a sport culture where men learn to ridicule 'queers' and debase women. It is not only through sport but also through social and 'locker room' cultures that men 'do gender' (Dunning, 1986; Curry, 1991; Messner, 1992; Parker, 1996).

In 1994 a special issue of *The Advocate*, a popular gay magazine published in North America, explored gay males' experiences of estrangement in mainstream sport (cited in Young, 1995). One athlete recounted a coach's comment to him: "We don't want a fairy on our team". Another athlete stated:

> They always stuck me in the outfield and I always sat down and picked at the flowers. I couldn't relate to the competitiveness and macho mentality. I just didn't feel like I belonged. (both quoted in Young, 1995: p. 121–122)

Many gay men recount feeling 'out of place' or 'unworthy guests' (Wielder, 1998). Building on these experiences, it has at different times been assumed by members of the gay community, gay writers and academics that gay men and sport are incompatible. Some have claimed that gay men are disinterested in sport as they reject assimilation with narcissism, over-competitiveness and homophobia (Altman, 1992; Dermody, 1999). In this context, it is not surprising that gay men might come to believe that 'sport is not for them'. Hekma (1998: p. 3) aptly notes that "… for gay men, aversion to sports typically has a long personal history".

Sport and gay men have been viewed as 'opposites'. The athlete is viewed as the 'healthy', 'well-adjusted', 'go-getter' (Tatchell, 1996: p. 80, Dermody, 1998: p. 1). In contrast, Dermody (1998: p. 1) presents alternative cultural expressions of gay stereotypes:

> Bigots portray them as child molesters. G&L lifestyles celebrate 'drag' and 'S&M leather'…. Hollywood presents either comic queens, or sad effeminates.

The invisibility of gay male role models in sport, which has been noted elsewhere, does not provide a cultural counteraction to unhealthy stereotypes (Clark, 1992; Clarke, 1998). 'Not feeling at home', verbal harassment, derision of poor performance, invisibility of and lack of communication on homosexuality have all been cited as reasons for gay men's aversion to sport (Hekma, 1998). Likewise the discriminatory social protocol of heterosexist clubs is noted by a number of the athletes interviewed by Woog (1998a).

Paradoxical masculinity and gay sports clubs

So, in the face of discrimination and isolation, what is the attraction for gay men to participate in sports? There are conflicting views in the literature. A number of authors devote time to exploring the erotic element of sports (Pronger, 1990; Clark, 1992). Implications of homoerotic imagination and contact link sport to sexual relations. Likewise, the development of gay gym culture links sport to body control and presentation. As Clark (1992: p. 2) notes regarding the gym, "it was the sport's early base of gay participants striving for a more fuckable bod that put it on the map". These authors suggest stereotypical attractions: ascetic and sexual motivations. Is there a desire to display an inverted masculinity? Are gay men in fact caught in a contradictory love affair with sports? Sport participation may demonstrate paradoxical masculinity. A gay athlete may filter the traditional signs of heterosexual masculinity, through 'ironic gay lenses'. Young gay males are attracted to sport out of desires to construct male identities, but the undercurrent is a desire to attract other men (Pronger, 1990).

The desire to construct a different masculinity may have forced a number of gay athletes out of the 'straight' sporting environment. Perhaps this explains the growing interest in separatist gay sports clubs and teams. As Woog (1998b: p.30) explains, most clubs have a social role within the gay community: "In many ways gay sports have taken over the role once played by bars as gay community centres". The reasons why gay men join a gay sports club are diverse. In addition, the preference for 'gay sport' varies, as Hekma (1998: p. 19) suggests:

> ... because they dislike the competitiveness or macho culture of regular sports, and because they enjoy participating in gay activities or the eroticism of being among gay men. Others opposed gay sports because they enjoy competition of variation, or because they dislike the 'faggotry' of other gay men.

Perhaps these comments demonstrate that gay clubs do not fit the mainstream definitions of sport. If masculinity and athleticism are products of social construction, they should be amenable to contradiction, change and renegotiation. In reality, the way in which these clubs have been organised is sometimes radically different to the dominant institutions of sport. Many of the clubs have spurned the idea of what sport means to the dominant heterosexual culture. Aggressive competition has often been replaced with an 'explore and enjoy the experience' sensibility as clubs have sought to replicate the Gay Games ideals of universal participation (Young, 1995). This is based on an inclusive culture for 'all sexualities' and support of all athletic abilities.

Gay sports clubs in the UK

The initial lack of support from governmental institutions to various types of 'Gay Games' has been noted by Young (1995) and Hekma (1998). As participants have been shunned from straight clubs, likewise the wider sport network has at times ridiculed gay clubs and games. In addition, media commentary has done little to help dispel heterosexist views of gay sport (Pronger, 1990; Woog, 1998a). One journalist's report on a plan for the BGLSF to host the 1999 EuroGames in Manchester is an example of extreme hostility to gay sport: "Woofters chasing each other round a track.... Shirtlifters weightlifting ... For three weeks this city's population is to be subjected to an invasion of thousands of foreign deviants..." (quoted in Clarke, 1998: p. 155). Subsequently, lack of commitment from the local authorities and financial problems were cited as the reasons for the collapse of the 1999 bid (Clarke, 1998). Examples such as these suggest limited support from mainstream sport institutions.

Where then do these alternative clubs sit within sport? Pronger (1994) suggests that attempting to change dominant institutional sport from the inside is conspiring with 'fascism':

> ...the issue becomes not one, then, of including more people in sport, but of trying to exclude as many as possible from its fascist project. (1994, p. 10; and quoted in Messner, 1996: p. 229)

Responding, Messner (1996) contends that sport can be reinterpreted and resisted. Is, then, the gay sport club an alternative, offered outside the dominant sport institutions, or does it offer the chance to change sport from within the network? At the start of this paper, we saw a glimpse of the interaction between gay sport and the network in practice. Briefly, we need to examine any inclusion of gay sport in recent policy documents.

Two recent policy strategies from Sport England and the Department for Culture, Media and Sport (DCMS) respectively endorse the ethos of 'Sport for All'. *The Value of Sport* (Sport England, 1999: p. 8) states that sport:

> ... must look for innovative ways of reaching the disenchanted and socially excluded to ensure that real progress is made towards the ideal of Sport for All.

The inequities highlighted are 'gender, ethnicity, disability and social class': 'sexuality' is notably absent. *A Sporting Future for All* (DCMS, 2000) details initiatives for local authorities, sport development units and clubs to tackle 'inequities' and 'social exclusion' from society and sport. The initiatives of gay sports clubs could act as prime facilitators of this strategy, yet gay sport and sexuality again receive no mention although the document is a generalist presentation.

What then is the situation at the local level? Are gay sport clubs resisting an exclusive, dominant heterosexual sport culture? Has the dominant culture acknowledged or supported their role? Do gay clubs represent social inclusion, or a perpetuation of social exclusion from mainstream sports? Would true social inclusion involve catering for gay men within mainstream sports? These are questions we will take up later.

Method

This paper forms part of a larger research project funded by a research grant from the University of Northumbria at Newcastle, undertaken to look at the "participation patterns and organisation of 'openly' gay male sports activities, in the UK". The data used in this paper were collected in two parts. Initially surveys were designed for club organisers. After gaining a general quantitative picture of gay sports clubs in the UK, follow-up interviews were to be conducted with some of the club organisers. (This would also allow 'snowballing' of a members sample, for a second set of surveys on members' experiences of sport, in and out of gay clubs. This latter on-going stage of data collection will be presented elsewhere.)

The initial survey questions covered the following key areas:

- club history and purpose;
- sport activities and delivery;
- participation/competitive structures;
- staffing and finance;
- membership demographics, recruitment, reasons for participating;
- relationships with other sport organisations.

The subsequent interviews probed the areas above in more detail and examined:

- club role in the gay and wider community;
- stereotypes associated with gay sports clubs and gay men's participation;
- differences between alternative and mainstream sport culture.

Initially, the BGLSF had agreed to distribute surveys to their total club membership (50 clubs approximately Clarke, 1998). The surveys were to be distributed with the BGLSF newsletter. A poor response was received, with only 7 clubs replying. Subsequently, it became apparent that a local authority had agreed to administer the newsletters and surveys for the BGLSF, and clubs had received the survey after the 'cut-off' date for replies. Whilst the low return was disappointing, those who did respond provided insightful comments on club purpose and culture. Surprisingly, 6 of the 7 respondents were willing to take part in all further stages of the research. (Before and after interview a number of respondents directly phoned or wrote to the researchers, to express further interest in helping with the research. This perhaps suggests the novelty, within gay sports, of being researched.)

At this stage Peter Thompson joined the research project. Peter was to conduct interviews with the six club organisers already identified and attempt to make further contacts with other clubs elicited from gay magazines, internet searches and gay switchboards (we did not expect the BGLSF to release contact details due to confidentiality). Before interview all the newly recruited club organisers completed the survey. As interviewing commenced and the sample recruitment went on, it became apparent that there was a London / non-London club divide, based on the degree of support from and integration into a gay sport network. In response, the researchers deliberately tried to obtain club details from outside of London. Control of sport types sampled was not intended, although the researchers tried to avoid repeating sport types among the clubs interviewed.

Sample details

In total, 12 interviews were conducted with male organisers of gay sports clubs. At the time of writing only 10 transcripts were available. Table 1 (page following) provides the sample details. The geographical locations of the clubs were London (5), and Brighton, Bristol, Leicester, Manchester and Newcastle (1 each).

Table 1:   Sample details

Sports offered	Interviewee's Position	Membership		
		Total	Male	Female
Swimming, Badminton, Cycling	Chair	200	177	23
Outdoor activities	Regional Contact	22	20	2
Swimming	Secretary	144	115	29
Football	Chair	20	15	5
Football	Chairman/ Membership Secretary	250	215	35
Badminton, Tennis, Cycling	Chairman	65	54	11
Karate	Chair	60	40	20
Rugby Union	Chair	40	39	1
Rugby Union	Secretary	80	77	3

Although the sample involved male organisers of gay sports clubs, the clubs were not 'male only' but had predominantly male memberships. Both Hekma (1998) and Clarke (1998) have commented on the quantitative dominance of males in gay sports clubs. Considering this, it is perhaps not surprising that the organisers were all male. Using a male sample was of benefit when asking organisers to describe the culture created for gay men, since the club leaders could draw on their personal experience of joining and organising the sport club.

Research administration

Interviews were conducted by telephone, in order to cope with the geographical scattering of clubs. The interviews lasted approximately 40 minutes. This resulted in 'rich data', as the interviewer had the participant's written responses to survey questions, to probe further. There were initial concerns about the impersonality of telephone interviewing with potentially sensitive topics. However, a pilot interview proved successful and interviews flowed freely. All respondents agreed to the tape-recording of the interviews which were later transribed and subjected to content analysis.

Researcher identities

The research team was careful to consider their relative involvement in data collection. The initial research idea was developed by Lindsay King, a straight female. However, owing to other work pressures it was necessary to recruit a research administrator. By coincidence the researcher, Peter Thompson, was a gay male.

Lindsay's story:

> *Several colleagues and friends raised the now-familiar question, 'how and why are you researching sport and 'gay males', when you're not either?'. I am straight but I spend a great deal of time with a gay male friend, who's an avid sport participant. My interest in the research developed from seeing the trouble my friend had in trying to find a gay sports club to join, on moving to the UK from Canada. On subsequently joining a gay badminton club, he would often describe the different stages of gay sport, club and league development, between the UK and Canada.*

Peter's story:

> *Having already completed research in the area of homosexuality I was interested in the study. I hoped to be able to contribute to the research both in terms of the actual research process and with my knowledge of gay men and the issues that surround them. The interviews were very much reciprocal and I felt that the respondents were comfortable talking to a gay man (with experience of interviewing other gay men) who could understand and relate to their feelings. Considering that all of the clubs are always looking to recruit new members I was surprised that the process of identifying clubs and contacting them proved quite difficult. I had some success through adverts in gay newspapers but most of the clubs I used were identified through web pages on the Internet. Although not all the clubs were willing to be interviewed I had a 100% response to the surveys that were sent out after the initial telephone call to establish contact.*

On reading the following discussion the reader should consider the researchers' value positions. As a white, straight, female, Lindsay has perhaps felt less 'discrimination' than gay colleagues. Debate on the question, 'Is a straight female authorised to speak about gay men and sport?' has arisen elsewhere. Messner (1996), for example, has been accused of reproducing the hetero-homo binary, by Davidson and Shogan (1998):

> His "studying up" is an unproblematised "authoritarian speech about a gay subject" in which it is not noticed "who is authorised to speak, to whom, and with what truth effects... (Davidson and Shogan, 1998: p. 365).

In the context of this paper, the position of power the first author occupies within a 'straight' discourse is acknowledged. In conjunction, one needs to consider how far outside personal social circles the researcher can go, before she/he can no longer 'report for' the researched? This debate has been taken up with race, gender, age etc. Readers here are aware of the researchers' identities and should take these into account. Using empathy and letting the club organisers speak for themselves were key elements in the treatment of data, for both researchers. Whilst the discussions raise the issues brought to the fore by respondents, the conclusions and policy questions are purely the researchers' own.

Results

UK Gay sport is somewhat in the shadow of the faster developments in North America. The clubs within this research are relatively young, with only two formed before 1989. The two formed in the 1970s were sport-generalist in nature, reflecting perhaps an earlier, greater emphasis on being a social rather than sport club. The clubs set up in the 90s are all sport specific, with the exception of one. The primary focus of activities varied between clubs. Four of the clubs presented themselves as social/recreation groups; three saw competition as their focus; and three catered for recreation and competition.

Membership is heavily biased towards men. The Karate club had the highest proportion of female members, but this was low at 33.3%. Only one of the organisers interviewed raised unprompted concerns about low female membership. Two organisers stated that their clubs catered for gay men only, in their account of club purpose and constitutional documents. In both cases, the clubs provided a team sport considered to be traditionally male. Interestingly, within both clubs there were a couple of straight female members, but lesbians were absent [according to the statements of the organisers: members may not be 'open' or 'overt' regarding their sexuality]. All the organisers stated that straight members could join. Although clubs would not actively recruit 'straight' members, promotional material made it clear that non-gay members were welcome. As one organiser said, "Our events are open to everyone. Gay participants often bring non-gay friends or relations on walks". Most clubs saw accepting straight members as a chance to consolidate their role in the wider sport network and in the social circles of members. Likewise, they often operated in local authority and community facilities, so expected the facilities to be open to all. There was an expectation that straight members or guests would be socially attached to and 'vetted' by a gay member. In addition, it was anticipated that 'straight' members would need to be 'gay friendly' and willing to participate in a gay environment.

Reasons for setting up gay-separatist sport clubs

Clubs were set up for a variety of reasons. Three themes were apparent:
- a feeling that gay men were denied opportunities to participate elsewhere;
- a safe space, non-judgmental of sexuality, could be created;
- clubs could act as an alternative way of socialising with and/or meeting other gay men.

Organisers argued that straight sport was often associated with competition and lacked any focus on personal or skill development. In the context of the alternative clubs, men could play at any standard. As one respondent explained:

> Most of the people that we get aren't particularly good at football… They might be wary about joining a football team, thinking that they weren't good enough… We advertise it as a fun social group, rather than being serious.

The organisers acknowledged that many members had a personal history of alienation from sport. Some organisers ran evaluations where typical comments illustrated this point: for example, "playing rugby is so much fun, I wish I would have realised this 20 years ago". Others felt that men were denied the opportunity to play within the rest of the community because of the social hostility of a 'straight' environment. From a club with one hundred active members, an organiser commented that only a couple of members had played sport since leaving school. There was a strong implication that many members would not play sport, if a gay club did not exist.

A number of organisers felt a need to create a safe space for gay men to participate in sport. The 'space' they believed they had created was physically and socially safe. An organiser elaborated:

> [This] leisure centre is used for our swimming group and it is fantastic, it might not be like a gorgeous new swimming pool but because it is secure because of the area that it is in, people feel safe when they go in. There have been cases of homophobia from the general public and it has been dealt with very well by [this centre].

The gay clubs aimed to be friendly and non-threatening. A social environment was created where a gay man could disclose information about himself, any partners and sexuality, without fear of 'retribution'.

Many of the clubs were set up by groups of friends or individuals, with the aim to create social opportunities for 'like minded' people. At the present stage, all of the clubs saw themselves primarily as 'sport' rather than 'social' clubs. The clubs presented a health and fitness orientated environment in which to meet people, in contrast to 'bar hopping' and 'clubbing'. Many of the organisers felt that the traditional gay social scene was unappealing to some of the gay community. They catered for those seeking alternative social outlets:

> As somebody who at the time was in their late 30s I found that the concept of meeting gay people in clubs and those sort of places, the traditional way of meeting people didn't appeal to me and I was thinking that I wanted to meet people in a context where we have something in common and you can still have fun because you are doing something you want to do.

This need was felt more strongly in a number of the clubs outside London. They felt a need to self-organise because of the lack of gay sport opportunities in their area.

One club had been formed under quite different circumstances from the others. In the context of gay men's health promotion work (local authority funded), a needs assessment had taken place. Gay men's perceptions of illness, health and, subsequently, sport were evaluated. In response to the assessment, low level and higher level activity groups were set up. Initially the club was driven by an individual worker, but it developed a 'voluntary club' focus to its organisation and delivery.

Changes in purpose?

Over time clubs have grown and changed and consequently discussion of direction arises. A number of clubs commented on the implications of growing membership size. Members' needs were more wide ranging. Participation levels and demand for different sports were often diverse. In turn, this had implications for the levels of organisation. Some clubs operated in an informal self-help style, others were highly structured.

Club committees had been struggling for some time with a number of debates centred on three themes:
- the need to cater for competitive athletes;
- political roles in the gay community, wider sport community;
- questions around inclusion of lesbians and heterosexuals'

Clubs were operating under a philosophy of inclusion of all abilities. At times, conflict between the desire to 'field' a competitive side and the need to include everyone was apparent. One organiser illustrated a common problem:

> The tennis teams are quite competitive as well but the problem is that as you start something like this, it is supposed to be all inclusive and that sometimes means that the good players think 'well I don't really want to play with beginners so I won't play'.

Many clubs felt a need to challenge stereotypes, by proving themselves through this competition. They wished to make more obvious the contribution of gay athletes to sport.

This semi-political motivation links to club roles in wider challenges. Clubs saw themselves, foremost, as facilitators of activities for gay men. However, they did feel a responsibility to challenge stereotypes and change people's attitudes towards gay men in sport. For many clubs their resistance was seen as indirect. They anticipated that through playing they could make a difference. Two organisers expressed this:

> Any gay person or gay organisation would feel that the fact that they are there, the fact they are doing what they are doing, in an open way, is going to effect straight people's attitudes if they come across them.

> ... we do feel that we are confounding a few stereotypes, like gay men don't like football and they are all a bit mincy queeny, that sort of thing.

Many of the clubs felt that their relative success in including sections of wider society, was a matter for reflection and future action. A number of clubs, although promoting themselves as open to gays and lesbians, felt that lesbians believed they were a 'gay' club. Three of the clubs integrated with 'straight' clubs to different degrees e.g. for training. Many of the clubs had played 'friendlies' against straight clubs, but fewer took part in 'mainstream' leagues. One club had endless debates at committee meetings on how to get more straight members involved. For another club, the decision to be an 'exclusive' gay-only club had been a contentious one. In practice, their policy was not actively upheld, as the following example illustrates:

> We don't really exclude although it is a contentious issue. Our coach is straight and his two sons play with us. We did agree that a lot of people wanted to contribute and support gay clubs that aren't actually gay, so we thought that should be a discretionary decision rather than an absolute. In terms of our aims and objectives, a lot of our strength comes from the fact that we are clear that the club is there to promote [itself] for gay men.

Club culture

Organisers were asked to describe the culture within their club. With the exception of two, they claimed the environment was different from 'straight' facilities. The culture catered for needs in a way that 'straight' sport clubs are not able to do. Clubs were seen as less competitive, more private and less family-orientated. In particular, the environment provided by clubs protected men from the attention and hostility they might face in mainstream sport:

> ...they [mainstream sports clubs] don't provide a welcoming atmosphere if you are gay. It is like anything gay. If you go into a gay pub or something, you know that you are going to be accepted, you can relax and be yourself. Whereas if you go into a straight pub and start camping it up you might get beaten up or chucked out, it is the same in a football group.

The clubs in our research sample catered for a broad range of abilities (in contrast to straight clubs which were perceived to cater for a particular participation level). Organisers estimated that the largest proportion of their members fell into lower ability and participation levels. However, beginners were still expected to participate in the sport. Club philosophy centred on personal development, and members were encouraged to set their own personal goals:

> People have this perception of swimming being very competitive and very hard, but people can come along and compete in a London competition, in our competition, just by putting a time in and they just have to do 50 metres as fast as they want and then next time they can just do it better and train to do it better.

Clubs that played a sport offered competitive opportunities. Whilst a number of highly successful athletes were noted; only two clubs appeared to prioritise training and competition before recreation and fitness activities. One club organiser said:

> We are definitely a sports club first, because that is what we spend all our time with, we don't do social, everything is not geared around that sort of stuff, it is geared around getting faster times and improving fitness.

Nevertheless, club culture involved welcoming new members and offering opportunities for members to make new friends. Organisers, by virtue of the length of their involvement, had seen club and team developments. Many spoke of a 'family' of members, based on strong relationships and trust. Others noted emotional attachments and pride in club affiliation. Whilst organisers noted that "...there is always an aspect of relationship hunting going on...", some clubs felt that members actively discouraged this occurring.

Respondents talked of accepting environments and noted that people would not 'bat an eyelid' at sexual orientation, mannerisms, or demonstrations of affection. The club provided a culture where gay men could 'be themselves'. For example:

> ... you can completely be yourself in a gay sports club, if you want to make a camper mark then you can do so. If you belonged to a straight club, even if they knew that you were gay, I don't think that they would expect you to be coming out with very camp or bitchy remarks.

Organisers felt that participants need not feel any of the awkwardness associated with mainstream sport:

> The biggest thing is swimming, a lot of partners and couples go. If they want to go swimming then they go together like a family would, but they can feel comfortable in that if they did touch each other or something like that then it wouldn't matter. There is none of the uncomfortableness and paranoia and guardedness that they would perhaps have within a general swimming session.

The gay club also affords men the chance to be open. Clubs do not force men to explain their sexuality, yet there is the absence of any pressure to disguise it. Clubs recognised that the culture offered men the opportunity to 'be out' which they might not have in everyday life. Likewise the problems of heterosexist social protocol are avoided:

> It really is just saying we are gay, we don't want to join a straight club because we can't necessarily be out. Or if we want to be out then we have to go through this situation of coming out, you go along and you get to know people and then you have to go through this thing of "oh by the way my partner is a man", and that's a bit cringeworthy, whereas here you turn up and it's just accepted or expected or whatever, it's not an issue.

The gay club culture allowed athletes the chance to talk about sexuality and other players in a sexual way if they desired. As one organiser aptly illustrates:

> A gay man going to a straight club, there are going to be certain subjects that are off limits. I am not saying that we all stand around talking about players' legs but it does occasionally crop up in the conversation. It's just a different culture.

Gay sports clubs in the wider sport network

It is perhaps now apparent that gay clubs have developed a distinctive ethos. The overall club culture is based on inclusion, regardless of ability. However, in order for gay men to feel at ease, an element of exclusivity is required to protect privacy. Generally, the research sample clubs provided for gay men and their friends (who could be straight). The clubs are providing for those who may have previously felt socially excluded from sport. Considering the recent statements of the Sports Council and the UK government (Sport England, 1999; DCMS, 2000) on social inclusion, the clubs would appear to fit the strategy ethos, as they provide inclusion for gay men. We now explore the position of clubs in the wider sport network. Do the club organisers believe they are recognised, valued and treated as equals?

Links to other gay sport clubs

The organisers frequently commented on the geographical dispersity of gay clubs in the UK. To compete against other gay clubs requires significant travel and associated costs. It was recognised that London and continental Europe acted as a focus for many gay events or leagues. Some clubs had been able to counteract the expense of competing in Europe when host clubs offered accommodation; however, expense could be a barrier to interaction with other clubs. Likewise a number of clubs were aware of few, if any, other gay clubs in their sport. In contrast, some sports such as badminton and volleyball benefited from considerable popularity in European gay clubs.

It is not only the chosen sport, but location that effects the opportunity for inter-action with other gay sport clubs. Organisers noted a London versus non-London divide — as one said:

> ...but it is like Londonitis, the focus is always around London. Things are more likely to happen in London, clubs are more likely to get together because there are more gay men living there.

Organisers accounted for the larger number of London clubs and informal networks, with comments on the wider catchment of gay men, the ease of club contact and awareness of each other. In areas with lower catchments and less developed gay communities, some organisers struggled to establish clubs. As one said:

> ...particularly outside of London where gay sport is hardly organised at all. There must be gay sports people out there, they just don't know any other gay sports people so they never form clubs or anything.

Likewise, London was the focus of events and festivals, which were often co-ordinated by the BGLSF.

The British Gay and Lesbian Sport Federation (BGLSF)

Clubs had different expectations of the role of the BGLSF, including co-ordination of the gay games and other festivals, communication with government bodies and offering a general support structure for clubs. Expectations of (or desires for) BGLSF support varied according to the size of the club. One of the largest clubs recognised that a small staff of two or three could do little more than any of the member clubs individually. However, the 'sway' of a co-ordinating body was seen to be important in negotiations with other organisations such as the Lottery Sports fund, and with gay event organisers such as London Pride. As one respondent said:

> If an organisation such as the BGLSF come forward and say that we are representing all the gay and lesbian sport clubs in Britain and we would like a presence in mardi gras, then no matter how small they are because of their standing they are able to get things done that as a club we couldn't.

The BGLSF received criticism from clubs for its London focus, work with London clubs and London events; and for lack of direct communication and slow response to getting information out. This is not uncommon for many small, resource constrained, voluntary organisations. One organiser said of BGLSF:

> ...there is no real direct communication with the clubs, certainly nothing in writing to say we are doing this and we want to find out about that and who are you, and what's your contact details and all that sort of stuff. It's a bit fragmented...

Some organisers felt the committee was formed by individuals with their own agendas and the approach was uncoordinated. There appears to be some animosity and frustration over the organisation of events, where clubs appear to desire more consultation. A number of organisers said their clubs intended to obtain representation in the organisation, to instigate change. Improved communication, co-ordination and accountability were prime wishes for the BGLSF. Clubs wanted practical support, e.g. in promotion and publicity training, plus contacts for international competition. All clubs who were members wanted to hear of other clubs than Stonewall football club which, they reported, dominated newsletter coverage:

> A good forum for communication so we know when other clubs are holding their events and we can support them and that kind of stuff.

Links to the gay community

Many of the interviewees commented on their desire to "uphold honour" for the gay community. For some this was a positive feeling, endorsed by the support and congratulations they received.

> A lot of people know who we are and are talking about us. I remember, at the times of the last gay games, reading about [the club] in the pink paper and

even though I hate football having a real sense of ownership because they were Manchester and I think that is what a lot of people are getting back.

Others felt a sense of pressure to compete to a high level, as losing would mean 'letting yourself, team and community down'. A number felt this pressure was greater than for straight clubs, a consequence of the feeling that stereotypes should be challenged and more attention given to some clubs by the media.

> I think that there is that feeling sometimes by some people, that being in a league for example is such a responsibility because we are not just like any other club, we get more press coverage as a rugby club than any other rugby club in Britain apart from those in the premiership.

Despite any pressure, clubs want to be involved in outreach and promotion of sport to the gay community. On a practical level, the annual London Pride offered an opportunity for the BGLSF to set up a sports tent and stalls, with demonstrations planned for 2000.

Playing with 'straight'[3] clubs

Due to their lower number, most gay clubs accept the need to compete against 'straight' clubs. Some would prefer gay leagues, but many do not have a preference.

Some clubs had problems getting games, but this appeared to be linked to club inexperience. Concurrently, whilst there was no direct discrimination, it was felt that it might be 'lurking' behind the closed doors of some straight clubs who declined the invitation to compete. The following two quotations illustrate different experiences:

> ...one of the difficulties that we did have was getting games and I think that is inherent within sports clubs anyway and I also suspect that it's because we are gay men.

> ... we have a waiting list of clubs who want to play us and we can't play them because we don't have time.

Other noted incidents of homophobia were infrequent. There were some derogatory comments used during competitions, but for competitive clubs this was felt to be the way of the game. Organisers recognised that a number of their members continued to play for straight clubs because of higher competitive levels and the availability of more games. There was one clear example of integration. A straight club had approached a gay club, inviting them to play with them on a permanent basis and have their own games. It was noted that the inviting club were sensitive to the gay club's need to maintain their own identity and have not attempted to hide their participation as a gay club:

> It has been really positive so far, [although] everybody is guarded on both sides and they are still very polite but the feedback has been very positive and

people have got drunk together and had a good time. It is not just that we are using their facilities, they make us very welcome.

Local Authorities and Governing Bodies

At facility level, assistance received praise. Services varied: one facility sent forward possible members; one club were protected in the service contract; another facility wanted to organise a gay tournament. Development officers were reported to be less helpful, with the exception of offering inclusion in Sport Directories. Several organisers had taken the initiative to visit leisure services and invite development officers to attend meetings, with no results. A number of clubs were frustrated with the lack of developmental help.

> ... bearing in mind that we live in a catchment area of over 20,000 gay people, the local council was not very supportive and it has since proved to be the case that the council spends a very small amount of money on gay and lesbian issues in the area.

There was an exception to this pattern. As previously illustrated, one club had received direct support from the Health Authority and Health Action Zone, for research on health/sport and some development work. Support was appreciated where received, and a number of organisers felt that local sport development and facilities could do more to promote sport access for gay men. As one said:

> ...they have women-only sessions and Muslim-only sessions. I am not saying that specialist services are the only answer but it is important to look at the needs of lesbian and gay men, within the structure and the framework of your organisation.

Whilst support was desirable, clubs did not want to lose their autonomous identity.

There were limited comments on governing bodies. Some recreational clubs did not have membership. Observations varied from the positive to neutral. Some clubs felt they were treated like any other club, while one club felt they were over-scrutinised as an indirect result of being a gay club. The governing body, in the latter case, received media attention because of the gay status of the club and, hence, wished to be able to justify their membership. Few clubs were aware of training available, yet desired to develop competitively and in membership size.

Conclusions and policy issues

The aim of this paper has been to present an over-view and to offer an insight into the data collected. We have presented the results with few links to existing literature because of the novelty of the research subject. Areas touched on here will be addressed in more detail in future papers. However, considering the views of Pronger (1994) and

Messner (1996), discussed earlier, the paper will end with a focus on the role of the sport club as a reaction against or an alternative 'playmate' of the dominant sport network. This follows-on from the discussion of the practical position of the gay sports clubs in UK sport.

Are the clubs challenging social exclusion by being inclusive of the recreationally disadvantaged? Or should they seek to challenge social exclusion of gay men from sport by operating as close as possible to a mainstream sport club model? Dermody (1998: p. 4) presents a 'fun' model, a picture of the practice of the 'Golden Gate Wrestling Club' (of which he is coach) as "... *strictly* athletic, very mainstream, less elitist, more recreational and very inclusive". This model suggests that clubs should 'integrate' by providing a culture similar to that of mainstream clubs. But, if clubs were to operate under mainstream models, then equal support would be required from higher institutions. Our research shows that some clubs feel supported by their governing bodies and some by local authorities; however, there is a feeling that more support could be given generally. Whilst this would be an issue for any voluntary sport club, the invisibility of gay sports clubs in national sport policy and discussions does not bode well for a 'trickle down' of further support.

A perennial dilemma faced by minority groups is that the degree of support offered from the mainstream may be influenced by the actions of the minority groups themselves. The clubs may effectively contribute to discrimination (or lack of support from the outside) in the very process of providing for their own. Dutch government-commissioned research conducted by Hekma (1998) illustrates this problem in the Netherlands. When the team of researchers advocated gay-separatist clubs, the Government response was negative, with fears of 'ghettoization' and 'social splintering'. The government reacted in a similar manner to the successful bid to host the Gay Games in Amsterdam, 1998, since social integration policies in Holland require activities to be open to everyone. However, support was later received for the games when it was affirmed that "straights [would] not be excluded" (Hekma, 1998: p. 22). Dutch politicians have not encouraged autonomous forms of organisation for minorities. In the UK we have a similar situation.

The position of the gay sports clubs in terms of inclusion and exclusion is not clear-cut. Are they within the mainstream or outside it? Where are they located on a continuum? At one end, clubs may be sympathetic to gays and all sexualities; at the other they may be "...separatist G&L culture orientated..." (Dermody, 1998: p. 4). At the same time most clubs would not actively recruit straight members. Perhaps clubs are offering a real alternative to mainstream sport. Although they say they will cater for anyone who wants to join, they do this within a gay culture, and on a practical level this may be regarded as socially exclusive. It has been acknowledged that, collectively, sport contributes to the reification of heterosexuality within the sporting world (Pronger, 1990; Hargreaves, 1994). So are separatist clubs resisting the dominant patriarchy, or are they 'buying into' it? Clubs need to be inclusive to match their philosophy, yet they need to be exclusive enough to attract gay men. Pronger (1994) and Messner (1996) do not see such alternative clubs as challenges to dominant sport institutions; perhaps the challenge they make is more subtle.

The sport clubs discussed in this paper serve a socially 'excluded' group — gay males. In order to serve this group, they need to be seen by their members as operationally 'exclusive', at least to some extent. Can they be seen as 'exclusive' and also be seen as part of the inclusionist movement in sport?

Consider the absence of gay groups in policy documents. In response to the English Sports Council's omission of homosexuals from their list of groups facing recreational discrimination (ESC, 1997), Gill Clarke (1998: p.156) urged that:

> By remaining silent on issues of sexual and social justice the English Sports Council colludes with others in the legitimising of a particularly narrow and stereotyped discourse of sexuality and sporting participation....

The ESC's response was that not all groups could be listed, and that the final statement — "The challenge is to ensure that sport is openly accessible to *everyone* ..." — was deemed to include all groups facing discrimination (ESC, 1997: p. 6.).

But, to add to Clarke's (1998) concerns, the policy document and others following continue to miss out the contribution made by the gay sports clubs, discussed in this paper. These questions require debate. Do policy-makers wish to encourage the development of more gay-separatist clubs? Alternatively, will they rise to the challenge of actively recognising the detrimental and exclusionist effects which are caused directly by homophobia and indirectly by sport and sport policies entrenched in hegemonic, heterosexual masculinity?

The questions this paper raises are many. It is the intention to put them forward for debate and response from academics and policy-makers. The research programme has created further data, not discussed within the remit of this paper, and subsequent data collected on gay members' experiences of club sport will also be released.

It is felt appropriate to conclude with comments from one of the organisers to summarise the issues, for the reader's consideration:

> I think that it is an unfair criticism of gay men to expect them to just go out and get over it, that is one of the worst criticisms that gay men should be able to just go into a straight environment and feel comfortable in terms of challenging that. We do recognise that lots of gay men are quite happy playing in straight teams, on whatever level. We have comments like 'why do you have to have a gay-only team? My friend is gay and he has come out and he has had no hassle'. Obviously that is people's experiences. Gay-only teams are not the answer, they are just part of it. We are just getting to a level where we are having our gay-only teams, but the day will come when we start to challenge sport generally, in terms of everybody should have a right to access it, and sport is there for everybody.

Acknowledgement

The assistance of David Hindley in initially reviewing literature for the overall research programme was greatly appreciated.

Notes

[1]   The British Gay and Lesbian Sport Federation (BGLSF) is a voluntary, non-profit making organisation, originated in 1994. It acts as a support group to approximately 50 gay sports clubs (Birch, 1996 cited in Clarke, 1998). At the time of this writing, the most up-to-date statistics had not been obtained from the BGLSF (Personal correspondence, 2000).

[2]   The first Gay Games in 1982 attracted 1,350 participants. By Amsterdam, 1998, the number of athletes was over 14,000 (Clarke, 1998).

[3]   The label 'straight club' is used to categorise clubs that do not promote themselves as providing for specific sexualities: it is acknowledge that this label is problematic.

References

Anon. (2000) 'Teaching from the closet', *The Advocate* April 11: www.advocate.com/html/stories/809/809_anon_persp.html

BBC Radio 5 (1998) Interview with Stonewall Football Club.

British Gay and Lesbian Sports Federation (2000) Personal correspondence.

Clark, J. (1992) 'The locker as closet. Queer activists say, "We are everywhere". So where are the gays in high-performance sports?', www.fawny.org/roundup.html

Clarke, G. (1998) 'Queering the pitch and coming out to play: Lesbians in physical education and sport', *Sport, Education and Society* Vol. 3, No. 2: pp. 145–160.

Curry, T. J. (1991) 'Fraternal bonding in the locker room: A profeminist analysis of talk about competition and women', *Sociology of Sport Journal* No. 8: pp. 119–135.

Davidson, J. and Shogan, D. (1998) 'What's queer about studying up? A response to Messner', *Sociology of Sport Journal* Vol. 15, No. 4: pp. 359–371.

Dermody, G. (1998) 'American wrestling: A success story for gays and lesbians'. Unpublished paper presented at the *European Gay and Lesbian Federation* Meeting. October, Lisbon.

——— (1999) 'Why Gay Games?'. Unpublished paper presented at the Federation of Gay Games Forum, April.

Department for Culture, Media and Sport (2000) 'A sporting future for all', www.culture.gov.UK/sport/index.html

Dunning, E. (1986) 'Sport as a male preserve: Notes on the social sources of masculine identity and its transformations', *Theory, Culture and Society* Vol. 3, No. 1: pp. 79–91.

English Sports Council, (1997) *England, the sporting nation*. Ipswich: Ancient House Press.

Hall, A. (1998) 'Is NASSS homophobic and racist?', Sociology of Sport On-line at www.brunel.ac.uk/depts/sps/sosol/vlila2.htm

Hargreaves, J. (1994) *Sporting females*. London: Routledge.

Hekma, G. (1998) 'As Long as They Don't Make an Issue of It…:' Gay Men and Lesbians in Organised Sports in the Netherlands', Journal of Homosexuality Vol. 35, No. 1) pp. 1–23.

Kruger, A. (1999) 'The homosexual and homoerotic in sport', in J. Riodan and A. Kruger (eds) *The international politics of sport in the 20th century*. London: E & FN Spon.

Laberge, S. and Albert, M (1999) 'Concepts of masculinity and of gender transgressions in sport among adolescent boys', *Men and Masculinities* Vol. 3: pp. 243–267.

Lenskyj, H. J. (1990) 'Power and play: Gender and sexuality issues in sport and physical activity', *International Review of Sociology of Sport* Vol. 25, No. 3: pp. 235–243.

——— (1991) 'Combating homophobia in sport and physical education', *Sociology of Sport Journal* 8: pp. 61–69.

Messner, M. (1992) *Power at play: Sports and the problem of masculinity*. Boston: Beacon Press.

——— (1996) 'Studying up on sex', *Sociology of Sport Journal* 13: pp. 221–237.

Messner, M. and Sabo, D. F. (eds) (1994) *Sex, violence and power in sports: Rethinking masculinity*. Freedom: The Crossing Press.

Parker, A. (1996) 'Sporting masculinities: Gender relations and the body', in M. Mac An Ghaill (ed) *Understanding masculinities: Social relations and cultural arenas*. Buckinghamshire: Open University Press.

Pronger, B. (1990) *The arena of masculinity: Sports, homosexuality and the meaning of sex*. London: GMP Publishers.

Rotella, R. J. and Murray, M. M. (1991) 'Homophobia, the world of sport, and sport psychology consulting', *The Sport Psychologist* Vol. 5: pp. 355–364.

Squires, S. L. and Sparkes, A. C. (1996) 'Circles of silence: Sexual identity in physical education and sport', *Sport, Education and Society* Vol. 1, No. 1: pp. 77–101.

Sport England (1999) *Best Value through sport: The value of sport*. London.

Tatchell, P. (1996) 'A queer way of re-defining masculinity', Heroes and Heroines, *Soundings* Vol. 3, pp. 79–84.

The Federation of Gay Games (2000) Federation member Organisations, www.gaygames.org/comorg.htm

Wielder, J. (1998) 'The gift of the gay athlete', *The Advocate* August 18: p. 11.

Woog, D. (1998a) *Jocks: True stories of America's gay male athletes*. London: Turnaround.

——— (1998b) 'Fields of teams', *The Advocate* August 18: pp. 30–31.

Young, P. D. (1995) *Lesbians and gays and sports*. New York: Chelsea House.

Benchmarking of Public Leisure Services: A Tool for Efficiency, Effectiveness or Equity?

Susan M Ogden
Glasgow Caledonian University
David Booth
South Lanarkshire Council

Introduction

In the increasingly competitive leisure and recreation sector, continuous improvement of service quality is necessary. Unfortunately, 'competing for quality' (HMSO, 1991) encouraged an emphasis on inputs rather than outcomes such as customer satisfaction and social inclusion (Bailey and Reid, 1994), and was found to inhibit service development (DETR, 1998). This led to the replacement of compulsory competitive tendering (CCT) — introduced to leisure services in 1989 — by the policy of Best Value (BV), implemented in Scotland from 1997 and, in England and Wales via the Local Government Act 1999. The policy of BV has charged local authority leisure providers with the double challenge of further developing their commercial orientation (i.e., so as to be less reliant on public subsidy), while more fully demonstrating their commitment to effectiveness in terms of customers and wider stakeholders, including non-users or those with limited voice/spending power — the recreationally deprived (ILAM, 1997; Coalter *et al.*, 1988). In other words, local authorities must demonstrate efficiency, effectiveness and equity in the delivery of services. The BV mantra is "Challenge, Compare, Consult and Compete" (DETR, 1998) in order to ensure that the objectives of accountability, transparency, continuous improvement and ownership are fulfilled (Scottish Office, 1998). To fulfill these ends, benchmarking is advocated both as a way of ensuring that a wider perspective is injected into strategic service reviews required under BV (DETR, 1998) and as a way of helping authorities identifying where and how performance improvements in service delivery can be made (Accounts Commission, 1999). Using the BV language, benchmarking can be seen as a way of 'comparing' service outcomes and outputs in order to 'challenge' both what services are delivered and how they are delivered (see Figure 1). By doing so, benchmarking should foster 'continuous improvement' and should help an authority to demonstrate the competitiveness of public service provision against alternative service providers.

The aim of this paper is to explore the role and limitations of public sector benchmarking in delivering best value and, in particular, discuss the key issues surrounding its implementation in local authority sport and recreations services. As Robinson (1997) suggests managerial techniques such as total quality management (TQM) and benchmarking must be adapted to the public sector context. Thus, the extent to which benchmarking is a useful tool for measuring and improving performance relating to efficiency, effectiveness and equity dimensions of leisure service provision is investigated. The paper first provides an overview of the manner in which Best Value is being implemented in Scotland and explains how this differs to the English approach. This leads on to a discussion about the role of benchmarking in delivering BV, and, in particular, a debate relating to the extent to which social inclusion effectiveness (a) affects benchmarks, and (b) can be improved by applying process benchmarking. These issues are then examined via a case study of the South West of Scotland Benchmarking Group (SWSBG), which formed in 1998 as a forum for investigating and improving performance of its member authorities in relation to the provision of sport and recreation services. This paper follows on from earlier work which highlighted the importance of managing inter- and intra-organisational relations in order to ensure effective public sector benchmarking (Ogden and Wilson, 1999; Ogden and Wilson, 2001).

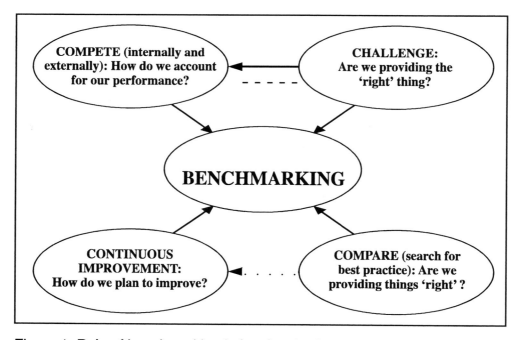

Figure 1: Role of benchmarking in local authority sport and recreation

Best Value: the Scottish approach

Following the announcement of a commitment to the BV policy by the Blair Government after its election in 1997, the approach to the implementation of BV has differed across the UK. This is in light with the ideal that practice should feed directly into policy. In line with this philosophy, the Scottish approach to BV has attempted to avoid a highly prescriptive approach. In June 1997, all 32 Scottish local authorities were granted a 12 month extension to the CCT moratorium which had been put in place in 1995 to allow authorities to concentrate on local government reorganisation. A Best Value Joint Task Force, comprising The Scottish Office, the Convention of Scottish Local Authorities (COSLA) and the Accounts Commission, was also set up at this time to advise, after appropriate consultation and analysis, on the approach to the implementation and monitoring of BV in Scotland. The Task Force recommended a three stage Best Value appraisal process (Scottish Office, 1998).

The first tranche of Best Value Appraisal rounds have now been completed. The first stage required all authorities to produce a timetable and plans for the implementation of BV. Following appraisal of these plans, the Scottish Executive Best Value team (with input from COSLA and the Accounts Commission), granted all authorities an extension of the CCT moratorium. During 1998, the BV team and various service inspectorates appraised a sample of the strategic service reviews undertaken by each authority. Four authorities received an appraisal of their leisure and recreation strategic service review (South Ayrshire, South Lanarkshire, Renfrewshire and Stirling). The final stage in the Scottish BV appraisal process involves Performance Management and Planning (PMP) audits of a sample of three services in each local authority. These audits examine the extent to which a rigorous performance management approach has been developed in terms of establishing clear strategic and operational objectives and targets for all activities, monitoring these performance measures and identifying where and how improvements can be made (Scottish Office, 2000). In the first round of PMP audits organised by Audit Scotland[1] during 1999/2000, eight authorities received audits of their 'leisure and libraries' function (Aberdeenshire, Dundee City, East Lothian, City of Edinburgh, Fife, Glasgow City, Perth and Kinross, and Scottish Borders) (Audit Scotland, 2000). At the same time, the BV team at the Scottish Executive has been following up progress on a sample of the BV reviews conducted in 1998.

In England and Wales, the initial approach to BV has been less inclusive that the Scottish approach. In 1997, English and Welsh authorities had to bid to get the chance to become BV pilots. Only 41 (36%) authorities (38 in England and 3 in Wales) were given pilot status and were therefore exempted from CCT legislation from 1997/98. The remaining authorities remained subject to CCT regulations for their defined services until a legislative base for Best Value was introduced via the Local Government Act 1999 (England and Wales), the details of which will be discussed later. The

Beacon Award for outstanding local authority service delivery has also been introduced to encourage the dissemination of good practice. In 1999, its first year of operation, 44 councils were given Beacon status under which they have an obligation to take steps to spread their best practices until 2001 (DETR, 2000). Although it is recognised that Scottish authorities are continuing to develop and deliver BV without a legislative framework, the final report of the Scottish Joint BV Task Force Report has recommended that a legislative base for BV is required to remove barriers to its full development. For example, they point to the need to remove Part 1 of the Local Government Act 1988 and amend Part II in order to allow non-commercial matters (e.g. workforce and equality issues) to be taken into account when awarding contracts. In addition it is suggested that the Local Authorities (Goods and Services) Act 1970 should be amended to give authorities flexibility to pursue joint ventures and other delivery mechanisms consistent with BV. It remains to be seen how different in tone or in effect, the Scottish legislative framework will be from that contained in the Local Government Act (England and Wales) 1999 (HMSO, 1999). The next section draws on both the English and Welsh legislation and the Scottish non-statutory framework to illustrate in more detail the role benchmarking plays in delivering BV.

Benchmarking for Best Value

The benchmarking tool can be defined as a process of identifying and sharing best practice with the overarching goal of achieving continuous improvement. The nature and effectiveness of benchmarking activities is governed by what your benchmark, against whom, and the extent to which lessons learned are incorporated into the organisation (Accounts Commission for Scotland, 1999). In the quality management literature, benchmarking is seen as a complementary tool to TQM which provides an "external dimension that can accelerate improvement and galvanise change." (Hutton and Zaire, 1995: p. 399). The facilitation of change is partly what the BV policy aims to encourage. For instance, the overriding duty expressed in the Local Government Act 1999 is that:

> A best value authority must make arrangements to secure continuous improvement in the way in which its functions are exercised, having regard to a combination of economy, efficiency and effectiveness. (clause 3.1)

Thus, it is clear that the benchmarking technique is worthy of consideration as one way of meeting this duty. Regarding 'what' is benchmarked, BV requires authorities to demonstrate not only efficiency, but also effectiveness in terms of both service quality and equity. Therefore, the benchmarking process to be fully effective may be used to develop comparative data benchmarks on a wide range of performance indicators, possibly encompassing measure of economy, efficiency and effectiveness. However, developing benchmarks is only the first stage in the process. In order to deliver continuous improvement, the benchmarking process must include an investigation into the causes of disparities in the data benchmarks — this activity is termed process benchmarking. The final, but most important stage is to adapt and implement the lessons learned into the organisation.

The BV legislation supports the use of benchmarking as a tool to "assess the competitiveness of its performance in exercising the function by reference to the exercise of the same function, or similar functions, by other best value authorities and by commercial and other businesses" (The Local Government Act (England and Wales) 1999, clause 4 (e)). Similarly, in the conducting of the strategic service reviews in Scotland, authorities are expected "to show progress in conducting rigorous reviews by applying transparent option appraisal and benchmarking processes" (Scottish Office, 1998: p. 8). The fuller purpose of benchmarking is recognised by Scottish authorities since it has been reported that:

> Performance measurement is fundamental to BV and should be generated as far as possible as part of routine management information. In their submissions, every council accepted this tenet and confirmed that they are actively seeking to improve performance information and develop meaningful benchmarking arrangements." (Scottish Office 2, 1998: p. 6)

However, the same report also notes that:

> too often commentators focus on the benchmarks as numbers or indicators, without regard to the processes and circumstances that explain them. (Scottish Office, 1998: p. 9)

Bovaird (1999), in his study of 41 BV pilot authorities, suggested that although authorities were positive about the role of benchmarking, it was still relatively rare to find examples encompassing the full range of benchmarking activities, i.e., data benchmarking, process benchmarking, functional benchmarking, strategic benchmarking. Similarly, a recommendation from the Scottish PMP Audit (2000: p. 6) was that "most services need to refine their approaches to benchmarking, to ensure comparison of processes as well as data". Factors hindering its full use include the time and resources required in collection of 'new' and/or comparable data, and the challenge of ensuring "transferability of the lessons learnt to the 'home authority'. Thus, as Davis (1998: p. 76) observes:

> Whilst the scope for learning through benchmarking in local government appears high, past failures and limited financial resources to engage in what is a complex and often double-edged technique continue to inhibit development.

This underlines the need to move beyond data benchmarking to process benchmarking to deliver insights into reasons for disparities and, as a consequence, suggestions as to how performance gaps can be closed. The inter-relationships between benchmarks can also be gauged through process benchmarking. For example, unit costs which are higher than other authorities in similar circumstances may be justified under BV if it can be explained in terms of higher quality or greater local need (section 5.17: Failures of substance, DETR, 1998). In this way benchmarking may provide authorities with information which both challenges what they already do and how well they do it. However, in order to ensure that benchmarking takes place in the spirit of continuous improvement and organisational learning, benchmarking needs to be decoupled from any association with reporting of Performance Indicators by Accounts Commission (Stephens and Bowerman, 1997). In addition, to maximise the benefits of this technique, processes under considerations for benchmarking should be prioritised according to "their future strategic importance, economic importance, perceived ability to change and the ease with which the processes can be benchmarked effectively" (Hutton and Zaire, 1995: p. 403). Clearly, within the public sector, equity is a key strategic priority which must be considered when benchmarking. This is discussed further in the next section.

Benchmarking for sport and recreation

Demonstrating BV in sport and recreation services will involve moving beyond the efficiency based performance indicators often used under CCT to demonstrate effectiveness in the delivery of outcomes. The Sports Council (1995) breaks effectiveness down into three categories: excellence/customer satisfaction indicators; sports development indicators; and indicators relating to the equity of distribution. The last factor — equity in distribution — is argued to be necessary to address issues of social exclusion. Tony Blair has defined social exclusion as "a shorthand label for what can happen when individuals or areas suffer from a combination of linked problems such as unemployment, poor skills, high crime environments, bad health and family breakdown" (Scottish Office, 1999: p. 2). It is argued that sport and recreation can play a role in tackling both social exclusion and the problems which come with it (poor health and shorter life expectancy, high crime, and so on).

In local authority leisure and recreation services, social inclusion objectives relate to either: (a) ensuring that all sections of the community benefit from the services — 'distributive' equity; and/or (b) that the most disadvantages sectors benefit from the services — 'redistributive' equity (Sports Council, 1995). To fulfill these objectives, authorities offer a diverse range of reduced price admission to leisure facilities via Passport to Leisure (PTL) schemes. They include "resident or registered user/loyalty schemes, providing low discounts; passport/card schemes targeting larger discounts at the deprived groups ... or two-tier schemes containing both elements" (Collins and Kennett, 1998: p. 131). It is estimated that such schemes are operational in around half of all local authorities. Targeted groups include: unemployed; low income groups; disabled users (plus carers of those with disabilities/learning difficulties); students/young people (including/excluding part-time students); and seniors (excluding those still in work or in private pensions). It is relatively easy to see how benchmarking of such schemes could play a role in monitoring the effectiveness of these schemes. Data benchmarking of these schemes could encompass, for example, examining:

- PTL uptake (e.g., percentage uptake for each target group and per activity);
- Administration costs (e.g., enrollment costs, marketing costs); and
- Fees charged and exclusions (e.g. offpeak only).

However, while this might seem a straightforward task, the extent to which such information can be captured will depend upon the sophistication of an authorities' I.T. system. Thus benchmarking the effectiveness of such systems may also be useful.

There is debate, however, on the extent to which mainstream sport facilities plays a role in social inclusion. Collins and Kennet (1998: p. ???) argue that "leisure income has a direct influence on the capacity of an individual and family to participate in leisure activities (since few are free), and this is an important aspect of community and social life". However, there is much debate on (a) the type of leisure that should be promoted (e.g. banning of sunbeds even though there is a strong demand); (b) the extent to which there is a want for what is currently provided; and (c) whether even free entry would dramatically increase involvement in the type of sport and recreation which is provided. A Scottish study of residents found that 'no interest' (23%), 'no time' (24%), or poor health (19%) was far more significant than 'price' (1%) in reasons cited by non-participants for not taking part (Kay and Jackson, 1991). These findings are in tune with those of a recent study which reported that "a multiplicity of physical, social, economic and attitudinal barriers impede the full involvement of individuals in society" (O'Connor and Lewis, 1999: p. 1). The effectiveness of support strategies aimed at promoting involvement was found to be curtailed by factors such as inappropriate delivery and focus, and barriers to access due to lack of information about services. A key conclusion, therefore, was that "the dissemination of good practice in service development and delivery between voluntary, community and statutory organisations should be encouraged" (Lewis, 1999: p. 1). This last point suggests that there may indeed be a role for benchmarking networks across traditional service boundaries. For example, using lateral benchmarking to make comparisons between different services, e.g., museums services or library services, could provide lessons as to how to monitor and improve social inclusion.

Given the complexity and inter-relatedness of social exclusion problems, the role of Social Inclusion Partnerships (SIPs) in overcoming some of these barriers is currently being promoted. As the Scottish Minister for Culture and Sport commented at a Sports Development Conference:

> The area presenting the most challenge to Scottish sport is participation. I am fully committed to providing opportunities in sport for everyone, regardless of age, background, income and ability. I urge sports development officers to

connect with Social Inclusion Partnerships across Scotland to ensure that sport's contribution to this agenda is not overlooked. New partnerships need to be formed if we are to create a socially inclusive and cohesive Scotland. Sport is part of the answer. (News Release, 3 November, 1999)

Recent examples of the use of Sport Development initiatives to tackle social disadvantage within Social Inclusion Partnership zones include the opening of community based facilities such as the 'Stepford Sports Park' in Easterhouse, Glasgow (News Release, 12 August 1999) and the Dundee Youth Sports Development Project which "provides the opportunity for young people living in the city's SIP areas to participate in a variety of sports on their doorsteps' as a stepping stone to integrating them into city wide sports programmes (News Release, 1 February 2000).

Benchmarking the outputs of these and other 'joined-up' initiatives, for example GP Referral Schemes, can take place using simple measures such as, for example, referral take-up rate, continuation rate, or costs of scheme. Process benchmarking could then take place to investigate whether better performing councils and partnership programmes are more successful due to, for example, more effective promotion, price or the design of the service itself. This could lead to strategic benchmarking to challenge whether the 'right' services are being delivered.

Although there are problems inherent in the comparative analysis of strategies (or, more accurately, policies) in UK local government, as Davis (1998: p. 264) suggests, the heterogeneous and diverse nature of local authorities in principle provides great scope for "'learning by looking' at one another in terms of policy. It might challenge the implicit assumptions in policy and promote 'unlearning', if it can be demonstrated to councillors that the range of alternatives that have been considered have been narrow or constrained. More problematic, however, is any attempt to monitor the effectiveness of partnership schemes in terms of delivering social outcomes such as reduced crime or better health (physical or psychological). This area is fraught with methodological problems associated with the need for a longitudinal approach and difficulties in isolating causation. As Coalter *et al.* (2000: p. 1) suggest, the lack of systematic monitoring and evaluation of the outcomes of sport or physical activity-based projects on social issues is explained "by the complexity in defining and measuring outcomes, the short term nature of many projects, a lack of expertise and limited funding".

The benchmarking tool can, therefore, provide a tool for performance monitoring and improvement of efficiency and effectiveness. However, it can only tackle equity in a simple fashion. The remainder of the paper explores the complexity of actually implementing benchmarking to deliver these challenges, as experienced by a local authority leisure benchmarking group.

Research methods

The benchmarking group selected for study is the "South West Scotland Benchmarking Group — Leisure" (SWSBG). The case study can be described as an exploration of a "bounded system" (Creswell, 1998: p. 61), in terms of both time and place, i.e., the 'case' being examined is a study of a process unfolding over time and across multiple sites. The Group was selected as, at the commencement of the research project, it was the first local authority leisure benchmarking group in Scotland to be formed in response to Best Value. The Group also made a suitable longitudinal case study as, at the commencement of the project, it was in the early stages of its development thus enabling the benchmarking 'process' to be adequately followed throughout its lifecycle. The aim is to collect data corresponding to the following key stages

1. Formation phase (set up, devising rules, developing trust);
2. Operational phase (collation and exchange of information);
3. Implementation phase (facilitating change within each organisation); and
4. Evaluation phase (review benefits of continuing/regrouping).

These stages are similar to the steps in the benchmarking process recommended by Camp (1989) or Cook (1997). Many commentators agree that the implementation or integration phase is the most challenging as it involves communicating and gaining acceptance of findings, developing action plans and implementing and monitoring progress. As Ross (1997: p. 429) comments, benchmarking will not improve performance if "the proper infrastructure of a total quality programme is not in place".

The case study data presented below has been compiled primarily from semi-structured interviews conducted in February and March 1999 during, what has been described above as the operational phase of the benchmarking process. Some further data has also been gathered from follow up discussions with group members in February and March 2000 and an evaluation questionnaire distributed to each of the members in June 2000. This has suggested that many members feel that they are just entering the implementation phase of the project.

Characteristics of group

The benchmarking group is made up of representatives from nine Scottish local authorities, located in the South West of Scotland and focuses solely on the leisure function — in particular the performance of indoor sport and recreation facilities. They vary in size, both in terms of geographical area and density of population. Differences existed between members in terms of "net subsidy per user" for leisure services — the lowest being £0.11 per user, with the remainder ranging from £1.24 to £3.14 per user. In terms of leisure policy, at the time of the research, two authorities had leisure facilities provided by a Charitable Trust. None of the members had contracted out leisure services to the private sector as a result of CCT, but one member had recently entered into a Public-Private Partnership agreement whereby the private sector leisure company were funding a health suite, children's soft room and dance/aerobic studio in an existing 'flagship' facility in return for a guaranteed return per annum. It was hoped that the rest of the facility would benefit from spillover usage. Another member had been successful in its application for lottery funding for refurbishment of a leisure facility and was planning more lottery applications in the future. This authority had recently experienced closure of one of its facilities as a result of budget cuts, with staff and equipment being transferred to another facility.

The Group evolved from an Inter Authority CCT Working Group comprising client managers from three authorities. A bond of reciprocity in sharing information in an informal manner had developed between these authorities during preparations for the second tranche of CCT in 1997. Following the publication of the initial BV Guidance, a decision was made to formalise the existing networking arrangement via the creation of a formal benchmarking group. As one member explained, "the Group was a Client Group which expanded into a Benchmarking Group". The Group expanded gradually during 1998, with the last two members joining in summer 1999. Membership was achieved mainly by 'core' members inviting individuals from neighbouring authorities with whom they had previously networked within the geographical location. To a certain extent, the experiences of the "core" members in dealing with the Scottish Office "family groupings" had contributed to the desire to invite members from a limited geographical area with whom they had previously networked. However, as illustrated above, sufficient disparities exist between members to provide scope for inter-organizational learning.

The representatives of each member authority have a variety of different backgrounds in terms of client/contractor roles, degree of specialism in leisure management, and level of seniority. This diversity in experience is seen to be a positive aspect of the group:

> "there is a good mix which makes discussions very interesting because you get to look at benchmarking and Best Value both from a hands-on, operational perspective and a strategic, policy perspective." (SWSBG member)

Members who were on the client side of service delivery felt that managers in their organisations on the contractor/facilities management side may initially be suspicious of imparting information to them during the benchmarking exercise. This is partly due to the defensive culture that had developed under CCT where the focus of the client was mainly on the issuing of non-compliance and rectification notices, rather than on service development. In some authorities there was said to be a high level of anxiety at the operational level that BV service reviews would result in a transfer of facilities to Trust status. Thus, those authorities facing budget cuts and potential uncertainties of transferring to Trust status, getting benchmarking lessons implementing may be more challenging.

Motivation for membership

The key impetus for joining the Group was to prepare for future audit by the Scottish Office, as well as to deliver service improvements:

> My motivation is that I know I am going to get audited by the Scottish Office so, not only are we hopefully going to improve the service by doing it, but it will also enable us to provide evidence of benchmarking. (SWSBG member)

Member authorities were at various stages in their preparations for BV, with three having been selected by the Scottish Office for audit of their BV service review for indoor leisure. Learning about the BV audit process was, therefore, clearly an added benefit of membership. Members believed that benchmarking was an essential part of the new BV culture in terms of delivering continuous improvement:

> I think the majority of members are looking on it as a valuable exercise whether it is part of BV or not, because it is good practice to look at what others are doing. (SWSBG member)

Part of the recognition of the need for continuous improvement came from an awareness of the highly competitive external environment. Members were aware that customers were becoming more mobile and therefore more able to travel for improved value or simply for new experiences. However, despite the fact that there is an element of competition between 'flagship' local authority facilities, two member authorities liaised closely in their provision of leisure by allowing citizens with leisure 'passports' in either authority to get reduced price access to facilities in both authorities. The increasing number of private sector leisure clubs was seen as more of a threat than cross boundary inter-authority competition from other group members. It was felt that private sector operators were capturing the lucrative hi-tech gym club memberships, which can subsidise the less lucrative wet and dry-side activities used to encourage wider access from non-traditional/target user groups. There was also a fear that once the private sector had saturated the top end of the market, they would target the middle and lower income brackets, thus making them direct competitors for the local authority providers. Some respondents emphasised a wider view of external threats, feeling that the service was competing for the discretionary income and 'leisure time' of customers.

The member who managed a Trust felt that group membership was a useful way of demonstrating to the trustees of the board that they are providing value. His main impetus for joining the group was to gauge how competitive they were and to gain valuable feedback on their initiatives for service improvement. The Trust manager also felt that their experience of trust status would be useful to SWSBG members who were considering this option as part of their BV service reviews.

Most members had tried out different approaches to benchmarking such as attending the Scottish Office benchmarking family groupings, and by completing the Scottish Association of Direct Labour Organisations (SADLO) Performance Indicator questionnaire [now renamed APSE (Association for Public Sector Excellence)].

Two members were members of the SADLO benchmarking group for leisure involving nine authorities and one member had taken part in a national ADLO benchmarking exercise involving 44 authorities from across the UK. Experience of these benchmarking initiatives was mixed, and members had generally become more skeptical of this form of benchmarking as the SWSBG's benchmarking activities revealed the extent of data comparability problems (see below). There was a general lack of understanding as to the rationale for how the Scottish Office had grouped the authorities into their "families". It was also felt that physical distance between members in these grouping would make it difficult to develop the level of trust necessary for process benchmarking.

Benchmarking activities

Group leadership and management

A clearly defined leadership role has been key to the successful management of the benchmarking activities. Again this was informed by experiences of the Family Groupings where it was felt that a lack of clear leadership and common objectives had led to impasse: "we all wanted different things". A Chair has been appointed from the core members of the group. Described as the 'benchmarking champion', the Chair has been instrumental in putting in place an agreed code of conduct; a cycle of regular meetings programmed for a year in advance, and a mechanisms for collecting, comparing and redistributing information.

The agreement to install a benchmarking code of conduct, signed by the Head of Service for Leisure in each of the Authorities, can be seen as marking the end of the set-up phase in terms of familiarisation and trust-building activities. One member made the point that although benchmarking had taken place at a very informal level prior to BV, they had been "loathe to divulge financial information to other authorities in case it got into the wrong hands". The BM code of conduct is seen as key to ensuring both confidentiality and reciprocity within the Group. For example, it states that each member will not be given information from other authorities, until they have provided the equivalent data for their authority. The agreement was also important to facilitate the intra-organisational trust required to gather information from the operational level, as one member put it "it gives you clout in the authority to collect whatever information is required". Even so, in some authorities information was passed to the benchmarking representative via the Head of Service. The dissemination of benchmarking findings was also undertaken via the Head of Service or Senior Management team.

Benchmarking for efficiency

Benchmarking activities began with an examination of differences between Group members in relation to the management and organisation of the leisure function within their respective authorities. This demonstrated the wide diversity which existed in terms of basic factors such as what departments were responsible for leisure management and consequently what objectives they were constrained by. To examine the extent to which lack of comparability was a problem, the Group spent a significant time discussing how each authority calculated statutory performance indicators (SPIs) for leisure facilities demanded by the Accounts Commission for Scotland. These include average attendance per opening hour for (a) leisure pools, and (b) traditional pools; attendance per square metre for indoor sport and leisure facilities (excluding pools); percentage total operating expenditure met from customers income for pools, other indoor facilities, and outdoor sports pitches and tracks. This exercise suggested that, although the guidelines issued governing the calculation of attendance had been followed, the data was not totally comparable.

To simplify the benchmarking process and to avoid information overload, the Group agreed to select one leisure facility in each authority (usually the flagship facility) and to each provide performance information with respect to this "nominated facility". The objective is that, by looking at performance in a microcosm, they will be better able to identify and understand the reasons for any differences. To further aid familiarisation and understanding, the benchmarking meetings have been held in each of the member authorities nominated facility on a rotational basis, scheduled in advance for a year at six weekly intervals.

In relation to the nominated facility, the Group first considered the SADLO performance indicator questionnaire data (which gives details of labour costs, energy costs, support services costs, etc.). Again, it became apparent that the guidance produced by SADLO still allowed significant variation to take place between authorities. Consequently, the Group devised a detailed set of guidelines to establish exactly what costs should be included within each category of data. Areas first selected for further study were labour costs and energy costs (the two areas of greatest revenue expenditure). For example, members were required to submit the following details for labour costs:

(a) total number of employees by type and grade;

(b) hourly rates, enhancements and bonuses;

(c) details of overtime payments;

(d)   details of payments made to teachers and coaches;

(e) a description of the use made of casual staff including the rates of payment; and

(f) explanatory notes for the above.

A similar process was then undertaken in relation to the calculation of the attendance performance indicators. For example, should purchase of a joint activity ticket (e.g., sauna and swim, or aerobics and swim) be counted as one or two? Once the information was in a standard format a detailed Inter-Authority analysis enabled process benchmarking to take place to identify how authorities achieve good performance in each of the categories.

As a result of these findings, for example, one authority set up of dedicated sales team for leisure memberships. Given the budget cuts faced by members, it is understandable that, efficiency and income was the first area tackled.

Benchmarking for effectiveness

Following the evaluation of efficiency, benchmarking priorities for effectiveness were selected using the Quest self-assessment questionnaire (SAQ) (AQS, 1996). Developed in 1996, Quest is the first UK quality assurance system devised specifically for the leisure and recreation sector and supported by a wide range of organizations within the industry including Sportscotland, ILAM, ISRM, and SPRITO. The QUEST framework includes categories such as 'programming and sports development' which are specific to the industry (Table 1).

Table 1: Quest Assessment Criteria

Assessment Categories	Management Issues Covered
1. Facility Operation	Service Planning, Delivery and Control Cleanliness Housekeeping Maintenance of Buildings, Plant and Equipment Equipment Environmental Control Changing Rooms Health and Safety Management Inspection of Service Quality
2. Customer Relations	Customer Care Research Customer Feedback Advertising and Promotion Reception One-off Booking
3. Staffing	Supervision and Staff Planning People Management Management Style
4. Service Development and Review	Programming and Sports Development Objectives Measurement and Review Usage Awards Achievement Service Development

(Source: derived from AQS (b), 1996: p. 8.)

The results of the SAQs have been summarised on a spreadsheet thereby illustrating which authorities have scored most highly for each particular Quest management issue. From this, authorities have been able to identify the areas which require most improvement. Authorities scoring most highly for each issue demonstrate, at benchmarking meetings, how they have achieved their score by describing the processes and mechanisms used to achieve the results. The intention is that this process will provide a direct pathway for the dissemination of best practice.

In an attempt to widen the scope of benchmarking beyond the nominated facilities, a Facilities Directors has been created with the aim of enabling facility managers from across the nine authorities to be put in contact with other facility managers. The non-nominated facilities were also encouraged to complete the SAQs, where they had not previously done so. In addition, the SWSBG has arranged for a pool of representatives from each member authority to be trained to undertake mystery customer visits, using the Quest methodology. The mystery customer visit programme is now well underway and members are receiving valuable feedback on the service quality outcomes from the customer perspective. The feedback is returned on a confidential basis to each benchmarking member and then processed internally. For example, in one authority the benchmarking member and the Area Manager for the facility which has been mystery shopped, have highlighted the items which require to be addressed and have produced an action plan to address each item "where possible within the resource constraints". In addition, a copy of the report has been distributed to other Area Managers so that they can similarly address the issues it raised if relevant to the other facilities. The exercise has, therefore, also been effective in raising the profile of the role of the group internally.

The Group have also invited various private sector organizations to give presentations to the Group. For example, a private sector retailer gave a presentation to the Group on Customer Services. Unfortunately private sector leisure organisations had declined invitations to become involved in the Group's activities. Some members were very enthusiastic about private sector benchmarking and had identified pricing, income generation, marketing and customer consultation as areas where they could learn from the private sector. However, some members expressed a lack of enthusiasm about benchmarking with private sector leisure organisations, particularly with companies who were in the gym sector. The experiences of one member in undertaking a small benchmarking exercise with a key private sector player in the English leisure market rather confirmed their anxieties. It was felt that the exercise had to be carefully managed as the motive of the private company was "to see what areas they could move in on and operate either along with us or independently". The authority had been interested in "seeing how they operate as a business when it is not so tied down by political direction". However, the reciprocal information they received had been disappointing.

Benchmarking of equity

The most recent addition to the SWSBG agenda has been to begin an examination of the challenge of benchmarking social inclusion effectiveness. It is felt that benchmarking of this area is important to raise the internal profile of the contribution of sport and recreation to the social inclusion agenda. In member authorities, performance measurement systems which had evolved during the years of CCT, had generally neglected the measurement of 'equity'. For example, prior to joining the SWSBG, some of the member authorities had not been monitoring performance data relating to total number eligible for 'reduced price' leisure passports and percentage uptake of this eligibility. The SWSBG is therefore, encouraging members to embark on this agenda. However, as one member commented:

> As budget cuts continue, the people who actually collate this information are being displaced, and it is becoming increasingly difficult to maintain even existing PIs. (SWSBG member)

Again the Quest framework is proving helpful in highlighting how this may be tackled as it contains performance criteria on 'usage' (SDR4) as well as the 'programming and sports development' section (SDR1). The Quest guidance notes state "the programme of use is fundamental to meeting both business and community objectives and there should be a direct link." (p. 58). It suggests ways in which the effectiveness of the programme can be analysed are by age group, by activity; by user group (e.g., unemployed, people with disabilities); by skill level (foundation to excellence); or by type of use (e.g., casual, coaching course). The Quest programming and sports development category is also being used to review 'what' is provided. The SWSBG feel that a broad definition of sports development is required, one that promotes inclusiveness. Thus, as well as evaluating sports development effectiveness (in terms of attendances and continuation rates) in relation to target sports (such as hockey, swimming or badminton), the group also intend to evaluate the effectiveness of community development and play activities (such as, line dancing or plays schemes for under-5s, 5–12, etc.). One group member was also monitoring the uptake of specialist schemes which offer, for example, free access to local swimming facilities to residents in SIP areas. However, the research findings have, so far, not provided data on the extent to which process benchmarking had taken place to investigate issues underpinning uptake figures such as levels of awareness of, or interest in, what is on offer.

Conclusion

Part of the impetus for the creation of the SWSBG came from a need to demonstrate commitment to BV in light of the pending Scottish Office Strategic Service Reviews. However, the group emerged from a small informal network which had existed as a support system prior to BV. The ongoing commitment to the process over a period of over two years has remained due to the need to make efficiency savings (in light of budget cuts), to raise service quality and marketing effectiveness (in light of increasing private sector competition), and to raise the profile of the service (by demonstrating achievement of social objectives). Inter-organisational learning about how to respond to BV strategic reviews and PMP audits was also a clear motive for ongoing membership.

The case of the SWSBG suggests that, in the immediate period following the introduction of Best Value, there was a preoccupation with efficiency measures of performance. This is consistent with the emphasis on output controls and financial performance indicators found in the authorities studied by Robinson (1999). The need to monitor outcomes has now been recognised as being equally important by SWSBG, but information gaps within some authorities have slowed this process. Given the resource constraints faced by many public leisure managers, it is hardly surprising that the measurement of effectiveness was not tackled as a first priority. However, it can be argued that benchmarking of effectiveness is essential to the full understanding of simpler efficiency based data benchmarks. As discussed above, the level of social inclusion effectiveness can be a key reason for differences in efficiency. For example, income will be lower in a facility which attracts a high proportion of reduced-price/ target group customers. In such circumstance, process benchmarking should reveal whether there are valid reasons for lower efficiency benchmarks. Indeed, it may be that the less efficient facility can pass on lessons on social inclusion effectiveness to the 'more efficient' facilities!

Although the evidence from the SWSBG suggests that lessons and insights into service delivery improvements can be made, implementation remains a challenge. This appears to be partly due to the local authority environment where reporting mechanisms slow down the process. In some member authorities, the reporting structure has led to a time lag as approval and implementation of improvement plans developed by benchmarking members rests with the Head of Service or Senior Management team. For example, at the time of the research, one benchmarking member was waiting Council approval to collect 'new' performance data on the number of concessionary cards processed, number of actual concessionary users for the range of categories, geographical areas, and types of benefits. There is also evidence that some authorities have been unable to free up the amount of time and resources to reap major benefits, partly because of preoccupation with strategic service reviews, and other pressures of work, sometimes caused by under-staffing due to budget cuts.

The SWSBG now appears to be acting more as a 'quality network' forum than a benchmarking club and is, therefore, in a good position to facilitate inter-organisational learning. The benchmarkers are adopting a wide range of methods to compare data and processes with a view to improving. For example, the invitation of the private sector to learn from best practice and the implementation of the inter-authority mystery customer audits demonstrates a genuine commitment to organisational learning.

Members have also been thoroughly inducted into the merits of the Quest quality award and, as a result, some are choosing to go through the accreditation process. For example, one authority is currently in the process of undertaking in-house Quest internal assessor training for 28 sport and recreation staff. However, other member authorities are stopping short of full Quest accreditation. This is partly due to the perceived costs of adopting this system (at a time of continued budget cuts). It could also be argued that, unlike during CCT when quality awards such as ISO9002 were adopted as a "useful tactical ploy by local authorities keen to win their contracts" (Robinson, 1999: p. 212), under BV authorities are taking their commitment to continuous improvement more seriously. The evidence from this research study also suggests that the BV policy is succeeding in raising the importance of the social inclusion agenda and, in this regard, benchmarking can be a useful tool in highlighting the interlocking nature of the three performance criteria — efficiency, effectiveness and equity.

Note

1 Audit Scotland is a statutory body set up in April 2000, under the Public Finance and Accountability (Scotland) Act 2000. It provides services to the Accounts Commission and the Auditor General for Scotland.

References

Accounts Commission for Scotland (1999) *Measuring up to the best: A manager's guide to benchmarking*. Edinburgh: Accounts Commission for Scotland.

Audit Scotland (2000) 'Making progress with Best Value: a national overview of the Performance Management and Planning Audit 1999/2000'. Edinburgh: Accounts Commission for Scotland.

Bailey, S. and Reid, G. (1994) 'Contracting municipal sports management', *Local Government Policy Making* Vol. 21, No. 2: pp. 55–65.

Collins, M. F. and Kennett, C. (1998) 'Leisure, poverty and social inclusion: The growing role of leisure cards in public leisure services in Britain', *Local Governance*, Vol. 24, No. 2: pp. 131–142.

Bovaird, T. (1999) 'Achieving Best Value through competition, benchmarking and performance networks', Warwick/DETR Best Value Series, Paper No. 6, February, www.local.doe.gov.uk.

Camp, R.C. (1989) *Benchmarking: The search for industry best practices that lead to superior performance*. Milwaukee: ASQC Quality Press and Quality Resources.

Cook, S. (1997) 'Practical benchmarking: a manager's guide to creating a competitive advantage. London: Kogan Page.

Coalter, F., Allison, M. and Taylor, J. (2000) *The role of sport in regenerating deprived urban areas*. Centre for Leisure Research, University of Edinburgh, The Scottish Office Central Research Unit (June).

Coalter, F., Long, J. A. and Dufflield, B. (1988) 'Recreational Welfare: the rationale for public leisure policy. Aldershot: Avebury.

Cresswell, J. W. (1998) *Qualitative inquiry and research design*. London: Sage.

Davis, P. (1998) 'The burgeoning of benchmarking in British local government: the value of "learning by looking" in the public services', *Benchmarking for Quality Management and Technology* Vol. 5, No. 4: pp. 260–270.

DETR (1998) 'Modernising local government: improving local services through Best Value', Consultation Paper, www.local.doc.gov.uk/cct/improvbv/preface.htm, 19 March.

DETR (2000) 'The Beacon council scheme: where to go and what to see', www.local-regions.detr.gov.uk/beacon/where/1.htm

HMSO (1998) 'Modern local government in touch with the people', White Paper.

HMSO (1999) 'Local Government Act 1999', www.hmso.gov.uk/acts/acts1999.htm.

Local Government Benchmarking Reference Centre (LGBRC) (1997) *Benchmarking clubs: A good practice guide*. Pembrokeshire: LGBRC.

Hutton, R. and Zaire, M. (1995) 'Effective benchmarking through a prioritization methodology', *Total Quality Management* Vol. 6, No. 4: pp. 399–411.

News Release (12 Aug. 1999), 'Football tackles social inclusion in Easterhouse', No. WE0287/99, www.scotland.gov.uk

News Release (3 Nov. 1999) 'New Era for Sport in Scotland', No. SE1166/1999, www.scotland.gov.uk

News Release (1 Feb. 2000) 'Youth sport development can be community development', No. SE0231/2000.

Ogden, S. M. and Wilson, P. (2000) 'Bridging the quality gaps: implementing benchmarking to delivery best value', *Public Management: an international journal of theory and research*' Vol. 2, No.4: pp. 525–546.

—— (2001) 'Beyond data benchmarking: The challenge of managing a benchmarking network in the UK public leisure sector', *Managing Leisure* Vol. 6: pp. 1–14.

O'Connor, W. and Lewis, J. (1999) 'Experiences of social exclusion in Scotland', Research Programme Research Findings No. 73, www.scotland.go.uk

Robinson, L. (1997) 'Barriers to total quality management in public leisure services', *Managing Leisure* Vol. 2: pp. 17–28.

—— (1999) 'Following the quality strategy: the reasons for the use of quality management in UK public leisure facilities', *Managing Leisure* Vol. 4: pp. 201–217.

Scottish Office (1998), 'Best Value task force report No. 2', www.scotland.gov.uk.
———— (1999) 'Social inclusion — opening the door to a better Scotland: Strategy', www.scotland.gov.uk
———— (2000) 'Best Value in Local Government: Final Report — Best Value Task Force', www.scotland.gov.uk/bestvalue
Sports Council (1995) 'Performance Indicators', Recreational Management Factfile 1995/1.
Stephens, A. and Bowerman, M. (1997) 'Benchmarking for best value in local authorities', *Management Accounting* Vol. 75, No. 10: pp. 76–77.

Home Zones for Play Space:
A Community Planning Perspective

Debbie Hinds

Division of Management, Glasgow Caledonian University

Introduction

In its transport white paper "A New Deal for Transport, Better for Everyone"(DETR, 1998), the UK Government outlined proposals for consideration on ways to achieve a healthier, safer and sustainable community environment. This paper examines one of these proposals, the development of home zones.

The UK concept of a home zone is based on the European approach to 'living streets' where very low speed restrictions of 10mph or less, enables legal priority to be given to pedestrians while drivers are held automatically responsible for any accidents caused. By changing road priority, the streetscape becomes social space for people to meet and children to play providing a safer, sustainable community and the basis for a home zone. These areas provide a more "forgiving environment" (Wang and Smith, 1997) where danger and risk is minimised and pedestrian freedom and community interaction is maximised.

In examining the development process of home zones, and drawing on the author's previous research, this paper focuses on three main aspects. First, the concept of home zones in determining the use of street space, in particular the use of this space for encouraging "real play" for children. Second, the requirement for home zones to be a community led initiative if the wider social benefits are to be gained. Third, the essential legal changes which are required if home zones are to be more than elaborate traffic calming projects.

The paper concludes that home zones can provide valuable space for children's play, but can only be considered as safe if legislation is changed in favour of the pedestrian. In addition a nationally recognisable road sign is essential to warn drivers of the change in road priority and to expect and accept that children have the right to play in the streets. Secondly they should not be used for traffic calming initiatives to reduce road accidents, but should emphasise the overall benefits of social inclusion, neighbourhood interaction and environmental improvements which can be gained by the adoption of a new approach to residential living. Finally home zones are not suitable for, or desired by all communities, emphasising that community planning is fundamental to the success of these schemes and cannot be imposed on residents.

The no win situation: no grass, no place, no space, no play

In many residential areas the street was traditionally considered by children to be their outdoor play territory, providing space for play and a place for socialising, away from immediate parental gaze. Today as traffic levels continue to increase, the space for pedestrians in general and children in particular has been usurped by the car, reducing their space to unsuitable and dangerous pavements or to the confines of their homes. The adverse consequences of restricting play space in order to accommodate the needs of a car based society has resulted in reducing children's physical exercise, increasing their social isolation and restricting the development of "progressive personal auto-nomy" (Hillman, *et al*. 1990):

> The need for independence, in the sense of capacity to satisfy one's material and spiritual needs by oneself is common to all children and that, in this com-plex age, the loss of private life and the diminishing psychological identity have merged as fundamental problems. (p. 80)

In order to address these social impacts caused by increased car dependency, the Gov-ernment has identified the development of home zones as a means of curbing traffic and reallocating road space to pedestrians, creating sustainable community environ-ments "where it is safe for children to play and get around on their own" (Children's Play Council, undated). The dramatic increase in the use of the car and the freedom and speed of movement which it provides to many people has also brought about restriction of movement for others, particularly children. Traffic dominated streets has resulted in a loss of place and increased parental fears of road accidents, child abduction, murder and general stranger danger. Consequently, an over protective environment is being created for many children by adults, engendering an inherent fear of the outdoors:

> Wrapping children up in cotton wool at a very young age means it is more likely that they will struggle to cope or have accidents as teenagers when they are finally allowed out. Reducing exposure to risk can actually make children more vulnerable. (Hillman, 2000: p. 98)

This belief is endorsed by Cunningham (2000) who concurs that more and more youngsters are not developing social and interactive skills as a result of not being allowed out to play. Instead of street play, adults design and construct " safe " play areas with danger parameters being decided by their interpretation of children's play needs based on their own paranoia. Moorcock (2000), Knight (2000) and Hillman (2000) all endorse the concept of "real play", advancing the argument that children cannot learn to deal with the outside environment of they are not allowed to develop their own natural instinct to real danger and sensory motor capacity limits (Knight, 2000). A home zone can provide such an environment.

In addition to parental fear of the associated dangers of children playing, there is also a level of intolerance of play and fear and suspicion of "gangs" of young people by the adult community, especially the elderly. Yet much of this fear is based on the media's tendency to maximise bad news associated with a minority of young people while overlooking the positive contributions they can make to a community (Penny-cook and Ovens, 2000). This has led to "zero tolerance" policing schemes and curfew initiatives to keep children off the streets. Children's freedom to stand around the streets, socialising with friends has been interpreted as loitering, while shouting and swearing is considered anti social and intimidating behaviour. Implementing the curfew implies that children are automatically treated as guilty in law of anti social behaviour and their freedom restricted with no right of appeal. Children just 'hanging around' are considered dangerous or in danger (Waiton, 1998). As a result of these attitudes and initiatives, many children are being alienated from society; their needs, views and actions are either ignored or their intentions misinterpreted. Pennycook and Ovens (2000) identify that the views of children regarding social exclusion from their neighbourhoods leaves few opportunities for children to meet socially or play locally. Consequently they feel no ownership or involvement in their community and their actions and behaviour have been used as arguments to curb their freedom to play in the streets — i.e. 'kid free' streets are safe streets. However, the majority of children consider street space as free space, without the restrictions of anti play signs of: "No Ball Games" and "Keep off the Grass". This, for them, has becomes a 'no win' situation of 'no grass, no place, no space, no play'. Therefore, to create a home zone where shared space is to be enjoyed by all requires a shift in attitudes and increased understanding between all sectors of the community:

> ... what is needed is inclusionary strategies which encourage the incorporation of young people into communities, empower their voices in environmental decision-making, and challenging the hegemony of adulthood upon the landscape. (Matthews *et al.*, 1999: p. 1713)

This emphasises the importance of adopting a community planning approach to develop a home zone. Further, it focuses attention on the issue that home zones through a process of community interaction provides the potential to establish cohesive community networks and foster understanding between residents. To consider them as elaborate traffic calming schemes is to misunderstand the concept of home zones.

Community participation

The concept of home zones requires a greater community awareness by local authorities, more far reaching than the traffic engineers terms and references of spatial and statistical measurements. Consequently, they have to take a facilitating role in order to reconcile the various needs of competing and conflicting groups and individuals. Sensitive leadership is required to unite and mobilise diverse communities in determining the issues through social inclusiveness. This is a complex process, but if a solution can be found through community partnership, then the outcome will be more appropriate to community needs (Ryden, 1998). By removing social exclusion a level playing field for all parties is created and influential imposition minimised. In order to promote formalised public participation and awareness of new and sustainable living environments such as home zones local networks have to be established through good information systems, well managed public relations and lobbying of key stakeholders, including children. Successful initial awareness campaigns are required, incorporating communication techniques through proactive participation which will in turn deepen understanding and motivate community involvement which will trigger change (Hamer, 1998).

Community planning for home zones will therefore increase local democracy and accountability providing residents with a level of choice, within the financial constraints of the local authority. The approach compliments the Government's commitment to Best Value principles of accountability, transparency, continuous improvement and ownership in responding to community needs. In this way communities will be consulted and have a level of discretion over the environment in which they live.

Legality of home zones in the UK

Fundamental to the European approach of creating home zones in providing a safe and sustainable environment is a recognised legal framework which recognises and protects the priority of the pedestrian within the zone. However, UK legislation does not empower local authorities to introduce more stringent measures:
- to reduce speed limits to below 20mph without Secretary of State approval (a crucial factor in home zone development)
- to return streets to the people/community (once they have been formally adopted by the Highways Department.)
- to change road use priority to pedestrians
- to erect home zone signage to alert drivers that they require greater care and attention.
- to find drivers automatically guilty for any pedestrian accident within the home zone.

Consequently local authorities are compelled to use a combination of physical speed constraints reinforced by the available traffic legislation and designations of:

- 20mph zones,
- traffic calming schemes,
- access-only streets
- resident-only parking restrictions
- designated play streets.

The 'mix and match' approach of the above designations will result in a fragmented, cobbling-together of existing legislation in an attempt to change impersonal empty streets into elaborate traffic calmed areas masquerading as home zones.

Therefore a prerequisite to home zone development requires a new change in legislation if the objectives of socialising the streets and providing play areas for children are to be achieved. It is ironic that the UK law precludes the implementation of home zones because drivers who are involved in a street accident are innocent until proved guilty yet with the implementation of curfews, children on the streets are found guilty with no opportunity to prove their innocence.

Methodology

Throughout the literature review for this research no definition of a home zone or criteria for defining the boundaries of a "zone" was evident, therefore the development of the these settlements is depended on the interpretation made by the local authority's and community. To further explore the concept and subsequent development of home zones a comparative case study approach was adopted with four community settlements being selected on the pre requisite that each area required to have previous or existing experience of home zone development to enable contrasts to be identified. These settlements ranged from a "one street" to a "ten street zone" drawn from urban, suburban and rural environments (see Table 1, following page). Although the DETR were advocating the creation of home zones in the 1998 transport white paper few local authorities at the time of the initial research in 1999 had little, if any knowledge of the term "home zone", which considerably limited the sample size. Therefore the scale of the research is not adequate to draw firm conclusions but the approach does further the understanding of the concept and although cases studies in general may be considered anecdotal, they do provide the basis from which causal evidence can be examined (Gummesson, 1992). Personal interviews with the key stakeholders in each location provided the foundation of these studies in order to explore the rational for, and understanding of home zone developments and assess the level of participation between local authorities, housing associations and community/ neighbourhood groups. The samples analysed provide only a limited insight into home zones but serves to illustrate probable cause and effect issues during the development process.

Table 1

	Type	Size	Community Participation	Reasons for Home zone	Comment on development
1.	Private; Terraced (Leeds)	10 streets	Community Initiative; Strong Leadership; Media based resident; Child Participation	Better quality of life; Freedom for children	Home zone incorporated within regeneration plans
2.	Housing Assoc. Tenements (Glasgow)	6 streets	Housing Association Initiative; Strong Leadership Child Participation	Child road accidents; Regeneration	Remains a 20mph zone; no plans for home zone development
3a.	Mixed semi-detached	1 street	Council Initiative Little participation	Child road accidents; Political	Home zone rejected by community
3b.	Council semi-detached (Luton)	1 street	No Child Participation		Home zone accepted without play area
4.	Council terraced housing estate (Thurso)	8 streets	Community Initiative; Strong Leadership; Media based resident; Child Participation	Child road accidents; Regeneration	Home zone incorporated within regeneration plans

Case 1: Leeds

The Leeds housing area is a well-established city suburb which forms a boundary between a desirable suburban, residential area and a less desirable city area. It is not classed as an inner city area, nor does it, in the opinion of the City Council have the problems associated with them. The social make up is of middle class families and young professionals either owning or privately renting their houses. The houses are built in a unique back to back terraced design, with little or no garden space either to the front or the rear of each property (see Figure 1). As a result, space is at a premium with what little there is being increasingly impinged on by the car. It was the physical and demographic characteristics of the area that brought about a set of circumstances and actions which lead to the home zone initiative. The concept was very much community-driven by the Neighbourhood Action Group, formed in 1994, with the aims of improving the environment, giving play areas to children and preventing crime.

To gain publicity for the initiative and establish a strong neighbourhood the Group, with the assistance of one of the Group who was a freelance theatre producer, organised an imaginative public relations campaigns to attract attention to home zones by re-claiming the streets for the residents, However, once streets have been adopted by Public Highways Department they cannot be "given back" to the community. The

Figure 1   Leeds (Source: Children's Play Council)

group's request for the home streets was refused on the grounds that the area did not have a high enough incident of child road accidents to qualify for priority funding for the necessary traffic calming and streetscaping required for a home zone. The Group organised the children to lobby the Council, emphasising their right to be provided with an area to play under the UN Convention of the Rights of the Child (1989), and urging that it was within the Council's powers to designate a play street. In addition, children travelled to London to petition the House of Commons, with at least some effect:

> In December 1997 I found it especially moving and touching to hear these children describe to the House the difference that the trial (10mph limit) made to their lives and all the activities they could now safely engage in. (Brinton, 1998)

These events were short-lived and transient in nature. They were also dependent on a community willing and able to work within the complexities of the public policy system but constrained by fiscal regulations and financial budgets.

The case provides an example of a neighbourhood which is committed to change and is prepared to campaign vigorously and imaginatively to improve their living environment. However, as the area is not classed by the local authority as suffering from inner city deprivation, nor high child accident rates it is not considered a priority for funding. It could be argued that the upgrading of this suburban area is using public money to increase the value of the private housing stock by improving the surrounding environment. Therefore community-led initiatives can be thwarted by local authority priorities and financial budgets. Through the Millennium Green Fund, the home zone development will receive assistance from the Council and will be incorporated into an environmental regeneration scheme.

Case Study 2: Glasgow

Home zone development is not a new concept in Glasgow, having been introduced during the regeneration and upgrading of city's housing stock during the late 1980s (see Figure 2). It was not a local authority initiative but one which originated with the members of the an inner city housing association. Community involvement and participation was aimed at stimulating the awareness of both adults and children through consultation, leaflet distribution, questionnaires, discussions and debates. The local authority were reluctant to develop the scheme due to the estimated costs, however, the high number of child road accidents which were linked to non residential traffic forced the project through. The advantages of the consultation and development process encouraged a higher level of socialisation of the streets with increased numbers of children playing outside yet with fewer car accidents. However the development has not been a total success as streetscaping, although elaborate and expensive, has not weathered well and there is inadequate local authority funding for maintenance.

Figure 2   Glasgow (Source: Strathclyde Regional Council)

Figure 3   Glasgow (Source: Strathclyde Regional Council)

The streetscape design. although of high quality. suffered from a number of drawbacks, but primarily that little if any consideration had been given to the cost of ongoing maintenance of the scheme. Parked cars have returned to the neighbourhood as
there is little demarcation between pedestrian and car parking areas (see Figure 3). In
the absence of double yellow lines, police are unable to enforce parking restrictions.
The Council has rejected a community request to make the neighbourhood residential
parking only, although a 20mph pilot zone has been granted. Consequently, a development which was intended to improve the living environment of the community has
resulted in providing space for indiscriminate, non residential commuter traffic.

Case Study 3: Luton

The initiative to develop home zones within the city was enthusiastically undertaken
by the local authority, actively assisted by two constituency Labour MPs. The area
chosen by the Council was a 1950s housing estate of mainly 2–storey prefabricated-
type houses with mixed occupancy (Figure 4). The area is bordered by a high-rise
housing estate comprising mainly of transient immigrant families.
The principle criteria for choosing this area for a home zone were:
•   child accident levels (there had been 5 child fatalities in 5 years);
•   the street had to lend itself to an easily enforceable 20mph limit;
•   the street had to be no longer than 500meters;
•   there had to be an existing grassy area;
•   streets with through traffic had to be avoided.

Figure 4   Luton (Source: Luton City Council)

To involve the community and assist in the participation process, exhibitions were held in libraries and supermarkets, questionnaires delivered to all residents in an effort to inform, consult and elicit responses to the home zone initiative. The response was disappointing with only 33% of the questionnaires returned, an indication that the residents were not fully committed to the scheme. They were keen to have some form of traffic calming to dissuade joy riders but they were not supportive of the grassy play area or the street being used as play space. The perception was that the scheme would encourage children from the nearby high rise flats to come and play in the street resulting in vandalism to property. There was also the question of who would pay for and maintain the upkeep of the area.

The scheme was eventually abandoned by the Council due to the residents strong opposition based on the fear of children from the neighbouring high rise flats playing in the home zone. Therefore, location is of primary importance to the development and it is insufficient to identify an area without considering the wider environment and the issue of displacement. Further it could be argued that without incorporating children into the debate through active participation, the requisite level of understanding, community integration and social commitment could not be achieved. However, funds were earmarked and political will still existed to develop a home zone resulting in the designation of another street as a home zone. (see Figure 5)

Figure 5   Luton (Source: Luton City Council)

Again the consultation process was undertaken with the local MPs personally contacting 25% of the residents on door to door visits, and a further 25% being issued with postal questionnaires. The tenants association accepted the 'principle' of home zones, but with modifications — the major modification being the removal of the children's play area. Once again there was a perception that children playing outside in the street or in the designated play area would cause vandalism and attract other children from outside the street. Another modification was the guarantee that the Council would maintain the streetscaping.

In order to alert drivers to the home zone development, the Council produced a sign modelled on the official EU sign (not legally recognised in the UK). This is an attempt to use the existing road designations of 'access only' and '20 mph' limit to create within the UK legislation a safer pedestrian environment by limiting car speeds and movement. However, a 20 mph zone does not provide the safe and forging environment essential for home zone living. Once again, the development has become a traffic-calmed street but with a home zone sign. To date the scheme is considered by the residents to have little impact on their living environment.

Case Study 4: Thurso

The residents living on this rural housing estate (see Figure 6) experience similar problems associated with many urban areas — mainly those of poor housing design, layout, decay and deprivation through neglect and lack of resources — to the extent that it has been identified as within the 10% of Scotland's worst housing schemes for urban deprivation.

The quality of the living environment is poor. It is ironic, but not surprising, that road traffic here is recognised as a problem. Only one in three households own a car, but high walls obscure vision, token sized gardens restrict freedom to play, and playgrounds are sited across main roads that do not have pedestrian crossings. The home zone initiative here originated after a child was knocked down by a car. This ultimately spurred the tenants to form an association which would be inclusive of all residents, including children, to work towards their "Planning for Real" initiative with the aim of providing safer play areas, improving road safety and softening and greening the environment.

Local councillors, MSPs, residents and children have all become actively involved in the initiative which has focused attention, not only on the road problem, but on the social conditions. All residents are members of the Association which is led by a local journalist who has raised the profile of the home zone initiative. It is community planning in action, where the origin for the initiative at grass root level has brought residents and the local authority together to address the years of neglect experienced by the tenants.

Figure 6　　Thurso (Source: Case)

The home zone scheme has been designed and costed with funding actively sourced through the Lottery, the Tudor Trust, Children in Need, EU Objective One funding, in addition to the local authority and enterprise money. Consequently, a 1980s, decaying housing estate is being transformed through extensive redevelopment into a home zone, where community planning provides for increased resident participation in order to secure a safer and greener living environment.

Case study summary

The above home zone case studies provide evidence of approaches used by community groups and local authorities from which probable cause and effect can be inferred. The main motivating factor in all but one of the cases was the effect of road traffic on the community and the threat to child safety. The studies demonstrate that due to the diversity of communities, home zones may not be desirable or applicable to all neighbourhoods nor can their boundaries be identified from a local authority plan. Communities form their own boundaries based on demographic, social and geographic factors, and it is often a common agenda which provides the basis for increased interaction (Carley, 1999) and not official planning boundaries or child road accidents figures. Consequently, where communities are involved and have a level of ownership and influence, schemes are more likely to succeed than those which are initiated through political will. It is also noteworthy that strong leadership and publicity can influence local authorities acceptance of home zones, although budgetary constraints are considered to be the main barrier to development.

In addition, the omission of any reference to play policy statements or strategies is apparent. At the time of these separate home zone developments, only Leeds had a definite play strategy (Glasgow published *A Strategy for Sports Recreation and Play* in 1999), but at no time during this research was any reference made to a play policy or the need to consider adopting any play policy prior to or during the developments. If such strategies had been available, or if greater collaboration had existed between local authority departments, a wider and more diverse professional input to the developments could have resulted, with greater emphasis and understanding placed on children's claim to play space in residential areas.

It is also evident that there are disadvantages which may be incurred by communities if the wider surrounding areas are not taken into account:
* displacement of cars to nearby inappropriate streets;
* overuse of street amenities;
* honey pot attractions to children and teenagers;
* increased use for unrestricted parking.

The general concept of environmental improvements associated with home zones is generally acceptable to residents, while the provision of play space for children compromises the development. Therefore they may not be desirable or applicable to all due to the diversity of neighbourhood characteristics and the implications of existing surroundings and housing layout — important factors which could be overlooked during the quest for a home zone.

Conclusion

As the car continues to encroach on children's' freedom, it is increasingly obvious that the use of streets for play space and community activity has been overlooked by planners and developers. Play territory is marginalised in residential areas to sites which are often unsuitable yet streetscape which has been traditionally the outdoor play area, is being restricted. Based on the European experience, home zones can bring life onto the streets by drawing together sectors of a community by minimising danger and risks and maximising community interaction.

The case studies demonstrate that home zones can be created in residential areas, whether urban or rural, through community consultation and participation. Interest, co-operation and ownership are increased when residents adopt a proactive role and can see that their proposals and actions will make a difference. However, local authorities have to adopt good governance techniques in order to maximum inclusion, minimise influential imposition, establish a sound rationale for home zone development and access wider funding sources.

Therefore a community planned home zone initiative will assist in forming partnerships to improve community benefits by:
- increasing social interaction and sense of ownership, including a social arena for children and teenagers;
- increasing amenities including play areas for the young;
- increasing freedom for all including pedestrians and cyclists;
- providing for a safer and healthier living area;
- assisting in reducing crime;
- assisting in reducing pollution.

Rather than legal restraints, the dependence on and cost of physical streetscaping barriers required to limit traffic speeds will hinder the development of home zones. Without a robust and significant change in legislation home zones will remain as glorified traffic-calmed streets, where children's freedom will continue to be con-strained by the car and their safety compromised.

References

Brinton, H (1998) Home Zones, *Hansard Points of Order*, no 1774, 27th Jan., cols. 149–151.

Brown M, and Elrick, D. (1997) 'Best value from local government? A community development perspective', *The Scottish Journal of Community Work and Development*, Edinburgh: pp. 39–53.

Carley, M (1999) 'Neighbourhoods — building blocks of national sustainability', *Town and Country Planner* (February): pp. 58–59.

Cunningham, J. (2000) 'Prioritising free play', *Freeplay* (June), Glasgow.

Children's Play Council (undated) *Home zones: Reclaiming residential streets*. London: National Childrens Bureau.

Department of Environment Transport and the Regions (undated) *Places, streets and movements, A companion guide to Design Bulletin 32, Residential roads and footpaths*. London: The Stationery Office.

——— (1998) *A new deal for transportation, better for everyone. Government White Paper on the Future of Transport*. London: HMSO.

Department of Health (1993) *The right of the child: A guide to the U.N. convention*. London: HMSO.

Department of the Environment (1994) *Sustainable development: The UK strategy*. London. HMSO.

Giffard, R. (1997) *Home zones — reclaiming residents' streets*. London: Routledge.

Gill, T. (1997) 'Street kids and home zones', *Transport Retort* Vol. 4, No. 20 (Jul/Aug): p. 10.

Gummesson, E. (1992) Case study research. Stockholm University Publications.

Hamer, L. (1998) 'Changing travel behaviour: Raising awareness should be just the start', *Local Transport Today* issue 248, October 8: pp. 10–11.

Hillman, M. (2000) 'Children safer despite the worries of parents', *The Sunday Times* 11 November: p. 98.

Hilman, M., Adams, J. and Whitelegg, J. (1990) *One false move*. London: Policy Studies Institute.

Institution of Highways and Transportation (1997) *Transport in the urban environment*. London: Institution of Highways.

Knight, S. (2000) 'Welcome to the danger zone', *The Scotsman*, No. 15: p. 3.

Leeds City Council (1998) Leeds Unitary Development Plan, Internet (http://www.leeds. gov. uk/lcc/planning/planpoli/poli_fr. html. p. 2).

Luton Borough Council (1998) *Luton transport policies and programmes, 1999/2000*, Luton: Department of Planning and Development.

Matthews H, Limb M, Taylor M (1999) 'Reclaiming the street: the discourse of curfew', *Environment and Planning* Vol. 31: pp. 1713 –1730.

Moorcroft, K. (2000) 'Families for freedom', presentation at Play Scotland Conference (June), Glasgow.

Pennycook, J. and Ovens, N. (2000) *East Lothian strategy for children and young people 0–18*. East Lothian Council.

Preston B. (1990) 'Home zones — child's play for inner cities', *Town and Country Planning* (April): pp. 116–117.

Rydin, Y. (1998) *Urban and environmental planning in the UK*. London: Macmillan.

Sloman, L. (1996) 'Streets for people', *Town and Country Planning* (July/August): pp. 194–195.

Sturt, A. (1992) 'Going Dutch', *Town and Country Planning* (Feb): p. 1.

Waiton, S. (1998) 'Children in a bad light', *The Herald Magazine* (Glasgow?): pp 10–11.

Wang, A. and Smith, P.J. (1997) 'In quest of "forgiving" environment: Residential planning and pedestrian safety in Edmonton, Canada', *Planning Perspectives* Vol. 12: pp. 225–250.

Whitelegg, J. (1993) *Transport for a sustainable future*. London: John Wiley and Sons.

Including the Forty Percent: Social Exclusion and Tourism Policy

Ronnie Smith

The Scottish Hotel School, Glasgow

Britain led the world in the development of modern mass tourism. The growth of the 'holiday habit' among the industrial working class in the early twentieth century created both the traditional seaside resort and a national appetite for holiday-taking which continues today. In the twenty-first century we see the continual emergence of new holiday products. Greatly increased levels of holiday entitlement, the deployment of new transport and information technologies, an increasingly sophisticated segmentation of tourism demand, the globalisation of travel markets (Fayos-Sola, 1995), and wide coverage of holiday ideas in the media all contribute to the dynamics of a market place in which the British are amongst the most enthusiastic international customers.

It remains the case, however, that in any given year some 40% of the UK population do not take a holiday of any kind of four or more nights away from home (Department of Culture, Media and Sport, 1999). This figure has been constant for some decades, and suggests that there may be a lot of people who are involuntarily excluded from taking holidays and are consequently denied the personal and social benefits of doing so. The aim of this paper is to explore the relationship of this deficit in holiday activity to the government's stated aim of generating new ideas and new approaches in order to combat social exclusion.

Since the 1920s United Kingdom governments have accepted a role in supporting the indigenous tourism business sector. This responsibility to provide funding for tourism promotion and development was enshrined in the Development of Tourism Act of 1969, still the only substantive piece of legislation relating specifically to national tourism organisation structures and funding support. The marketing, visitor service and research activities of the British Tourist Authority (BTA), the English Tourism Council (ETC), and the Wales and Scottish Tourist Boards (WTB and STB) continue to be conducted at arm's length from their lead government Departments. Central funding for BTA, WTB and STB has been increased substantially in real terms in recent years. In this sense (the treatment of the English Tourist Board is an exception), the UK government and the newly devolved administrations in Scotland and Wales have held to the general approach of most developed countries in terms of a continuing commitment to national tourist organisations (Smith, 1998).

There is also, of course, very substantial additional funding being channelled from central government sources into the development of tourism-related infrastructure. National museums and galleries, the work of English Heritage and other conservation agencies, National Lottery-funded projects etc., all sustain on-going innovation which has the effect of underpinning and enhancing the core heritage product which Britain offers in the international tourism market place.

At a supra-national level, the European Union has not been allowed to develop a significant central tourism policy which could influence member governments in the formulation of national tourism objectives or make much of an impact across the member states. The influence of DG XXIII-inspired schemes to promote rural, youth tourism etc. has been at best marginal. Even so, the EU has had a profound influence on tourism development. This has been felt primarily in the broad fields of single market legislation, consumer rights, liberalisation of transport policy, harmonisation of statistics and environmental protection measures (Robinson, 1996). Also, the UK has been particularly adept at accessing EU structural funds, generally to support infrastructural developments in designated regions such as the Highlands and Islands of Scotland.

Government at local authority level has a long-standing involvement in tourism development and promotion, stretching back to the era of spas and the initial emergence of seaside resorts in the eighteenth and nineteenth centuries. It is still the case that a large proportion of Britain's tourist attractions are owned and operated by local authorities, who often choose to be highly active in marketing activities, culture and leisure support, visitor service provision and a wide range of urban regeneration, countryside conservation and economic development strategies which are crucial to the functioning of the tourism system in the UK (Davidson and Maitland, 1997).

However, the underlying rationale for nearly all of what has until recently been a vaguely defined UK national government policy for tourism has been formulated almost exclusively in terms of the economic benefits which can accrue from a flourishing tourism sector. The focus has been on stimulating the supply side. Thus the passage of the 1969 Act was largely justified in terms of the unrealised potential for more overseas visitors to Britain to ease the chronic national balance of payments problem (Heeley, 1989). The Act introduced the Hotel Development Incentive scheme, which handed large sums of money to hotel developers so that they could improve the national hotel stock. Subsequent twists and turns in economic macro policy have seen the adoption of varying objectives. The encouragement of tourist facilities and the generation of tourist revenue in underperforming regions of the country was a key concern of the 'Shore guidelines', in force from 1974 to 1983. During the Thatcher years tourism was seen to have great potential to alleviate high unemployment, particularly in urban areas. At that time also much attention was focused on removing barriers to business growth. In recent years, more sophisticated urban regeneration approaches, market deregulation measures, the rationalisation of public organisations with moves towards partial privatisation and the promotion of partnership working, have all come to the fore in attempts to encourage a more efficient and competitive tourism industry.

It remains the case, however, that nearly all of government thinking about tourism is focused on approaches to remedying some aspect of 'market failure'. In a typical example the Scottish Office-commissioned 'Prior Options' study of the Scottish Tourist Board (The Scottish Office, 1998) confirmed the economic rationale for the continued existence of the STB in terms of:

- the diffuse nature of the tourist industry;
- domination by small businesses;
- lack of vertical integration;

and saw continuing public intervention as justified in relation to: general marketing efforts; efforts to minimise seasonality; efforts to increase the spatial spread of tourism expenditure; efforts to improve quality; and efforts to disseminate research and provide guidance. The 'social rationale' identified by this study relates only to the benefits of not concentrating all tourism-related economic activity in one part of the country. No attempt is made to assess the potential social benefits of more people being enabled to take holidays.

This is not to say that no thought has been given to encouraging the wider participation of the population in tourism activities. In the 1980s the English Tourist Board and the charity Holiday Care Service produced a report with a string of recommendations about measures which could be taken to help several disadvantaged groups gain access to holidays (ETB, 1989). However, the ongoing activity of the Holiday Care Service has been focused on providing information about holidays and meeting the access needs of disabled people. And although in the subsequent period some research was undertaken by the English Tourist Board, the development of government policy in this area has essentially been to place increasingly stringent requirements on providers to ensure access for the physically disabled. The needs of other disadvantaged, non-participating groups have not hitherto been systematically analysed and they have largely been ignored by public tourism agencies.

An aggravating factor is that we are unmistakably moving out of the era of direct voluntary and local authority provision in this area. Holiday camps and other facilities run by trade unions for their members are largely a thing of the past. The Youth Hostelling Association has tended to move in the direction of providing more lavish and therefore more overtly commercial facilities with greater emphasis on new flagship developments in urban centres, designed to serve the needs of a relatively prosperous international backpacking clientele. Local authorities are also financially constrained and are finding it difficult to sustain the holiday support previously offered to children and families in crisis. For example, local education authorities have often found themselves compelled to dispose of outdoor recreation centres which were previously open to participating schools at minimal or no cost to pupils.

Thus tourism policy at UK government level has been focused on production rather than consumption issues (Hughes, 1991). The 'welfare reformism' identified by Richards (1995) for leisure policy in the period 1964 – 1976 actually failed to put in any significant appearance in the context of tourism. Since the early 1990s 'disinvestment and the flexible state' have done nothing to alter the basic position. Only the physically disabled have benefited in any substantial way from government moves to improve access to holidays. For the remainder of the excluded, small-scale charitable initiatives by voluntary agencies such as the Family Holiday Association, Gingerbread and the Round Table, and declining financial support from local government agencies are all that is on offer.

The current government could reasonably argue that much of its labour market regulation programme, including the establishment of a statutory right to paid holidays and the introduction of a minimum wage, as well as many changes to the benefits system, will have produced beneficial effects for low income earners and some other excluded groups. Yet the 'public good' argument which underpins the UK government's support for national tourist organisation activities has not been extended to attempting to spread the benefits of holidays to those groups which are unable to participate for reasons other than physical disability. This refusal to intervene or even encourage self-help approaches is in contrast to several countries in Europe, where tourism as social welfare has been a long-standing concern.

The people likely to experience difficulty in participating in current holiday opportunities are not difficult to identify. Apart from the physically disabled and their carers, they comprise: the frail elderly; the unemployed; low income groups; lone parent families; large families with young children. The term in widespread international use to characterise efforts on their behalf is 'social tourism'. Thus the recent declaration of the World Tourism Organization, under the heading 'Right to Tourism' includes the clause:

> Social tourism, and in particular associative tourism, which facilitates widespread access to leisure, travel and holidays, should be developed with the support of the public authorities. (WTO, 19++: p. ++)

There is also an international organisation, the Bureau International du Tourisme Social (International Bureau of Social Tourism), which brings together member organisations from some 25 countries with the stated aim of furthering the idea of organising and bringing improved tourism within the reach of the majority (Bureau International du Tourisme Social website).

Little of this can be expected to influence UK government thinking. The UK government has traditionally shunned involvement in bodies such as the World Tourism Organization. Its response to the 1995 EU Green Paper on the role of the Commission in tourism was to oppose the strengthening of Community actions and/or the establishment of a formal competence for tourism in the treaty structure.

It is therefore all the more unexpected that the Department of Culture Media and Sport in its 1999 strategy document, 'Tomorrow's Tourism' should have identified as one of 15 key action points 'initiatives to widen access to tourism for the 40% of people who do not take a long holiday' (DCMS, p. 4). Taken at face value, this marks an unheralded and strikingly radical departure from the traditional British set of parameters governing tourism policy. The most likely motive for this unexplained change is surely that the New Labour government, in wishing to extend its social inclusion agenda across Departmental boundaries, saw the coincidental preparation of a tourism strategy for England as a suitable opportunity for the Department of Culture, Media and Sport to come up with some new thinking.

As a result of this development the English Tourism Council was commissioned to carry out some research into holiday non-participation and the barriers to holiday taking. The intention was to investigate the scope for creating products which could exploit new market opportunities or specifically tackle social exclusion. The findings of this study have not been published, but a summary of the results has been made available to the author. The study confirms the long-standing statistic (derived from the BNTS) that in any given year some forty percent of the population do not take a holiday of four or more nights either abroad or domestically. However, the apparently high level of non-participation needs some qualification. The BNTS does not take account of short breaks. And short breaks are becoming more common – some 86% of people have taken at least one short break in the last 3 years. ETC suggests that in order to establish a case for social exclusion a sustained pattern of non-holiday taking has to be established.

The ETC analysis of the forty percent revealed by the BNTS found that:

- 11% of adults do in fact go away to visit friends or relatives;
- 15% of adults had not taken a holiday that particular year but had done so relatively recently and may do so again;
- 14% of adults had not taken a holiday during the previous three years and did not plan to do so in the coming year.

Further analysis of focus group discussions organised for samples of the 14% long-term non-participants (equating to 6.6. million adults) found eight separate groups, characterised by ETC as:

- holiday motivated but poor;

- poor, large families;
- poor with little transport;
- just disinterested in holidays;
- holidays not a priority for expenditure;
- higher income workers, too busy for holidays;
- elderly disheartened, many disabled or with special needs;
- more affluent, older, interested, but recently stopped taking holidays.

The 11% VFR sector was also analysed and several separate clusters identified:
- just uninterested in paid/organised holidays
- young working singles
- old, nervous or infirm
- single parents
- older affluent but satisfied with visiting family and friends
- interested but ill or caring for someone else.

Although the study was not focused specifically on disabled people, further investigation showed that among the disabled respondents the main barrier to holiday taking was not the cost but the availability of products suitable for a particular type of disability.

ETC has concluded from these findings that a whole raft of different measures would be needed to facilitate and motivate non-holiday takers and argues that the market opportunities are limited and would be extremely costly to target. It is claimed that in the main non-participants do not wish to be stereotyped. While many are constrained by income, others prefer to stay close to home during their holidays, not believing that a holiday would enhance their quality of life. Ignorance of what is on offer is also thought to be a factor. Spending priorities often focus on home, family and health rather than taking holidays.

Yet other recent research undertaken by ETC shows that health professionals see holidays as having health benefits and that 91% of English GPs think that holidays can enhance quality of life. However, ETC sees this primarily as a strategic opportunity in what it terms 'the health market'. Although the Council is committed to further research into both the family market and the area of disabled people's holidays, the focus here is likely to be niche product development.

The broad conclusion drawn by ETC from the investigation of the non-holiday taking sector is that the findings are too complex to provide clear direction for product development or new initiatives. There might, it is suggested, be some scope for development of more appropriate accommodation, catering and transport solutions for many not susceptible to normal marketing. ETC also proposes that in addition to its work on the health and family markets, its work relating to seaside resorts, rural regeneration and strategic improvements in quality, attractions and accessibility all relate to social inclusion issues. The Council draws attention to the need for better communication about the range of products available, suggesting that promoting family-friendly holidays would impact on many sectors, including single parents, estranged parents, large families and the wider market of parents.

While this investigation of the non-participating sector by ETC should be welcomed, the complexity which it reveals should not be allowed to inhibit the development of some broader and more creative thinking on how holidays can contribute to the social inclusion agenda. The ETC is properly concerned to relate the study findings to its planned work programmes, themselves derived from the DCMS strategy for tourism in England and its Action Plan. But there is a danger that the focus on product development opportunities and marketing initiatives will preclude the 'joined up thinking' which the government claims to espouse. At issue surely are not just 'market opportunities' but also 'market failure' in a much broader sense? In other words, there is a wider social context into which holidays should be placed and which the ETC research findings should serve to illuminate. There is a danger that the undoubted difficulties of responding to the wide range of needs and attitudes revealed in the ETC findings will result in a lack of government support and public agency leadership other than in measures designed to help the physically disabled. The potential social benefits of tourism need to be considered in terms of a much wider social and educational agenda. This is particularly pressing in the context of an increasingly internalised consumerism of despair where low income families interviewed about their holiday preferences say they would prefer to spend spare funds on buying fashion footwear for their children, rather than save for a family holiday (ETC).

What the ETC research does not address and what might therefore go by default is a more wide-ranging exploration of opportunities for collective action to realise the health and other personal benefits which holidays can bring to those falling within the definition of social exclusion. One might speculate that beyond the personal benefits to be gained there are also likely to be potential benefits in terms of reducing anti-social behaviour and encouraging confidence and skills development among marginalised groups such as school truants, the consequences of whose alienation and disaffection from society impose heavy costs extending over decades. The need is to develop a research agenda which does indeed demand 'joined up thinking' and links input from public tourism agencies and tourism businesses to such fields as social and vocational education for students with special needs, social work provision for the socially and economically disadvantaged, while drawing additionally on the expertise of voluntary and charitable support organisations.

Two illustrations will be given here of how such approaches can work in practice. The Family Holidays Association (FHA) is a charity which provides grants for holiday breaks for families under pressure, mostly at UK caravan sites and centres on the coast.

The FHA aims:

* to provide a week of fun and relaxation for children and families who otherwise would have no opportunity to take a break;
* to give children new experiences, so raising their confidence and self-esteem;
* to give parents and carers the chance to recover their health and general sense of well-being;
* to promote greater family togetherness, happiness and stability and so improve children's lives;
* to reduce the social exclusion caused by living in poverty
* to give parents time away from day-to-day problems to reflect on how they could improve their lives;
* to provide something to look forward to and look back on with happy memories;
* to support both statutory and voluntary agencies working for the welfare of children and families by giving them something positive to offer (Family Holiday Association).

The FHA has developed a 'family holistic holidays' concept which it piloted in February 2000, organising a holiday at a stately home in Dorset for families under pressure, with activities laid on for the children and different kinds of therapies offered to the parents. The holiday was intended to fit not just with FHA's aims but also a wider perspective on health, which sees health promotion in a relationship with quality of life issues. The concept also ties in with concern for family support and with community building and regeneration starting at the level of those most disempowered. The broad strategy here, derived from the American-inspired 'Communities that Care' project, is to take action to address the 'risk factors' in young people which lead to criminality, social problems, poor parenting, abusive relationships and school failure. The 'risk factors' include low income and poor housing, family conflict, parental attitudes condoning problem behaviours, availability of drugs and low school commitment. The project aims to build up 'protective factors' which will have an impact over time, including family attachment, social skills, healthy values and opportunities for social involvement. This is seen to embrace breaks away from a bleak environment (Family Holiday Association, 2000). What follows here are the unpublished findings of the FHA's own review of the pilot scheme (Family Holiday Association).

The pilot holiday scheme invited referral of families from three sources:

* KIDS in Camden, a project for parents with children with special needs;
* WELCARE parent and children Centre based in Twickenham;
* Social Services in Richmond.

Some twenty families took part, most of which were on income support and had not had a holiday for some years, if ever. Ten trained therapists, a doctor (GP), facilitators and teachers joined the group to run specific workshops and one to one individual sessions. Staff from FHA also visited and talked to the families. The workshops included parenting skills, health advice (with the doctor), reflexology, massage, counselling, music and drumming (for children and adults), dance and exploring nature. Children were offered sessions in creative arts and drama and in the evenings games were organised for them and relaxation, singing and dancing for families (Family Holiday Association).

Follow-up semi-structured interviews and participant questionnaires established a highly positive response, all those taking part agreeing on particular benefits as:
- feeling greater family 'togetherness';
- less stress as a result of 'getting away from it all';
- 'getting to know the children'.

Much of the feedback was concerned with expressing what positive things both children and adults would take with them: the prospect of support, assertiveness, more self-confidence, more patience with the children and different ways of dealing with them when they were difficult, ways to end isolation, e.g. setting up support groups, friends; open-mindedness about opportunities for change; and ways to add value to their lives. More follow-up research is planned to measure the longer-term benefits of the break (Family Holiday Association).

A very different example of social tourism in action is provided by the activities of the French organisation, *Agence Nationale pour les Cheque-Vacances* (ANCV). Since 1982 this organisation, 'a public establishment with an industrial and commercial character', has been developing its system of holiday cheques. The key aims are to help less well off people to take holidays and gain access to a wide range of cultural and leisure activities (ANCV). An essential feature of the scheme is the facility whereby for a period of between four and twelve months an individual can pay into a savings fund which is topped up with an additional 25% contribution by a participating organisation (employers, social organisations such as staff committees, collective undertakings). Where the employer acts as the distributing agent entry to the scheme is limited by the level of the client's annual tax assessment. The fund is made available in 50,100 and 200 franc coupons valid for up to two years. According to the ANCV website, the coupons can be redeemed against services (specifically not consumer goods) provided by:
- camp sites, self-catering accommodation, youth hostels, 'villages de vacances', all categories of hotels;
- swimming pools, sports facilities, 'colonies de vacances' for children, theme parks, wildlife attractions;
- catering establishments of all types from gourmet dining to pizzerias;
- transport facilities, including rail, air and ferry tickets, also motorway toll payments;
- historic monuments, castles, museums, concerts, theatres, even cinemas.

In addition, in many cases the cheques carry money saving offers, providing additional value to the consumer.

ANCV claims 4.1 million beneficiaries of the scheme (i. e. participants and families), with 12,000 participating organisations and 90,000 tourism, leisure and cultural enterprises accepting the cheques at 130,000 outlets. In 1998 3.6 billion francs were issued in cheque-vacances. The scheme obviously commands growing public support — between 1993 and 1998 the average annual growth rate in cheques issued was 23.4%.

Another aspect of the scheme, in operation since 1987, is the payment of 'travel grants' to assist disadvantaged people to go on holiday for the first time. Some 7 million francs annually are devoted to this purpose. The beneficiaries may include young people learning to crew a tall ship and learning the value of joint effort, tolerance, respect for others, or families who have to overcome the fear of the unknown (saving, planning, managing a budget, getting ready for the trip). ANCV has close links with recognised charity organisations who participate in this work, for example by helping chose suitable recipients and offering support to families inexperienced in holiday taking. A further role of the ANCV is the disbursement of capital grants to operators specialising in leisure and holiday facilities catering for the disadvantaged.

This is therefore a highly flexible scheme, targeted on the less well-off employee and offering a wide degree of consumer choice in terms of leisure, daytrip or holiday expenditure. A study of participants carried out by ANCV (ANCV 1998) reveals the typical client profile:

- a white or blue-collared employee in their 40s
- married or living in partnership with two dependent children
- 67% have an income below 15,000 F per month
- 29% have an income below 10,000 F per month
- only 4% of participants did not take a holiday in the two preceding years, compared to a French national average of 28%
- in the preceding two year period they took an average of 3.36 holidays, compared to a national average of 2.31
- among blue-collar participants 7% did not take a holiday in the two preceding years, compared to a national average of 38%.

The rhetoric deployed by ANCV in its publications and website in support of its activities is interesting. In communications directed to the potential personal saver much is made of the cost-effectiveness of the scheme and the wide degree of individual choice which it offers. For elected members of staff committees (comites d'entreprise) the emphasis is placed on the freedom which they have to determine who should be permitted to take part, with the clear indication that the whole workforce can be included. For employers the message is partly reassurance about the possible fiscal consequences of signing up but also that the scheme offers means of creating a close link between the firm and its employees — it is presented as an easy and flexible means of implementing an innovative 'politique sociale'. To potential participating tourism businesses the emphasis is on how easy the payments are to administer and the increased business likely to accrue from membership (ANCV website). Elsewhere much is made of the 'social solidarity' aspect of the scheme and the partnership arrangements with charity organisations to implement the holiday grant scheme, but also the boost which the cheques-vacances concept provides for the national tourism economy, particularly rural tourism. It is even suggested that the scheme could be taken up as a model in developing countries (ANCV, n.d.).

Neither of these case studies presents examples of practice likely to be adopted wholesale in the UK. The 'holistic holiday' concept of the FHA is clearly extremely labour intensive and only suited to willing and self-selecting client groups. And it is highly unlikely that the UK government would in the short term consider it a feasible prospect to promote the French cheques-vacances model to British employers or even commend it to trade unions. French holiday-taking culture is very different from ours, as is the French tradition of workplace organisation and social welfare provision. Nevertheless, both these approaches exemplify a concern to retain some element of collective provision and social welfare in holiday-taking which is otherwise in danger of being quite lost to British society. The English Tourism Council is no doubt right in its conclusion that the non-participating 40% do not break down into easily accessible market niche groups, but that is not really the question which we should be addressing. We cannot consider the issue solely from the 'market potential' perspective. The whole purpose of having a social inclusion agenda is that the excluded should be helped to reach the point where they have the resources and can find the motivation to join the rest of society. If taking a holiday provides personal physical and mental health benefits, and thereby in aggregate produces demonstrable social benefits – and if holidays are now also seen by most of the population as a necessity, then we need to be imaginative enough to find ways of delivering those advantages to all who might wish to take them. The laudable intention of the current UK government to disregard traditional Departmental boundaries in pursuit of better welfare provision and greater social cohesion presents tourism practitioners and researchers with an opportunity to review what has been done elsewhere and devise a new agenda for further research in relation to social tourism. The aim should be to come up, not necessarily with products, but with solutions which are appropriate to our national traditions and modern circumstances.

Note

The author wishes to thank Katrina Voysey of the English Tourism Council and Jenny Stephenson of the Family Holiday Association for generously providing unpublished information for this paper. The views expressed in this paper are the author's own.

References

ANCV (Agence Nationale pour les Cheques Vacances) website, http://www. ancv. com/
    rc/rca/rca0. htm, visited 10 July 2000.
ANCV (1998) La gazette officielle du tourism, No. 1438, June 1998.
ANCV (n.d.) ANCV et Solidarite. Paris: Agence Nationale pour les Cheques Vacances.
Bureau International du Tourism Social, (International Bureau of Social Tourism)
    website, http:www. bits-int. org, visited 10 July 2000.
Davidson, R. and Maitland, R. (1997) *Tourism destinations*. London: Hodder and
    Stoughton.
Department of Culture, Media and Sport (1999) *Tomorrow's tourism*. London: DCMS.
English Tourist Board (1989) *Tourism for all*. London: ETB.
ETC (English Tourism Council), personal communication to the author, 16 June 2000.
Family Holiday Association, personal communication to the author, 26 June 2000.
Fayos-Sola, E. (1996) 'Tourism policy: a midsummer night's dream?', *Tourism
    Management* Vol. 17, No. 6: pp. 405–412.
Heeley, J. (1989) 'Role of national tourist organizations in the United Kingdom', in S.
    F. Witt and L. Moutinho (eds) *Tourism marketing and management handbook*.
    Hemel Hempstead, Prentice Hall.
Hughes, H. L. (1984) 'Government support for tourism in the UK. A different
    perspective', in *Tourism Management* Vol. 5, No. 1: pp. 13–19.
Richards, G. (1995) 'Politics of national tourism policy in Britain', in *Leisure Studies*
    Vol. 14, No. 3: pp. 153–173.
Robinson, G. (1996) 'Tourism policy', in R. Thomas (ed) *The hospitality industry,
    tourism and Europe*. Perspectives on policies. London: Cassell.
The Scottish Office (1998) *Policy and financial management review of the Scottish
    Tourist Board. Prior options study. Final report*. Edinburgh: The Scottish Office.
Smith, R. (1998) 'Public policy for tourism in Scotland', in R. MacLellan and R. Smith
    (eds) *Tourism in Scotland*. London: International Thomson Business Press.
World Tourism Organization website, http://www. wto. org, visited 10 July 2000.

A Disabled Leisure Studies: Theorising Dominant Discourses of the Employed Body, the Able Body and the Active Body?

Cara Aitchison

Cheltenham and Gloucester College of Higher Education

Introduction

This paper offers some theoretical reflections following the completion of an empirical study titled *Disability and Social Inclusion: Leisure, Sport and Culture in the Lives of Young Disabled People* (Aitchison, 2000a). The research project was conducted with Scope, the UK's largest disability organisation, and was undertaken following recognition of the limited amount of data and fragmented knowledge base relating to the leisure experiences of young disabled people with cerebral palsy. The purpose of the research was to provide data, analysis and recommendations to inform future leisure provision and advocacy by Scope and other disability and leisure organisations. The purpose of this paper, however, is not to provide a detailed account of the methods and findings of the research as these have been explained elsewhere (Aitchison, 2000b). Instead, this paper reflects on the results and analysis of the project, from which it became evident that the relationship between leisure and disability has received limited attention and remains an unproblematised and unsophisticated area of research within the subject field of leisure studies. In short, leisure studies has a codified set of knowledge within which disability studies has only a marginal place (Aitchison, 2001a).

The body of knowledge conceived and perceived as leisure studies has, as one of its central axes, an established discourse addressing the leisure lives of people deemed to be peripheral, marginal or excluded from leisure provision, participation and consumption. Disability, disabled people and people with impairments have, however, been rendered largely invisible from such a discourse. This paper attempts to offer a series of explanations for the continued marginalisation of disability and disabled people from the leisure studies research literature. Three explanations are proposed as having been mutually informing in developing what, in poststructural sociological terms, might be defined as an unsigned, non-disabled hegemonic discourse within the subject field of leisure studies. The three explanations put forward are: the orthodox origins of leisure studies as a subject field; the dominance of particular and hegemonic models of disability used in leisure research; and the maintenance of conventional, and perhaps outmoded, definitions of leisure within the leisure studies literature. The paper argues that each of these three discussions has informed a dominant discourse within leisure studies that emphasises the employed body, the able body and the active body.

This paper will first explore the orthodox origins of leisure studies. Secondly, it will examine the dominance of particular and hegemonic models of disability, and, thirdly, it will evaluate the influence of conventional definitions of leisure. Prior to this theoretical discussion, the research objectives, methodology and findings will be summarised briefly to provide a contextual underpinning.

Research context

The empirical research informing this paper took the form of a regional study designed to provide knowledge of the leisure consumption patterns of a group of young disabled people, their desires and demands for leisure provision, the extent to which these leisure aspirations were met by leisure providers, and the impact of current provision and participation on parents and carers of young disabled people. The research project therefore aimed to map the place of leisure in the lives of young disabled people and those who care for them. This mapping exercise was designed to explore the meanings attached to leisure itself, the leisure experiences of young disabled people and their carers, and the potential for meeting any demands for improved provision. The research was conducted in Scope's West Country Partnership Area, stretching from Bristol in the north to Dorset and the Channel Islands in the south, and from Wiltshire in the east to Cornwall in the west. The area has a number of urban centres including Bath, Bristol, Bournemouth, Exeter, Plymouth, Poole and Swindon but much of it is semi-rural and the population and services tend to be geographically spread.

The research combined the use of quantitative and qualitative methods in an attempt to generate data that would elicit details of the type, frequency and meaning of leisure in the lives of a group of young people and their parents. A combination of leisure diaries and focus groups was selected to achieve these research objectives. Twenty-nine leisure diaries and four focus groups were completed during November 1999. The leisure diaries provided data relating to the type and frequency of leisure activities undertaken by the young people and the leisure facilitation activities of the parents who also acted as the young people's main carers. Fifteen young people and fourteen parents completed leisure diaries over a period of four weekend days and ten school days in the two weeks prior to the focus groups. The young people all had cerebral palsy and their levels of disability ranged from moderate to severe: more than half of the group used walking aids or wheelchairs; the majority had moderate to severe speech difficulties; and a minority required assistance in writing their leisure diary. Four focus groups were held at a leisure event specially organised for the young people who had been keeping leisure diaries. Two focus groups were held with the young people and two with their parents. The young people were divided according to age with one group made up of 11–13 years and one of 13–15 years.

There were four main findings from the research. First, the young disabled people shared many of the same leisure priorities as their non-disabled counterparts. Secondly, the majority of leisure activities comprised informal everyday leisure with an over-whelming emphasis on electronic leisure media. Thirdly, where patterns of leisure participation differed between disabled and non-disabled young people was in the amount rather than type of leisure participation and in the social circumstances surrounding participation. This was illustrated by young disabled people's tendency to participate in leisure on their own or with their parents rather than with friends. For example, during the course of the two-week diary-keeping exercise, the young disabled people aged 11–15 averaged one visit to or from a friend. Social interaction, however, was emphasised strongly as an important feature of leisure, and this fourth finding served to provide insight into the meaning of leisure in the lives of the young people in the study.

The orthodox origins of leisure studies

The origins of leisure studies can be traced to a number of disciplines and subject fields that experienced increasing status within the academy during the 1960s and 1970s. Three multi-disciplinary areas in particular played an important role in the formation of leisure studies in the United Kingdom and can be seen in the origins of the Leisure Studies Association, formed in 1975, and the Leisure Studies Journal, founded in 1982. Within the UK, the sociology of work, physical education and human movement studies, and urban planning and countryside recreation were largely responsible for the development of the leisure studies canon. All three areas, however, have left an unwitting legacy from which disability and disabled people appear peripheral. The sociology of work has reified the employed body; physical education and human movement studies have valorised the able body and the orthodox aesthetic body; and urban planning and countryside recreation have validated the active body and the mobile body. Consequently, it can be argued that unemployed, disabled, non-aesthetic, inactive and immobile bodies have been displaced from the conventional leisure studies literature (Aitchison, 2001b).

It is perhaps more readily acknowledged that active leisure and sport presuppose the existence of an able body. But tourism, too, adopts an unsigned non-disabled hege-monic discourse and assumes an able body to be both mobile and seeing. Indeed, there is a sense in which both mobility and sight are deemed to be prerequisites for engaging with the tourist experience as conventionally constructed by the tourism industry and tourism studies. Nowhere is this emphasis on mobility to sites and ability to see sights more evident than in the writings of Urry (1990) who has focused upon 'touring cultures' and 'the tourist gaze' as signifiers of the importance of mobility and sight within tourism. To those who identify as blind or visually impaired, however, Urry's duality of tourism as 'site' and 'sight' is rendered problematic.

The marginalisation of disability from the leisure studies research agenda is, however, anomalous with the growing concern with inequity and social exclusion voiced by leisure scholars in the UK from the 1970s onwards. This concern is particularly evident in contemporary public policy and has been acknowledged within sport and physical activity research, although less so within leisure studies research. Moreover, the increasing social theorisation of the body, so evident in sports studies, together with sociology, social and cultural geography, cultural studies and gender studies, appears to have gone largely unrecognised in mainstream leisure studies.

Hegemonic models of disability

As identified above, one tenet of leisure studies research over the last thirty years has been that of identifying inequity and exclusion, within society in general and leisure in particular, as a precursor to achieving equity and inclusion. In contrast to the influence of structuralist sociology in the UK, the development of leisure studies in North America has been underpinned by a strong tradition of social-psychology in which the individual, leisure experience, disability and the disabled body have been central. Ostensibly then, it may appear paradoxical that North American leisure studies research has shown greater interest in disability than the European leisure studies community. On closer examination, however, it is apparent that much of the North American research on disability and leisure is informed by a medical model of disability that offers few possibilities for disrupting the paternalist discourse of therapeutic recreation. Whilst such research has undoubtedly made a positive contribution to physiotherapy and recreational therapy, its contribution to critical social science has been limited. Much of the literature emanating from this tradition has been written in relation to sport, where the injured body is seen to be disabled and in need of rehabilitation, therapeutic exercise and physiotherapy provided by others and performed on the disabled body. In other words, the disabled body becomes the blank canvas upon which ability can be re-inscribed.

The medicalisation of disability, sustained by the use of the medical model, emphasises the adaptations that need to be made to the body rather than to society. Through its denial of the social construction of disability and disabled people, the dominant medical model of disability has offered little scope for the contestation of leisure studies' unsigned non-disabled hegemony. In disability studies, although there is a range of models, two have dominated the discourse of the last twenty years: the medical model and the social model. Humphrey (2000: p. 63) explains the rise of the social model "as a reaction against the medical model of disability, which reduced disability to impairment so that disability was located within the body or mind of the individual, whilst the power to define, control and treat disabled people was located within the medical and paramedical professions". Both critical and poststructural theory have begun to question the dualised juxtaposition of the social and medical models as explanations and interventions in relation to disability. For example, Abberley (1997) cautions against the adoption of a simple materialist social model that fails to problematise the cultural and symbolic nature of oppression. In recognising the need to expand the social model to accommodate diversity of experience, Shakespeare and Watson (1997: p. 271) suggest that "the dominant version of the social model has favoured a materialist, if not Marxist, worldview. We argue it is possible (and indeed desirable), to retain the social model within a more nuanced worldview drawing on feminist and post-modernist discourse".

Thus recent discussions have referred not to one social model but to a range of competing and overlapping social models. Developments within disability theory have therefore begun to accommodate the increasing acceptance, within the academy, that grand narratives and simplistic models provide only general answers and superficial solutions to what are, in fact, complex issues and problems. Challenging the dualism of social-medical recognises that analyses of the interplay or nexus of the medical and social may offer more scope for a detailed understanding of both physical and attitudinal phenomena and the inter-relationships between material and symbolic realities in disabled people's lives.

Conventional definitions of leisure

Defining leisure has preoccupied leisure scholars since the inception of the subject field. Because it is more often defined residually by what it is not than by what it actually is, leisure remains an elusive concept. Thus, we know that leisure is not usually defined as employment, paid work or essential duties such as childcare and household chores. Although leisure can mean different things to different people at different times or in different places, it is generally agreed that it is the nature and composition of time, space, activity, function and level of freedom that constitute the meaning of leisure for both individuals and society. Commensurate with such a view, conventional definitions of leisure have focused on when people take part in leisure (leisure time), where leisure participation takes place (leisure spaces), what people do in their leisure (leisure activities), what purpose their leisure serves (leisure function), and the degree to which their leisure is freely chosen (leisure freedom). Although contested within the leisure studies literature, these definitions have not been critiqued in relation to disability.

Mainstream leisure studies literature assumes that leisure experiences represent positive choices with leisure frequently being seen as free time, freely chosen time or time free from the constraints of everyday life (de Grazia, 1962). But these definitions may be less meaningful for people whose freedom is relative freedom dependent on the care and support of other people. As the majority of disabled people is not engaged in full-time paid employment, defining leisure in relation to work is only useful for the minority and simply reinforces the marginal status of those who are not part of the labour force. Defining leisure in such temporal terms, albeit residual temporal terms, has formed a cornerstone of the leisure studies literature emanating from the sociology of work referred to above.

Conceptualising leisure in spatial terms is central to the leisure studies literature informed by urban planning and countryside recreation. Throughout the 1970s and 1980s the influence of geography was evident in leisure studies emphasising the significance of spatiality in shaping both urban and rural leisure patterns and relations (Aitchison *et al.*, 2000). But these early leisure geographies offered little acknowledgement or insight into the different ways in which leisure spaces are accessed by disabled people. In recent years, however, social and cultural geographies have begun to address issues of access and mobility in relation to disability and disabled people (Butler and Parr, 1999; Gleeson, 1999; Imrie, 1996; Kitchin, 1998). The recognition that space is both a relative concept and a physical actuality offers valuable insight into the ways in which spaces are accessed and experienced differently by people depending on their disability and/or impairment and society's approach towards disability, impairment and leisure participation.

Defining leisure as an activity has been central to the dominant discourse of physical education and human movement studies. In both of these fields, leisure pursuits in the form of sports are emphasised whilst physical activities such as walking and gardening, that may be of great physical and psychological benefit to some disabled people, are de-emphasised. It is only now, largely through Department of Health and Local Health Authority discourses and policies, that physical activity is beginning to be promoted as something quite separate, and with a much wider relevance, than sport and exercise *per se*. Paradoxically, it is the medical profession that is now informing the leisure profession and leisure academics of the social and psychological benefits of physical activity and leisure.

Seeing leisure as functional for society or the individual is often associated with the Victorian movement of rational recreation and notions of muscular Christianity through which active and directed leisure were seen to offer opportunities for capitalists to control the time, activity and spatial patterns of the working classes (Clarke and Critcher, 1985). Where leisure is seen as functional for disabled people, it is normally associated with a medical rather than social function. Emphasis on physical activity and physiotherapy thus seem to dominate less physically active leisure or social interaction as leisure (Leach and Bailey, 1995).

Defining leisure as freedom may be equally problematic as a number of 'leisure' activities may not be freely chosen by disabled people but may be part of prescribed physiotherapy or recreation regimes requiring facilitation by others. The involvement of other people, however, can serve to redefine some activities as leisure. For example, data from both the diaries and the focus groups informing this paper illustrated that, for some young disabled people, physiotherapy was viewed as leisure because it involved social interaction with the physiotherapist in an environment outside the young person's home. As most of the leisure activities recorded by the young people were home-based and often very solitary, the novelty of engaging with others was viewed as a highly desirable leisure pursuit.

For the young disabled people involved in the study, the findings therefore demonstrate that leisure was not defined so much by when they took part (leisure time), what they did (leisure activities) or where their leisure took place (leisure spaces), but by who they encountered and interacted with as part of their leisure. Any sense of freedom derived from leisure may therefore be influenced by the extent to which meaningful social interaction is experienced in leisure time, activities and spaces. Such findings raise important questions for leisure provision and highlight the importance of new leisure-related technologies for providing home-based virtual social interaction.

This paper has sought to identify and explain why the relationship between leisure and disability has received limited attention and remains an unproblematised and relatively unsophisticated area of research within the subject field of leisure studies. Three explanations were proposed as being mutually informing in developing what was identified and defined as an unsigned, non-disabled hegemonic discourse within leisure studies. These explanations were: the orthodox origins of leisure studies as a subject field; the dominance of particular and hegemonic models of disability used in leisure research; and the maintenance of conventional, and perhaps outmoded, definitions of leisure within the leisure studies literature. The orthodox origins of the subject field were identified as the sociology of work, physical education and human movement studies, and urban planning and countryside recreation. These sub-disciplines have emphasised the employed body, the able body and the mobile body respectively. In doing so, disabled people and their experiences of leisure have been rendered marginal to mainstream leisure studies discourse. In conclusion, the theoretical sophistication of leisure studies could be greatly enhanced by a wider appreciation of social and cultural exclusion together with a more reflexive critique of the role of academic discourse in reproducing or challenging dominant, and often exclusive, definitions.

References

Abberley, (1987) 'The concept of oppression and the development of a social theory of disability', in L. Barton and M. Oliver (eds) *Disability studies: Past present and future*. Leeds: The Disability Press, pp. 160–178.

Aitchison, C. (2000a) *Disability and social inclusion: Leisure, sport and culture in the lives of young disabled people*. Cheltenham: Cheltenham and Gloucester College of Higher Education/Scope.

Aitchison, C. (2000b) 'Young disabled people, leisure and everyday life: reviewing conventional definitions for leisure studies', *Annals of Leisure Research*, 3.

Aitchison, C. (2001a) 'Gender and leisure research: The codification of knowledge', *Leisure Sciences* Vol. 23, No. 1: pp. 1–19.

Aitchison, C. (20001b, in press) 'From leisure and disability to disability leisure: Developing data, definitions and discourses', *Disability and Society*, No. 16.

Aitchison, C., Macleod, N. and Shaw, S. (2000) *Leisure and tourism landscapes: Social and cultural geographies*. London: Routledge.

Butler, R. and Parr, H. (1999) *Mind and body spaces: Geographies of illness, impairment and disability*. London: Routledge.

Clarke, J. and Critcher, C. (1985) *The devil makes work: Leisure in capitalist Britain*. London: Macmillan.

De Grazia, S. (1962) *Of time, work and leisure*. New York: The Twentieth Century Fund.

Gleeson, B. (1999) *Geographies of disability*. London: Routledge.

Humphrey, J. (2000) 'Researching disability projects or, some problems with the social model in practice', *Disability and Society* Vol. 15, No. 1: pp. 363–86.

Imrie, R. (2000) 'Disabling environments and the geography of access policies and practices', *Disability and Society* Vol. 15, No. 1: pp. 5–24.

Kitchin, R. (1998) '"Out of place", "knowing one's place": Space, power and the exclusion of disabled people', *Disability and Society*, Vol. 13, No. 3: pp. 343–356.

Leach, M. and Bailey, H. (1995) 'Physical activities', in J. Hogg and J. Cavet (eds) *Making leisure provision for people with profound learning and multiple disabilities*. London: Chapman and Hall, pp. 86–96.

Shakespeare, T. and Watson, N. (1997) 'Defending the social model', in L. Barton and M. Oliver (eds) *Disability studies: Past present and future*. Leeds: The Disability Press, pp. 263–273.

Urry, J. (1990) *The tourist gaze*. London: Sage.

The Validation of Alternative Discourses in the Lifelong Learning Systems of Australian Appreciative Outdoor Recreationalists and Indigenous Peoples

Kim Polistina

School of Leisure Studies, Griffith University, Australia

Introduction

This paper will discuss the continued marginalisation, through the dominant social discourse and subsequently the leisure discourse, of the following community groups in Australia: 'appreciative outdoor recreationalists'[1] and Aboriginal and Torres Strait Islander peoples[2]. Information provided is drawn from a literature review and preliminary data collected through a collaborative work in progress with these two communities.

A brief overview of the current dominant social discourse is provided before focusing the discussion on the current discourses in the leisure field. Examples of how the dominant leisure discourse perpetuates the marginalisation and silencing of the voices of the two community groups will be provided. The lack of platforms, in both the wider social system and the leisure field, that allow for the validation of the world-views and lifelong learning systems[3] of these community groups is also discussed throughout the paper. Finally, the necessity for the scientific community to assist in providing platforms for validating alternative discourses is addressed. These platforms would not only provide avenues for these marginalised voices to be heard but would also ensure the coexistence of their worldviews with other dominant social systems, through acceptance and respect in this wider social forum.

Dominant social discourse

This section will briefly discuss the characteristic noted as indicative of the current dominant social system's discourse. The foundation of this discourse is one that finds its roots in the economic rationalist, and hence capitalist, philosophy of the Western world (Aplin, 1998). The values that underpin this discourse are those that espouse unrestrained market forces, the continual accumulation of wealth and an overemphasis on the importance of competitiveness and individualism (Burch, 1993; Knudtson and Suzuki, 1992).

Parker (1992: p. 5) commented: "Discourses provide frameworks for debating the value of one way of talking about reality over other ways." The outcomes of these debates appear to be biased, however, by the manipulation of available forums for alternative voices to enter into the discussions. At present this manipulation of public forums appears to be conducted by those controlling the dominant discourses, which tend to be the social structures promoting and perpetuating the economic rationalist philosophy of the Western world. Support for this philosophy, however, appears to be waning. This includes the belief that this philosophy is based on nothing more than articles of faith (Merton cited in Haralambos and Holborn, 1991), the decline in the belief of the adequacy of industrialisation theories (Mommaas and van der Poel, 1987) and the recognition that consequences of modern industry, technology and science are far from being wholly beneficial to society (Giddens, 1993). There also appears to be a lack of research providing evidence of widespread commitment to the values underlying this economic rationalism in Western society (Aplin, 1998; Haralambos and Holborn, 1991). This situation is exacerbated by the identification that the Western social system itself is yet to provide evidence that its economic rationalist foundation is a viable social system (Aplin, 1998). Therefore, the appropriateness of using the discourse of this dominant social system as the arbitrary discourse for all social systems (in particular, those marginalised by this system) may be seen to be biased and self-perpetuating. This follows the argument put forward by Parker (1990: p. 61) when discussing Foucault's notions of power and discourse, that:

> ...what counts as true knowledge is ostensibly defined by the individual, but what is permitted to count is defined by discourse. What is spoken and who may speak [that is who is provided a platform to voice their discourse], are issues of power.

Parker (1992: p. 13) also commented that "a critical reflection on a discourse will often involve the use of other discourses" with the analysis facilitated by the identification of contradictions between the different ways of describing something.

Drawing on the notion of 'discourse dynamics'[4] (Parker, 1992) the following section will provide a brief critical reflection on the dominant leisure discourse taken from the position of the two marginalised community groups previously mentioned. Their daily interaction with these dominant social and leisure discourses will provide the basis for gaining a better understanding of the issues that emerge when one holds a different worldview (and discourse) to that of the dominant social system. Examples will be provided of how the dominant social discourse continually stifles the voices of these two groups through a variety of mechanisms in the leisure field. These mechanisms tend to promote and elevate the leisure values of the dominant discourse whilst simultaneously silencing the voices and values of these marginalised communities.

Leisure and environmental discourse literature

From the outset it should be noted that the following sub-sections have been separated for the purposes of this paper. These elements, however, are seen to be interconnected to all other life elements by appreciative outdoor recreationalists and Aboriginal and Torres Strait Islander peoples and should be read in this manner.

The general characteristics and beliefs noted as present in the worldviews and values held by appreciative outdoor recreationalists and Aboriginal and Torres Strait Islander peoples are:
- human-nature interconnectedness and a high level of positive environmental values;
- holistic lifestyles and lack of compartmentalisation of life's elements;
- high communal values, non-competitiveness and lack of individualism;
- lifelong learning systems of knowledge transfer.

Discussion on these characteristics will be provided throughout the following sections. It would be remiss not to note, however, that the level of adoption of these worldviews and values by an individual will depend on their level of assimilation into Western culture[5] (Djagamara, 1975; Ewert, 1993).

Environmental values

As the main difference between the underlying philosophies of the two community groups and the dominant social system appears to lie in their environmental values, it is prudent to provide an overview of these differences. The characteristics of the environmental values of appreciative outdoor recreationalists and Aboriginal and Torres Strait Islander peoples include:
- high level of environmental knowledge and strong conservation ethic (Henley, 1996; Ibrahim and Cordes, 1993; McCullum and McCullum, 1975; The World Council of Indigenous Peoples — WCIP, 1984; Wearing, 1986),
- a strong connectedness with nature — leading to high positive environmental values[6] (Atkinson, 1990; Berndt, Berndt and Stanton, 1993; Chester and Chester, 1991; Foley, 1994; McDonald, 1995; Runtz, 1993; The World Council of Indigenous Peoples — WCIP, 1984) and,
- a high degree of spiritual value attributed to the natural environment (Foley, 1994; Fox, 1983; Hodgins and Benidickson, 1989; McDonald, 1995).

On the other hand, the environmental values identified as present in the Western social system have the following characteristics, which tend to be indicative of a negative or low level of environmental knowledge or concern:

- the separation of people from nature,
- the acceptance of domination, subordination and manipulation of nature by people,
- the view of nature as infinite,
- the view of nature as having purely extrinsic (for example, economic) value. (Almond, 1988; Dunstan, 1992; Matthews and Riley cited in McCabe and Wadsworth, 1994; Salleh, 1988–89; Sayne, 1993; Seshachari, 1992)

These underlying environmental values have been noted to have a direct effect on the continued degradation of our global environment (Devall, 1990; Higgins, 1996; Higgins, 1996–97; Phipps, 1985; Polistina, 1997; Wearing, 1986).

This highlights the ability of the economic rationalist philosophy, which underpins the dominant social and leisure discourse, to undermine the environmentalist discourse utilised by many appreciative outdoor recreationalists and Aboriginal and Torres Strait Islander peoples. For example, Aboriginal and Torres Strait Islander peoples identify themselves as one with, dependent on and derived from the land (Foley, 1994; Hodgins and Benidickson, 1989; McDonald, 1995). Bosselman (1978) noted in his study on Australian Aborigines at Uluru (Ayers Rock) that although the land was viewed as something that could be used, it was also shared and never entered the realm of a commodity.

These values and beliefs tend to be mirrored in the environmentalist values (Kluckholn cited in Simcox, 1993) which appear to be held by many appreciative outdoor recreationalists (Atkinson, 1981; Wearing, 1986). It is easy to see the direct contrast to the dominant discourse's utilitarian view, held by many Europeans, of the land as merely resources for human consumption (Aplin, 1998), or a commodity to be bought, sold and utilised for human consumption (Dunstan, 1992; Salleh, 1988–89; Sayne, 1993). As a "… resource is a cultural construct defined … by a particular group of people …" (Aplin, 1998) it is evident that the definition would therefore be dictated by the discourse of the dominant social system unless that group provides avenues for the voices of other social systems.

Given the dominant economic rationalist system's views on the environment, it is not surprising that the positive environmental values and knowledge discourses of these two groups are not provided a high level of coverage or exposure in leisure literature. Groups holding environmental worldviews espousing high positive environmental values also appear to be provided little overt encouragement or support from the dominant discourse. A review of the leisure and environmental sciences literature resulted in a scarce amount of information on the level of environmental impact from urban leisure — for example, studies on the environmental impacts of different sporting activities or the construction of sporting facilities — being found.

This is disturbing for groups such as appreciative outdoor recreationalists and Aboriginal and Torres Strait Islander whose lifelong techniques for knowledge transfer, in, for, about and with the environment, are implemented through leisure forums which are encompassed in their lifestyles. The invisibility of the environment in leisure research and discourse is thus highlighted.

An area that is starting to emerge in relation to the environment and leisure is encompassed in the environmental management literature and focuses on how leisure companies and organisations can 'save money' by being green. The opening introductory sentence in the new "Green Audit Kit: The DIY guide to greening your Tourism business" states:

> This kit is designed to help you save money and improve the efficiency of your business. ... As a tourism business, the environment is your most precious resource. (Dingle, 1993: p. 1)

Whilst the audit kit is commendable for its innovative attempts to promote environmentalism in the leisure market place, it does highlight the emphasis on money, as opposed to environmental consciousness, as the primary reason for researching and promoting environmental issues in leisure.

Some environmental impact research has been covered in the tourism fields and research into the environmental education benefits of eco-tourism has also been conducted. Environmental impact studies, particularly on outdoor recreation, however, tend to emphasise the negative impacts on the environment of these pursuits and tend to hold them responsible (either covertly or overtly) for the damage to and maintenance of the environment. For example, Liddle (1997) provides an extensive report on the negative impacts of outdoor recreation on natural areas and provides recommendations for the management of such activities. However, the report does not discuss the impacts that the manufacture of the leisure industry in general and other forms of urban leisure — for example, extension of urban pollution resulting from the manufacturing of urban leisure equipment — have on these same natural areas. If we are to look at leisure discourse in its entirety, it becomes ironically clear that the leisure activities that have the least amount of impact on the environment (for example, appreciative outdoor recreation) are those chosen for critique on the topic. For instance, bushwalking or even horseriding have a far lower impact on the environment than building a resort or sports stadium in any area (urban, rural or wilderness), as these facilities not only consume resources for their preparation and construction but are continuous consumers of resources in their daily operation.

In relation to literature on Indigenous peoples and the environment, the main source of information in the leisure literature is obtained through the related field of environmental co-management with Indigenous peoples of parks systems (primarily in Northern America, Canada, New Zealand and parts of Africa). We are only just beginning to see the importance of collaborating with Indigenous peoples in tourism (more specifically cultural tourism). However, it could be argued that this literature still requires the assimilation of Aboriginal and Torres Strait Islander peoples into the dominant Western leisure discourse, that is, the commodification of their culture for economic gain, to obtain verification and to prove its usefulness to the perpetuation of the dominant system.

The environmental values which underlie the worldviews of appreciative outdoor recreationalists and Aboriginal and Torres Strait Islander peoples are perpetuated through the environment's continual existence in their daily lives. These interconnected lifestyles involve a high level of interaction with the natural environment primarily through activities defined as leisure in Western society.

Leisure and lifestyle choices

From the outset we can see that these communities and the dominant social system are operating from opposing worldviews and value systems, and hence opposing discourses. This adversity is exacerbated with the preference and often adoption of lifestyles choices by the two community groups which are alternative to the dominant societal lifestyle. They appear to focus on a lack of importance of materialism and a high importance placed on the need for a healthy balanced lifestyle in a communal setting, including a high level of activities that promote creativity, physical activity and spiritual enlightenment. Many of these activities form the community and outdoor recreation components of Western leisure forums and tend be afforded a low priority due to what appears to be their lack of ability to produce high economic gains (this issue will be discussed further in the following sections).

Sklair (1996) commented that one form of silencing discourses that oppose the dominant discourse is through their marginalisation into obscurity. She provides the lack of social and governmental support for communal forms of living as one example of this marginalisation. Murray (n.d.) also provided examples of this marginalisation when identifying that these communal forms of living are often portrayed negatively through media texts as ferals, pests or social dropouts. These alternative lifestyles choices, however, are an important element of the perpetuation of the worldviews of appreciative outdoor recreationalists and Aboriginal and Torres Strait Islander peoples through lifelong learning systems (O'Rourke, 1998; Williams, 1994).

Many of the mediums for this lifelong learning rely on what have been defined as leisure activities by the dominant social discourse. They have also been defined by the dominant social discourse (particularly in relation to anthropological literature) as 'leisure lifestyles' with somewhat negative connotations. However, as Lynch and Veal (1996) commented in relation to traditional Aboriginal lifestyles, this should not be viewed as a label for a lifestyle in which leisure is the primary focus, but more as a lifestyle where leisure characteristics are important elements integrated into all activities. The negative connotations afforded this 'leisure lifestyle' are not surprising given the Protestant work ethic and economic rationalist foundations of the dominant social system (Clarke and Critcher, 1985) which Dunstan (1992) noted, views leisure as valued only for when work is completed or when it is economically viable.

Sport forum

This view of leisure as a disconnected component of life provides another area of difference between the discourses. The compartmentalisation of leisure in the dominant social and leisure discourse assists with placing a hierarchy of importance on its multitude of activities and pursuits. In the Australian context, in particular, sport and tourism are seen to be elevated to a level of importance above most other leisure activities, and this is reflected in the current governmental funding and provision policies. The manipulation through the dominant leisure discourse of the hierarchy of importance placed on sport and tourism serves as a means of silencing those leisure discourses that are seen to be a threat to this dominant discourse. This would appear to be at the expense of community-based recreation for both non-Indigenous and Indigenous Australians (Atkinson, 1991; Lynch and Veal, 1996; Polistina, 2000). Two examples may assist with highlighting how this biased leisure discourse operates to perpetuate itself.

Any mention of 'recreation' (which has slowly become the governmental umbrella covering all community leisure groups other than sport and tourism) other than 'sport' has been eliminated from the title of the current federal government portfolio[7] for leisure. This has the effect of erasing any terms of reference, for example outdoor or cultural recreation, other than those identified with sport, from the governmental discourse on leisure. With this major focus on sport (and tourism) in the governmental and public forums other leisure organisations are even finding it necessary to notify the minister of their existence within his portfolio. This was required of Queensland Outdoor Recreation Federation (QORF), the state body for outdoor recreation, in May 2000. Given that governmental funding and promotional support is distributed by the federal government, this invisibility is concerning for these two community groups.

A review of the state and federal leisure funding programmes for both Western and Aboriginal and Torres Strait Islander communities identified a major emphasis on the promotion and support for sport. This sporting emphasis is manipulated both explicitly and implicitly through the discourse utilised within these documents. For example, a current funding scheme[8] for community recreation provides grants for facility development projects. Given that the only facility that is generally required for outdoor recreation (in particular appreciative activities) and small-scale Indigenous cultural activities, is the access to large portions of natural environment, this title instantly sets up a funding barrier for these communities. No governmental funding schemes for the acquisition of natural areas by community groups were identified. This barrier is further strengthened by the priority given to built venues/facilities. "The development of an outdoor venue" (Queensland Department of Communication and Information Local Government Planning and Sport, 2000) is one of the three noted eligible projects for the scheme. Further investigation identified that the definition given to an outdoor venue was that it must be built. This further silences the needs and wishes of these marginalised groups, as one of the major elements of engaging in their chosen leisure activity is the non-existence of man-made structures. "With the towering monuments to the work ethic out of view, the outdoor adventurer is free to escape to nature for a renewal of the spirit" (Ibrahim and Cordes, 1993: p. 25). There is also no mention of eligibility for venues/facilities that would assist with engaging in Aboriginal and Torres Strait Islander cultural traditions through community activities in the natural environment.

When discussing the topic of sport, mention should also be made of its competitive and individualistic nature which opposes the non-competitive and communal focus inherent in the appreciative outdoor recreation sub-culture and Aboriginal and Torres Strait Islander cultures (Atkinson, 1991; Cooper, 1994; McKay, 1994; Noonuccal, 1992). This fundamental difference in these discourses highlights a possible source of alienation from the dominant social and leisure discourse for these two community groups.

Whilst outdoor recreation has been given some visibility in the media and leisure forums, it has generally been in the form of masculine traits that mirror sporting behaviours, for example, images of competitiveness, conquering and aggression[9]. These dominant leisure discourses can be seen in the images of the heroic, superhuman and invincible person (usually male) conquering the outdoors which are rife in the general literature and media coverage of any activities in the natural environment. There are various types of discourses that are being utilised to reinforce these notions of competitiveness, egocentricity and anthropocentrism, both overtly and subliminally.

The written texts abound with statements such as 'tough and harsh environmental conditions', and 'knowing the challenges of these environments'. The images that correspond to these statements are of superfit people traversing difficult terrain, often wearing the latest outdoor clothing. This picture presents the natural environment as a place to be dominated, but only by those select few who are strong enough to survive and who enjoy the adrenaline rush. An example of this is a recent publication on enhancing one's performance in extreme environments, which uses "Book Conquers Harsh environmental elements" as its marketing slogan[10].

The competitive, individualistic, compartmentalised, and somewhat egocentric leisure images and values promoted through the media are not only foreign to appreciative outdoor recreationalists and Aboriginal and Torres Strait Islander peoples, but are often the cause of much confusion, bemusement and concern. The behaviours previously mentioned are often alien to appreciative outdoor recreationalists and many Aboriginal and Torres Strait Islander peoples who view the natural environment as a place of peace, relaxation, comfortable interaction with the human and natural world and often spiritual enlightenment (Fox, 1983; Hodgins and Benidickson, 1989; Hogan, 1992).

These feelings are amplified by the fact that the activities that are utilised to promote personal reflection and spiritual connection with the natural environment, for example solo experiences or cultural rituals, are often ignored in the publicity for the outdoor recreation[11] field. The intention of this comment is not to condone inexperienced and ill-prepared individuals engaging in activities in the natural environment. It is, however, intended to identify that for individuals engaged in holistic lifestyles this lack of approval and acceptance by the dominant leisure and social discourse to engage in such activities denies the individual their freedom of choice that is purported to be inherent in leisure (Gunter, 1987). Particularly, since within these lifestyles the community members tend to conduct continuous lifelong learning that promotes a high level of attainment of environmental knowledge, values and skills before engaging in solo interaction with the environment. Hogan (1992) commented, in relation to the lack of environmental aspects in Western outdoor education and adventure programmes, that the wilderness should be viewed as a special place that individuals should earn the right to go to, through accumulation of appropriate skills and commitment to looking after environment. This does not appear to be occurring in current Western outdoor programmes (Polistina, 1997) although it does occur on a daily basis for appreciative outdoor recreationalists and Aboriginal and Torres Strait Islander peoples.

They are also discouraged in the wider leisure discourse through the norms of having three minimum in a bushwalking group and the use of litigation threats to deny approval for solo experience on outdoor education camps and excursions. Interaction with the natural environment is seen as continuous and many of these characteristics are what draw appreciative outdoor recreationalists and Aboriginal and Torres Strait Islander peoples back to the natural environment throughout life. This is done in an endeavour to learn from it through becoming a part of it rather than apart from it and viewing it as a place to conquer.

Whilst there are still many publications that provide for a reprieve from the more aggressive discourses on the outdoor recreation field they tend to be given far less coverage in public forums and, in particular, the media. As previously mentioned, those mirroring sport philosophies tend to hold priority, even with recent calls within the leisure field to reduce the level of aggression, competition and male-focused leisure in Aboriginal and Torres Strait Islander communities (Atkinson, 1991) and in Western leisure (Henderson, Bialeschki, Shaw and Freysinger, 1989).

The notion that sport provides a 'door opener' to a better quality of life for Aboriginal peoples is misleading as it does so only for a select few, whilst many Aboriginal communities still survive in atrocious living conditions. Tatz (1987) discussed the example of the concentration camp lifestyle on Toomelah Reserve in New South Wales. Fashanu (cited in Cashmore, 1982, npn) also noted, regarding the use of sporting role models for Aboriginal children:

> ... I don't think it's a bad thing because black kids can relate to someone who's good ... It helps, but, at the end of the day, the change that black sportsmen are going to make to the lives of everyday black kids is only marginal.

It should also be noted that the value attributed to elite sportspersons is very indicative of the Western social system value for the attainment of world prestige and status. The increase in pride and self-esteem (albeit in a Western context) could be viewed as a further assimilation of Aboriginal and Torres Strait Islander peoples into Western society through the covert imposition of Western elitist and individualistic values on their leisure.

Finally, the progressive elevation of the importance of sport and tourism over other forms of leisure could be linked to the social control mechanisms inherent in the dominant social political system. Historically, Australian leisure (to a large extent male sport) has been utilised as a social control mechanism for controlling the masses (Clarke and Critcher, 1985; Wilson, 1988). Hoch (1972: p. 8) also noted that "... sport is a mere instrument of capitalist domination designed to slough off energies or divert them into meaningless channels." Although this statement was made 28 years ago it could be said to still be relevant today. However, it is more likely to be the economic benefits derived from the sport and tourism industries which play a larger part in the value placed on them in a society where the accumulation of wealth is the main underlying value (Clarke and Critcher, 1985; Knudtson and Suzuki, 1992).

Whatever the reasons, the elevation of the importance of sport and tourism is perpetuated through the discourse found in all aspects of our social existence. Examples include: the media hype on the Rugby League football finals weeks (if not months) before the game is played; educational curriculums espousing the importance of physical activity predominantly through sport; sporting icons found on general clothing (from infant through to adult wear); and, even the use of sporting heroes as referent advertising to sell real estate. All of these social texts serve to reinforce the dominant importance placed on sport, and to a similar degree tourism.

Tourism forum

An example of the invisibility of outdoor recreation in the tourism forum is the inclusion of outdoor recreation participation figures (for example, bushwalking, rockclimbing, birdwatching, snorkelling) in the current tourism participation statistics (Blamey, 1995). These statistics are used to promote the idea that 'tourism' provides a high level of economic gains for the local community and therefore covertly justifying continued government funding to the area. Kelly (2000, npn) noted, "The data highlights tourism's vital significance to the economy and its key role in revitalising regional areas". Whilst this economic gain may be important, subsuming outdoor recreation participation into tourism statistics, particularly in relation to local people, is misrepresenting these groups and also misleading. It also jeopardises the government funding to outdoor recreation organisations through the possibility of its allocation being diverted to the tourism industry. Hence informal community-based outdoor recreation is reduced to a lower level of priority than that given to the economic gains of tourism.

At present the definition of 'tourist' given in the report is a person who travels outside a 40klm radius of their home to engage in their leisure (Blamey, 1995). Given that most natural environments in which outdoor recreation is engaged in are situated outside the 40klm radius of community members' homes, this perpetuates the silencing of outdoor recreationalists as it provides the avenue for misappropriation of their leisure participation statistics.

This also ignores the continuous travel back and forth to clan and community lands for Aboriginal and Torres Strait Islander peoples who are required to live away from their communities due to employment. To label these people as 'tourists' when travelling back to their own lands is misrepresentation, as community and family gatherings are an integral part of the extended family tradition and an important part of the communities' leisure and lifestyle and not a tourist activity. Whilst this might seem to be an argument based on semantics it is not viewed this way by those labelled with an identity with which they do not identify. Parker (1992: p. xi) commented that:

> Language is so structured to mirror power relations that often we can see no other ways of being, and it structures ideology so that it is difficult to speak both in and against it.

Given tourism's underlying economic rationalist philosophy, the benefits of tourism and cultural tourism policies tend to be reaped by the tourism organisations and the wider Western community, rather than by the Aboriginal and Torres Strait Islander communities. Tilmouth (1997) notes that millions of dollars are being made by tourism organisations from Aboriginal tourism in the Northern Territory, but many Aboriginal communities continue to live in Third World conditions.

According to Roberts (1997) tourism does little to address the many social issues within Aboriginal and Torres Strait Islander communities and simply generates more problems through the negative behaviour of tourists. Including Aboriginal and Torres Strait Islander culture into tourism programmes may provide tourist organisations with increased profits, and may in some cases give limited recognition and exposure to the Aboriginal and Torres Strait Islander community, but it also provides a forum for placing Aboriginal and Torres Strait Islander peoples and cultures into a museum context (Bosselman, 1978). Hence, it reduces their status to that of being a 'this is the way it was' culture, rather than their being accepted as part of a viable social system and culture in today's society.

The time pressures under which tours operate may not facilitate any depth of learning about Aboriginal and Torres Strait Islander cultures. Similar time constraints can be found in the number of cultural festivals being provided through Aboriginal and Torres Strait Islander communities (for example, the Cape York Dance Festival and the NAIDOC[12] celebrations). Their provision is indispensable to ongoing cultural education, acceptance and respect from mainstream society. They are, however, usually held only once a year and it could be argued that this reduces their provision to tokenism. Furthermore, the attention given to such festivals draws attention away from the poor provision of leisure to the community during the remainder of the year (Tilmouth, 1997). This issue will be further discussed in the following section.

Community values and lifelong learning systems

This overemphasis on competitive sport, and to some degree tourism, in leisure discourse tends to lead the individual into a false sense of community values, as it has the ability to disguise and ignore the lack of provision of alternative forms of community-based recreation. For example, the problem with assimilating Aboriginal and Torres Strait Islander peoples into this competitive Western sport culture is evident given their communal focus and high degree of group cohesion. Although temporary group cohesion among spectators may result from sporting events, it does little to address the non-competitive, non-individualistic and communal leisure needs of these spectators themselves.

Community-based recreational activities are generally those engaged in by women, older people, people with additional needs, people from cultures with a more communal focus and non-competitive youth and adults. This communal aspect to leisure is also a major component in both appreciative outdoor recreationalists and Aboriginal and Torres Strait Islander communities' leisure. The negative effects that a lack of communal activities has on community unity and cohesion was noted by Rojek (1987). He commented that, in general, regular community carnivals are being held as little as once a year and lack continuity and the [communal] 'spirit' generated by them goes once the event is over.

These community events tend to provide avenues for lifelong learning of specific cultural and social knowledge and values, especially for Aboriginal and Torres Strait Islander youth (Atkinson, 1991). This lifelong learning process concentrates on continual learning and development of holistic lifestyle knowledge, values and skills. This is opposed to the concentrated short courses that focus on a specific activity (for example, six month courses at adult colleges that purport to produce outdoor rockclimbing instructors on their completion) that are indicative of leisure training programmes in Western society. The absence of regular local community events results in the need to rely on other avenues for knowledge, values and skills transfer which usually tend to be the compartmentalised form of leisure training programmes of the dominant social systems.

This lack of avenue for lifelong learning has proven to be devastating for Aboriginal and Torres Strait Islander peoples as it is these avenues that have provided Indigenous peoples with a unique connection to the natural environment (Australia Today, n.d.; Capps, 1976; McKay, 1994). It has been noted that the way Indigenous peoples observe and understand nature heightens their sense of high intrinsic value, reciprocity and spirituality for the environment. This has been noted as primarily due to the lifelong interaction and learning, in the natural environment, engaged in by these cultures. Bosselman (1978: p. 84) gave an example of this spiritual and insightful understanding in Australian Aboriginal peoples of the Uluru (Ayers Rock) area:

> Where the indifferent observer sees a patch of lichen on the rock's wall, the Aboriginal sees the 'metamorphosed' smoke from the burning camp of the greedy sleepy-lizard.

This insight may only be described in Western language as the ability to see the soul of the object. Whilst similar notions have been identified as existing in the worldviews and lifelong learning engaged in by appreciative outdoor recreationalists (Ibrahim and Cordes, 1993), this imaginative vision has been noted as a major missing link in the positive environmental consciousness in Western culture as a whole (Capps, 1976; Knudtson and Suzuki, 1992; Levi-Strauss, 1966; McKay, 1994). The validation of these images, and hence discourses, could only serve to heighten the spiritual level of a social system flexible enough to provide platforms for such validation. The existence of this spiritual connection with the natural environment has been lost to a large degree within Western society (Hogan and Priest, 1996).

Indigenous peoples' spiritual connection with the environment has generally been developed by the knowledge transferred by clan and community elders through lifelong learning processes (Atkinson, 1991). Community recreation events are, therefore, particularly important to Aboriginal and Torres Strait Islander peoples in regard to access to extended families, which provides regular interaction with clan and tribal elders and other community members. This access and interaction forms the basis for lifelong learning and the transfer of cultural and environmental knowledge, values and skills (Atkinson, 1991; Djagamara, 1975; Robertson, 1975). To this end, the marginalisation into obscurity of communal lifestyles previously mentioned (see leisure and lifestyle choices section) has a deleterious effect on the ability for this lifelong learning to occur.

The danger of losing this community spirit and values is expressed by Loynes (1998: p. 35) in relation to the "McDonaldisation" of the outdoors and subsequent adoption of marketplace values in the outdoor education and commercial outdoor recreation fields. He identifies the major concern of this process is its ability to disassociate people "... from their experience of community and place" and hence leaving behind the "... values of the social movement that gave rise to the field", being community outdoor recreation. Once again this highlights the ability of the economic rationalist philosophy to undermine the communal and environmentalist discourse utilised by many appreciative outdoor recreationalists and Aboriginal and Torres Strait Islander peoples.

It is interesting to note that this communal responsibility for development and education of youth is only recently being identified as an important aspect in Western outdoor education forums[13], particularly in regard to 'at-risk' youth. This highlights the complex nature of this silencing of alternative discourses as it identifies the process of initial oppression into obscurity of these alternative discourses only to have the underlying values and techniques of these alternative social systems being 'discovered' as revelations by the Western social system. In effect misappropriating alternative cultural traditions and norms[14].

Education, training and lifelong learning systems

A review of the leisure, environmental sciences, anthropological and education literature produced very little on the beneficial characteristics of Aboriginal and Torres Strait Islander traditional and contemporary lifelong learning systems and leisure lifestyles. It is posited that it is inappropriate to discuss lifelong learning processes (as in Aboriginal and Torres Strait Islander cultures) in discourses, and subsequent texts, that engage the notions of levels of competency and assessment (as in Western education and training system). This denigrates the holistic lifelong learning nature of the knowledge transfer to one that compartmentalises time and learning and assumes expert status after completion of the education or training programme. This is also pertinent to the appreciative outdoor recreationalists' forum.

This compartmentalisation may be seen to weaken the foundations of lifelong learning, and, in regard to assessment, assumes the notion of an individual as an expert or of higher importance over another individual. These values of individual excellence and honour are inappropriate as these values are seen to be foreign, unethical and a great social risk to Aboriginal and Torres Strait Islander cultures (Cooper, 1994; McKay, 1994; Noonuccal, 1992: p. 69). The level of assimilation into Western culture may, however, affect the individual's perception of the degree of risk of adopting these Western values. The notion of assessment therefore results in the enforcement of the dominant discourse of leisure education and training, for example, teacher/student system as opposed to lifelong mentoring systems.

The holistic nature of Aboriginal and Torres Strait Islander lifelong learning knowledge transfer can be seen in relation to leisure activities undertaken in the natural environment. These include activities such as: canoeing, fishing, hunting, bush navigation, music, story-telling, art and crafts, kinetic skills (spear and boomerang throwing, running), bush food collection, social interaction and solo experiences (Djagamara, 1975; Foley, 1994; Fox, 1983; McKay, 1994) which were (and where opportunities exist, still are) an integral part of everyday life. Prior to colonisation and the implementation of assimilation and acculturation policies, all of these activities were integral parts of a holistic lifestyle and were used for, but not confined to, forms of travel, subsistence, education and spiritual enlightenment (Levi-Strauss, 1966; McDonald, 1995; McKay, 1994). Traditionally, these activities were also utilised to provide a context for the transfer of knowledge about economics, politics, domestic aspects, ceremonial rites, cultural identification and social integration (Salter cited in Robertson, 1975). Oodgeroo Noonuccal (1992) discusses the learning of skills for living with the environment being based on instincts and vast experience developed over years of interaction with one's natural environment. This holistic lifestyle and the activities utilised for perpetuating this lifestyle and environmental instincts are parallel with those undertaken by many appreciative outdoor recreationalists for developing similar knowledge, values and skills.

If we are to be serious about providing platforms for marginalised voices to be heard, and allowing them to co-exist in our social system, then the lifelong learning systems (with a strong outdoor leisure emphasis) would need to be accepted as valid systems for knowledge transfer. Therefore, they would need to be accepted and respected as being as equally viable as the Western education structure.

This is important as the Western education system — of which the leisure components of outdoor education, therapeutic recreation, adventure education, and indirectly, training for commercial outdoor recreation organisations are encompassed — is identified as a major perpetuator of the dominant social system (Haralambos and Holborn, 1993), and hence discourses. Education systems by their very nature have historically been utilised as social control and assimilation mechanisms particularly in regards to Indigenous peoples (Brady, 1997; Wong Fillmore, 1996). Examples of the negative and deleterious effects on Aboriginal and Torres Strait Islander cultures through processes of assimilation through the medium of Western education systems are well documented (Atkinson, 1991; Hegarty, 1999). It is argued that this same education system has tended to assimilate and hence ignore the knowledge, values and skills of appreciative outdoor recreationalists in an attempt to 'fit' the outdoor field into education curriculums, for example, through outdoor education. Therefore, the co-existence of alternative lifelong learning systems and associated cultures is essential for the demarginalising of these community groups.

A minimal amount of literature in regards to processes for Western cultures, or in fact any other culture, to learn from Aboriginal and Torres Strait Islander education systems was also evident in the above-mentioned literature review (Djagamara, 1975; Polistina, 2000). As previously mentioned (see environmental values section), co-management of natural areas is a strong area of education by Indigenous peoples even though it is still encompassed in the broader bureaucratic institutions of the dominant social system. These co-management agreements are primarily for resource management and focusing on visitor education and are not, to a large degree, attached to the dominant education systems in their respective countries. In fact, much of the education and leisure literature appears to focus on how Western institutions can incorporate programmes that will assist Aboriginal and Torres Strait Islander people to 'fit in' or cope with the system.

In regard to appreciative outdoor recreationalists and the slow maturation of knowledge and skills, we presently find ourselves in the midst of being coerced into adopting sports-based models of training and accreditation. The current Recreation Training Queensland (RTQ) model for outdoor recreation accreditation is derived from the model developed for the Australian Sports Commission (ASC). This model does not, at present, allow for the notion of continual lifelong learning through mentoring systems that do not encourage the demoralising techniques of assessments by so-called 'experts'.

The lifelong learning approach of appreciative outdoor recreationalists and Aboriginal and Torres Strait Islander peoples moves the transfer of knowledge into a more holistic lifestyle, which essentially encompasses leisure as an important medium for education (Levi-Strauss, 1966; McDonald, 1995; McKay, 1994). Therefore, the utilisation of a 'leisure lifestyle' as the forum for this lifelong learning approach to knowledge transfer requires the redefining of leisure to a more comprehensive and integrated element of life.

Clarke and Critcher (1985) identified the definition of leisure with the general processes of hegemony and power structures in society. They noted that in order to define leisure you must analyse who defines it, how and why they define it in this manner, their processes for reproducing their definitions and the resultant discourses which assist with this reproduction. It is argued, then, that this compartmentalisation assists with the perpetuation of dominant social structures and provides ease of monitoring and maintenance of these dominant definitive discourses. Mommaas (1987) posited that the academic interpretations defining leisure are an inherent part of the context in which it will exist. Therefore, leisure lifestyles based on the notion of a holistic lifelong learning processes would afford an alternative to the segregated definitions espoused by Western leisure scientists. For example, leisure as time (leftover from work and completion of life's practical necessities) (Godbey, 1990; May and Petgen, 1960), leisure as activity (in the sense of sport, tourism, community arts, outdoor recreation) (Dumazadier, 1960), or state of mind (for example, state of flow) (Csikszentmihalyi, 1975).

This section has sought to provide an overview of the different stances and ideologies found between two marginalised community groups in Australia (appreciative outdoor recreationalists and Aboriginal and Torres Strait Islander peoples) and the dominant leisure discourse. Whilst some of the comments aid a critique of the dominant leisure discourse, an attempt has also been made to start at a point outside of this dominant leisure discourse to prevent the strengthening of the stance of the prevailing ideologies by perpetuating their system of enquiry (Macdonell,

1987). This, then, leads our discussion to the necessity for the scientific community to assist in providing platforms for validating alternative discourses.

Necessity for platforms for validation of diversity of discourses

> ... to listen closely to the voices of those materially located within different leisure cultures in a society, and to theorise them, is to shift leisure studies some way from a bureaucratic technicism which has tended too often to misrepresent or betray the subjects for whom it has claimed to speak. (Tomlinson, 1989: p. 106)

The sentiments that are aptly expressed in Tomlinson's comment signify the revolutionary ways in which the diversity of cultures encompassed in wider social systems are beginning to be acknowledged. Blommaert and Verschueren (1998) noted, however, that the [dominant] social assumptions (ideology) both celebrate diversity and view it as a threat, danger and problematic. The systems that generate the knowledge underpinning this contradictory view of diversity (the scientific research institutions themselves) are an avenue that could be utilised to alter such viewpoints. One field noted as an avenue for this critical reflection is discourse analysis as it provides an informed critical attitude to social discourses and builds awareness of its constructive nature (Potter and Wetherell, 1990).

This is particularly relevant if we are to obtain strong social systems that accept and respect cultural diversity and the natural environment. As the dominant discourses of the scientific schools of thought underlie much of the rhetoric in social and leisure theories, the need for self-reflection and critique within leisure research is required. Potter and Wetherell (1990: p. 149) support this suggestion and extend it to include an analysis of the dimensions of the variety of repertoires an individual or group may hold, noting that:

> It is not, however, sufficient for analysis to simply identify these different forms of language in the abstract. We need to know, first, the uses and functions of different repertoires, and second, the problems thrown up by their existence.

Leisure research methodologies, therefore, need to utilise methods that allow for the collection and analysis of the variety of 'interpretative repertoires'[15] (Potter and Wetherell, 1990) that are utilised in the discourses individuals engage in, in their day-to-day lives. For example, the repertoires used in discourse when discussing a single topic may be different within their home (parents to children), work (colleagues) or community setting (parents to children's school teachers). By taking Potter and Wetherell's (1990: p. 121) discourse-oriented approach to leisure research and analysis we are able to provide a platform for people to both "… draw flexibly on preformed categories and construct the sense of categories as they talk". This is important to those community groups marginalised by the dominant social and leisure discourse through their differences in worldviews and subsequent discourses, and assists in their discarding the role of 'victim' of the dominant system's mechanical categorisation processes (Potter and Wetherell, 1990).

If leisure research is to engage in this endeavour, the definition and value of what constitutes 'text' in discourse needs to be extended from the dominant written form. Parker (1992: p. 6) comments that discourse is realised in texts and "Texts are delimited tissues of meaning reproduced in any form that can be given an interpretative gloss." Examples of texts that could be covered in leisure discourse analysis would include "… all forms of spoken interaction, formal and informal, and written texts of all kinds" (Potter and Wetherell, 1990) as well as other forms including images, pictures, symbols and the natural environment. This would provide us with discourse mediums that are relevant to alternative community groups like those discussed in this paper.

Tuhiwai-Smith (1998) also discusses the limitations and inappropriateness of Western research methodologies for research with Indigenous communities. She identifies such texts as claiming (processes for claiming or reclaiming histories, lands, and other cultural issues); to storytelling (particularly from elders and women); and, testimonies (presenting oral evidence to particular types of audiences) as not only appropriate, but necessary for authentic results to be achieved in research with Indigenous peoples. As many of these alternative 'texts' can be found in the community level leisure domain it is argued that the leisure field holds an appropriate setting for providing platforms for alternative discourses and voices to be heard, and rendered equal, in the wider social system. This is particularly relevant to appreciative outdoor recreationalists and Aboriginal and Torres Strait Islander given their focus on lifelong learning approaches through mediums of lifestyle education that utilise leisure characteristics and a high level of interaction with the natural environment.

Finally, a re-establishment of communal values is essential on all levels, in particular the field of leisure studies. A large portion of community-based activities which promote communal values are encompassed in the leisure forum (for example, community festivals, community theatre and arts). Therefore, the opportunity exists in leisure research to turn the tide on the promotion of individualisation, competitiveness, commercialisation and commodification values to more communal and environmental oriented values. These activities will align the leisure studies field more closely to the new age in scholarship which is more charitable towards disparate voices, sensitive to knowledge claims processes, has a heightened moral stance and is appreciative of the communal character of understanding (Shotter and Gergen, 1990).

Conclusion

This paper has provided a brief discussion on the dominant Western social discourse and its impact on the dominant leisure discourse. It was identified that this dominant leisure discourse may tend to assist in the perpetuation of the dominant social discourse. The economic rationalist philosophy underpinning this dominant social discourse was shown to be in opposition to the environmentalist and communal philosophy of two marginalised groups, appreciative outdoor recreationalists and Aboriginal and Torres Strait Islander peoples in Australia. Examples of the daily conflict these two community groups experience when interacting with the dominant social discourse were afforded. It is maintained that a shift in leisure discourses to those more able to accept and respect the voices of marginalised groups, such as the community groups discussed in this paper, may provide avenues for validation of alternative discourses in the wider social forum. The challenge for the leisure scientific community is therefore to develop and utilise research methodologies that are flexible enough to accept and respect alternative discourses, reducing the need to promote any one scientific discourse as more valid than others.

Notes

1 The dynamic definition used for appreciative outdoor recreationalists extends on the notion of 'appreciative outdoor activities' put forward by Dunlap and Heffernan (1975). Therefore, 'appreciative outdoor recreationalists' have been defined as people who engage in outdoor activities that are non-motorised, interact with an element of nature and where the acquisition of positive knowledge and values about that element of nature as desirable. These activities are then extended to form an integral part of an holistic lifestyle, interrelating all living things including humans.

2 The use of the phrase 'Aboriginal and Torres Strait Islander' serves the word limit of this paper, however, should not be taken as viewing these two very different Indigenous groups as homogenous.

3 Whilst a comprehensive explanation of lifelong learning systems is beyond the scope of this paper the following definition is provided for brief clarification purposes. Candy, Crebert and O'Leary (1994) define lifelong learning as a very broad and comprehensive idea that includes informal and formal learning, which occurs at any time across the lifespan, whether it is intentional or unanticipated. However, it must be accepted that there are a diverse array of views (particularly those specific to cultures adopting this knowledge transference approach) on the definition of lifelong learning and therefore this definition should not be held as the only 'true' definition of the notion.

4 Parker (1992) defines discourse analysis as deliberately systematising different ways of thinking in order to understand them, whilst discourse dynamics is the tensions within discourses, and between different discourses, and the way they reproduce and transform the world (p. 5).

5   It should be noted that the level of assimilation into the Western social system and culture may have a strong impact on the adoption and/or retention of high positive environmental values and belief in holism. Ewert (1993) in his study on ethnicity, culture and land ethics, identified a strong implication that acculturation and assimilation would modify an individuals behaviour and land ethic.

6   Are those that view the natural environment as having intrinsic value over and above the use of it by humans. Its preservation and conservation is valued as an essential requirement to quality of life, and it is seen as finite (Polistina, 1997). These values would be held by a person who has or is developing a strong spiritual connection with the natural environment.

7   The current Ministerial portfolio title, which is purported to encompass recreation and hence outdoor recreation, is 'Communication, Information, Local Government, Planning and Sport'.

8   QDCILGPS (2000). The Community Sport and Recreation Facilities Program 2001. Brisbane, Australian Government Printing Service.

9   For example, the eco-challenge, extreme games and the 'hard core' mountaineering expeditions.

10   Armstrong, L. E. (1999). Performing in extreme environments. Lower Mitcham, Human Kinetics Australia.

11   Current litigation threats also serve to exclude these activities from outdoor education and adventure education programmes, and could be viewed as detrimental to any form of holistic experience or education being obtained by the participants in these programmes. These litigation threats also serve to undermine and control the notions of inherent risks that are inherent in many outdoor recreation and adventure activities. To take away this inherent risk element reduces the outdoor experience to one that is somewhat contrived.

12   National Aboriginal and Islander Day Observance Committee.

13   Recent discussions on outdoor education, adventure therapy and camping research electronic list servers have identified that the youth's macro and micro environments are all important for their development. This is not a new concept to Aboriginal and Torres Strait Islander peoples or appreciative outdoor recreationalists.

14   For a good discussion on the misappropriation and misuse of Aboriginal and Torres Strait Islander intellectual and cultural property see Mansel (1997).

15   Potter and Wetherell (1990: p. 11) provide the notion of 'interpretative repertoires' as a useful tool for analysing the dynamics between the discourses (often tense) present in different groups. However, continue to caution the use of labelling phenomenon as a means of getting bogged down in formalism and seeking the positivist notions of totality in meanings.

References

Almond, B. (1988) 'Environmental values', in B. Almond and B. Wilson (eds) *Values: A symposium*. Atlantic Highlands, NJ: Humanities Press International, Inc., pp. pp. 163–177.

Aplin, G. (1998) *Australians and their environment: An introduction to environmental studies*. Melbourne: Oxford University Press.

Armstrong, L. E. (1999) *Performing in extreme environments*. Lower Mitcham: Human Kinetics Australia.

Atkinson, G. (1981) *The relationship between outdoor recreation participation and environmental concern*. Boston: School of Education, Boston University.

——— (1990) 'Outdoor recreation's contribution to environmental attitudes', *Leisure Today* (April): pp. 14–16.

Atkinson, J. (1991) *Recreation in the Aboriginal community*. Canberra: Australian Government Publishing Service.

Australia Today (n. d.) *Aboriginal Australians*. Alstonville: Visual Media Pty. Ltd.

Berndt, R. M., Berndt, C. H., and Stanton, J. E. (1993) *A world that was*. Carlton: Melbourne University Press.

Blamey, R. K. (1995) *The nature of eco-tourism*. Canberra: Bureau of Tourism Research.

Blommaert, J. and J. Verschueren (1998) *Debating diversity: Analysing the discourse of tolerance*. London: Routledge.

Bosselman, F. P. (1978) *In the wake of the tourist*. Washington, D. C.: The Conservation Foundation.

Brady, W. (1997) 'Indigenous Australian Education and Globalisation', *International Review of Education* Vol. 43, No. 5–6: pp. 413–422.

Burch, Jr. W. R. (1993) 'Culture, Conflict, and Communications on Leisure at the Wildland-Urban Interface', in A. W. Ewert, D. J. Chevez and A. W. Magill (eds) *Culture, conflict and communication in the wildland–urban interface*. Boulder: Westview Press, pp. 375–388.

Candy, P. C., Crebert, G., and O'Leary, J. (1994) *Developing lifelong learnings through undergraduate education*. AGPS: National Board of Employment, Education and Training.

Capps, W. H. (ed) (1976) *Seeing with a native eye*. New York: Harper and Row, Publications.

Cashmore, E. (1982) *Black sportsmen*. London, Routledge & Kegan Paul.

Chester, Q. and J. Chester (1991) *The outdoor companion: An environmental handbook for surviving and enjoying the outdoors*. East Roseville: Simon & Schuster Australia.

Clarke, J. and C. Critcher (1985) *The devil makes work: Leisure in capitalist Britain*. London: Tavistock.

Cole, D. (1993) 'Recreation practices of the Stoney of Alberta and Mohawks of the six nation confederacy', *Journal of Applied Recreation Research* Vol. 18, No. 2: pp. 103–114.

Cooper, R. (1994) 'Through the soles of my feet: A personal view of creation' in D. G. Hallman (ed) *Ecotheology: Voices from south and north*. Switzerland: WCC Publications, pp. 207–212.

Csikszentmihalyi, M. (1975) *Beyond boredom and anxiety: The experience of play in work and games*. San Francisco: Jossey-Bass Publishers.

Devall, B. (1990) *Simple in means, rich in ends: Practising deep ecology*. London: Green Print.

Dingle, P. (1993) *Green audit kit: The DIY guide to greening your tourism business*. Devon: West Country Tourist Board.

Djagamara, H. (1975) 'Harry Djagamara', in C. Tatz and K. McConnochie (eds) *Black viewpoints: The aboriginal experience*. Sydney: Australia and New Zealand Book Co., pp. 72–80.

Dumazadier, J. (1960) 'Current problems of the sociology of leisure', *International Social Science Journal* Vol. 12 (Winter): pp. 526.

Dunlap, R. E. and Heffernan, R. B. (1975) 'Outdoor recreation and environmental concern: An empirical examination', *Rural Sociology* Vol. 40: pp. 18–30.

Dunstan, D. L. (1992) 'The dance of the dispossessed: On patriarchy, feminism and the practice of leisure science', *Journal of Leisure Research* Vol. 24, No. 4: pp. 324–332.

Ewert, A. W. (1993) 'Research in land ethics: The problems of ethnicity, culture and methods', in A. W. Ewert, D. J. Chavez and A. W. Magill (eds) *Culture, conflict and communication in the wildland-urban interface*. Boulder: Westview Press, pp. 299–312.

Foley, S. (1994) *The Badtjala People*. Hervey Bay: Loorgine Educational and Cultural Centre Aboriginal Corporation Inc.

Fox, A. (1983) 'Kakadu is Aboriginal land', *Ambio* Vol. 12, No. 3–4: pp. 161–166.

Giddens, A. (1993) *Sociology*. Cambridge, UK: Polity Press.

Godbey, G. (1990) *Leisure in your life: An exploration* (3rd ed.). State College, Pennsylvania: Venture Publishing, Inc.

Gunter, B. (1987) 'The leisure experience: Selected properties', *Journal of Leisure Research* Vol. 19, No. 2: pp. 115–130.

Haralambos, M. and M. Holborn (1991) *Sociology: Themes and perspectives* (2nd edn.). London: Collins Educational.

——— (1993) *Sociology: Themes and perspectives* (3rd edn.). London: Collins Educational.

Hegarty, R. (1999) *Is that you Ruthie?*. St. Lucia: University of Queensland Press.

Henderson, K. A., Bialeschki, M. D., Shaw, S. M. and Freysinger, V. J. (1989) *A leisure of one's own: A feminist perspective on women's leisure*. State College, PA: Venture Publishing, Inc.

Henley, T. (1996) *Rediscovery ancient pathways, new directions*. Edmonton, Alberta: Lone Pine Publishing.

Higgins, P. (1996) 'Connection and consequence in outdoor education', *The Journal of Adventure Education and Outdoor Leadership* Vol. 13, No. 2 (Summer): pp. 34–39.

——— (1996–97) 'Outdoor education for sustainability: Making connections', *The Journal of Adventure Education and Outdoor Leadership* Vol. 13, No. 4 (Winter, 1996/7): pp. 4–11.

Hodgins, B. W. and J. Benidickson (1989) *The Temagami experience: Recreation, resources and aboriginal rights in the Northern Ontario wilderness*. Toronto: University of Toronto Press.

Hogan, J. and S. Priest (1996) 'Deep ecology: Toward eco-equalism', *The Journal of Adventure Education and Outdoor Leadership* Vol. 13, No. 1 (Spring): pp. 25–27.

Hogan, R. A. (1992) 'The natural environment in wilderness programmes: Playing field or sacred space', *The Journal of Adventure Education and Outdoor Leadership* Vol. 9, No. 1 (Spring): pp. 25–31.

Ibrahim, H. and Cordes, K. A. (1993) Outdoor recreation. Madison, Wisconsin: WCB Brown and Benchmark Publishers.

Kelly, J. (2000) 'Regional Queensland: A drawcard for domestic tourism spending'. Media Release. Brisbane: Ministerial Office — Sport and Recreation.

Knudtson, P. and D. Suzuki (1992) *Wisdom of the elders*. North Sydney: Allen & Unwin.

Levi-Strauss, C. (1966) *The savage mind*. Chicago: University of Chicago Press.

Liddle, M. (1997) *Recreational ecology, the ecological impact of outdoor recreation and ecotourism*. Melbourne: Chapman & Hall,.

Loynes, C. (1998) 'Adventure in a bun', *The Journal of Experiential Education* Vol. 21, No. 1: pp. 35–39.

Lynch, R. and A. J. Veal (1996) *Australian leisure*. South Melbourne: Longman.

Macdonell, D. (1987) *Theories of discourse: An introduction*. Oxford: Basil Blackwell Ltd.

Mansell, M. (1997) 'Barricading our last frontier — Aboriginal cultural and intellectual property rights', in G. Yunupingu (ed) *Our land is our life*. St. Lucia: University of Qld. Press, pp. 195–209.

May, H. and Petgen (1960) *Leisure and its uses*. New York: A. S. Barnes.

McCabe, R. E. and Wadsworth, K. G. (1994) *Transactions of the 49th North American wildlife and natural resources conference*. Washington, D.C.: Wildlife Management Institute.

McCullum, H. and K. McCullum (1975) *This land is not for sale*. Toronto: Anglican Book Centre.

McDonald, D. (1995) *A literature review of Native Americans and recreation: Cultural beliefs and outdoor recreation behaviour*. Minneapolis: Department of Kinesiology and Leisure Studies, University of Minnesota.

McKay, S. (1994) 'An aboriginal perspective on the integrity of creation', in D. G. Hallman (ed) *Ecotheology: Voices from south and north*. Switzerland: WCC Publications: pp. 213–217.

Mommaas, H. and van der Poel, H. (1987) 'New perspectives on theorising leisure', *Society and Leisure* Vol. 2, No. 10 (Autumn): pp. 161–176.

Murray, M. (n. d.) 'Ferals: the call of the wild', *Simply Living*: pp. 53–59.

Noonuccal, O. (1992) *Stradbroke dreamtime*. Pymble: Angus & Robertson.

O'Rourke, M. (1998) Personal communication (19th October). Brisbane, Australia.

Parker, I. (1990) 'Discourse and Power' in J. Shotter and K. J. Gergen (eds) *Texts of identity*. London: SAGE Publication: pp. 56–69.

———— (1992) *Discourse dynamics: Critical analysis for social and individual psychology*. London: Routledge.

Phipps, M. (1985) 'Adventure — an inner journey to the self: The psychology of adventure expressed in Jungian terms', *Adventure Education* Vol. 2: pp. 11–7.

Polistina, K. (1999) 'Cultural and environmental education by and for Indigenous Australians, through the medium of outdoor recreation and education', *Annals of leisure research* Vol. 2: pp. 100–19.

Polistina, K. J. (1997) *Environmental values and ethics in outdoor recreation and education: Bona fide practice or token gesture*. School of Leisure Studies. Mt. Gravatt: Griffith University: p. 174.

Potter, J. and Wetherell, M. (1990) *Discourse and social psychology: Beyond attitudes and behaviour*. London: Sage Publications.

QDCILGPS (2000) *The community sport and recreation facilities program 2001*. Brisbane: Australian Government Printing Service.

Roberts, J. (1997) 'Talking history' in G. Yunupingu (ed) *Our land is our life*. St. Lucia: University of Queensland Press, pp. 117–124.

Robertson, I. (1975) *Sport and play in aboriginal culture — then and now*. 10th National Biennial Conference of the Australian Council for Health, Physical Education and Recreation, Perth.

Rojek, C. (1987) 'Freedom, power and leisure', *Society and Leisure* Vol. 10, No. 2 (Autumn, 1987): pp. 209–218.

Runtz, M. (1993) *The explorer's guide to Algonquin Park*. Toronto: Stoddart Publishing Co. Ltd.

Salleh, A. K. (1988–89) 'Environmental consciousness and action: An Australian perspective', *The Journal of Environmental Education*: 20, 2, Winter 1988–89: pp. 26–31.

Sayne, P. L. (1993) 'Patriarchy, women's roles and human settlements', *Women and Environments* Vol. 13 (Winter/Spring 1993): p. 50.

Seshachari, N. C. (1992) 'Toward a holistic eco-vision: The infusion of the eco-feminine in eco-philosophy' in S. I. Zeveloff, L. M. Vause and W. H. McVaugh (eds) *Wilderness tapestry: An eclectic approach to preservation.* Reno: University of Nevada Press.

Shotter, J. and Gergen, K. J. (eds) (1990) *Texts of identity.* London: SAGE Publication.

Simcox, D. E. (1993) 'Cultural foundations for leisure preference, behaviour and environmental orientation', in A. W. Ewert, D. J. Chavez and A. W. Magill (eds) *Culture, conflict and communication in the wildland-urban interface.* Boulder: Westview Press: pp. 267–280.

Sklair, L. (1996) 'Australia in the global capitalist system', *Social Alternatives* Vol. 15, No. 1: pp. 14–17.

Tatz, C. (1987) *Aborigines in sport.* Bedford Park: The Australian society for sports history.

Tilmouth, T. (1997) 'Taking stock of land rights' in G. Yunupingu (ed) *Our land is our life.* St. Lucia: University of Queensland Press, pp. 18–27.

Tomlinson, A. (1989) 'Whose side are they on? Leisure studies and cultural studies in Britain', *Leisure Studies* Vol. 8, No. 2: pp. 97–106.

Tuhiwai Smith, L. (Ngati Awa, Ngati Porou) (1998) *Towards the new millennium: International issues and projects in Indigenous research.* Paper presented at the Te Oru Rangahau Conference Maori Research and Development, Massey University.

WCIP (1984) 'The World Council of Indigenous peoples', *Cultural Survival Quarterly* Vol. 8, No. 4 (Dec.): p. 14.

Wearing, S. (1986) 'Outdoor recreation: a catalyst for change', *Recreation Australia* Vol. 6, No. 2: pp. 18–21.

Williams, S. (1994) *Managing behaviour in a supportive school environment: Strategies for schools which have Aboriginal and Torres Strait Islander students — draft document.* Queensland: Queensland Department of Education.

Wilson, J. (1988) *Politics and leisure.* London: Unwin Hyman.

Wong Fillmore, L. (1996) 'What happens when languages are lost? An essay on language assimilation and cultural identity', in D. I. Slobin, J. Gerhardt, A. Kyratzis and J. Guo, (eds) *Social interaction, social context and language: Essays in honour of Susan Ervin-Tripp.* Mahwah, New Jersey: Lawrence Erlbaum Assoc., Publishers, pp. 435–446.

Leisure Studies Association
LSA Publications

An extensive list of publications on a wide range of leisure studies topics, produced by the Leisure Studies Association since the late 1970s, is available from LSA Publications.

Some recently published volumes are detailed on the following pages, and full information may be obtained on newer and forthcoming LSA volumes from:

LSA Publications, c/o M. McFee
email: mcfee@solutions-inc.co.uk
The Chelsea School, University of Brighton
Eastbourne BN20 7SP (UK)
fax: (+44) (0)1323 644641

Among other benefits, members of the Leisure Studies Association may purchase LSA Publications at highly preferential rates.

Please contact LSA at the above address for information regarding membership of the Association, LSA Conferences, and LSA Newsletters.

LEISURE CULTURES, CONSUMPTION AND COMMODIFICATION

LSA Publication No. 74. ISBN: 0 906337 84 4 [2001] pp. 171
ed. John Horne

Contents

JUST LEISURE: EQUITY, SOCIAL EXCLUSION AND IDENTITY

LSA Publication No 72. ISBN: 0 906337 83 6 [2000] pp. 195+xiv
Edited by Celia Brackenridge, David Howe and Fiona Jordan

Contents

JUST LEISURE: POLICY, ETHICS AND PROFESSIONALISM

LSA Publication No 71. ISBN: 0 906337 81 X [2000] pp. 257+xiv
Edited by Celia Brackenridge, David Howe and Fiona Jordan

Contents

WOMEN'S LEISURE EXPERIENCES: AGES, STAGES AND ROLES

LSA Publication No. 70.ISBN 0 906337 80 1 [2001]
Edited by Sharon Clough and Judy White ˙

Contents

MASCULINITIES: LEISURE CULTURES, IDENTITIES AND CONSUMPTION

LSA Publication No. 69. ISBN: 0 906337 77 1 [2000] pp. 163
Edited by John Horne and Scott Fleming

Contents

GENDER ISSUES IN WORK AND LEISURE

LSA Publication No. 68.ISBN 0 906337 78 X
Edited by Jenny Anderson and Lesley Lawrence [pp. 173]

Contents

SPORT, LEISURE IDENTITIES AND GENDERED SPACES

LSA Publication No. 67. ISBN: 0 906337 79 8
[1999] pp. 196
Edited by Sheila Scraton and Becky Watson

HER OUTDOORS: RISK, CHALLENGE AND ADVENTURE IN GENDERED OPEN SPACES

LSA Publication No. 66 [1999]ISBN: 0 906337 76 3; pp. 131
Edited by Barbara Humberstone

Contents

POLICY AND PUBLICS

LSA Publication No. 65. ISBN: 0 906337 75 5 [1999] pp. 167
Edited by Peter Bramham and Wilf Murphy

Contents

CONSUMPTION AND PARTICIPATION: LEISURE, CULTURE AND COMMERCE

LSA Publication No. 64. ISBN: 0 906337 74 7 [2000]
Edited by Garry Whannel

Contents

GENDER, SPACE AND IDENTITY: LEISURE, CULTURE AND COMMERCE

LSA Publication No. 63. ISBN: 0 906337 73 9 [1998] pp. 191
Edited by Cara Aitchison and Fiona Jordan

Contents

THE PRODUCTION AND CONSUMPTION OF SPORT CULTURES: LEISURE, CULTURE AND COMMERCE

LSA Publication No. 62. ISBN: 0 906337 72 0 [1998] pp. 178
Edited by Udo Merkel, Gill Lines, Ian McDonald

Contents

TOURISM AND VISITOR ATTRACTIONS: LEISURE, CULTURE AND COMMERCE

LSA Publication No 61. ISBN: 0 906337 71 2 [1998] pp. 211
Edited by Neil Ravenscroft, Deborah Philips and Marion Bennett

Contents

LEISURE PLANNING IN TRANSITORY SOCIETIES

LSA Publication No. 58. ISBN: 0 906337 70 4
Edited by Mike Collins; pp 218

Contents

LEISURE, TIME AND SPACE: MEANINGS AND VALUES IN PEOPLE'S LIVES

LSA Publication No. 57. ISBN: 0 906337 68 2 [1998] pp. 198 + IV
Edited by Sheila Scraton

Contents

LEISURE, TOURISM AND ENVIRONMENT (I)
SUSTAINABILITY AND ENVIRONMENTAL POLICIES

LSA Publication No. 50 Part I;
Edited by Malcolm Foley, David McGillivray and Gayle McPherson (1999);
ISBN 0 90633764 X

Contents

LEISURE, TOURISM AND ENVIRONMENT (II) PARTICIPATION, PERCEPTIONS AND PREFERENCES

LSA Publication No. 50 (Part II)
Edited by Malcolm Foley, Matt Frew and Gayle McPherson
ISBN: 0 906337 69 0; pp. 177+xii

Contents